International studies in the history of sport
series editor J. A. Mangan

Driving ambitions: an analysis
of the American hot rod enthusiasm

also available in the series

Nicholas Fishwick *English football and society, 1910–1950*
Richard Holt (ed.) *Sport and the working class in modern Britain*
Patricia Vertinsky *The eternally wounded woman: women,
    doctors and exercise in the late nineteenth century*
Eric Halladay *Rowing in England: a social history*

Further titles in preparation

Driving ambitions:
an analysis of
the American hot rod enthusiasm

H. F. Moorhouse

MANCHESTER UNIVERSITY PRESS

Manchester and New York

Distributed exclusively in the USA and Canada by St. Martin's Press

Copyright © H. F. Moorhouse 1991

Published by Manchester University Press
Oxford Road, Manchester M13 9PL, UK, England
and Room 400, 175 Fifth Avenue, New York, NY 10010, USA

Distributed exclusively in the USA and Canada
by St. Martin's Press, Inc., 175 Fifth Avenue, New York, NY 10010, USA

British Library cataloguing in publication data
Moorhouse, H. F.
    Driving ambitions: an analysis of the American
    hot rod enthusiasm. — (International studies in
    the history of sport)
    I. Title   II. Series
    796.7

American Library of Congress cataloging in publication data
Moorhouse, H. F.
    Driving ambitions: an analysis of the American hot rod enthusiasm
    H. F. Moorhouse.
        p.   cm. — (International studies in the history of sport)
    Includes index.
    ISBN 0–7190–2916–3
    1. Drag racing—United States—History. 2. Hot rods—History.
3. Automobile driving—Social aspects.   I. Title.   II. Series.
GV1029.3.M59 1991
796.7′2′0973—dc20   90–25264

ISBN 0 7190 2916 3 *hardback*

Photoset in Linotron Palatino
by Northern Phototypesetting Company Limited, Bolton
Printed in Great Britain
by Bell & Bain, Glasgow

Contents

Series editor's introduction

As he recounts wryly, when Bert Moorhouse decided to depart from ideologically sound and proper themes of legitimate professional concern such as 'initiation ceremonies of eighteenth-century French trade artisans' to investigate a matter of contemporary social importance through 'reading forty years of hot rod literature', he quickly discovered 'closed minds lurking behind the supposedly wide eyes of some of those who purported to study society'. Others, who have appreciated the significance of sport for modern cultures and communities, have had a similar experience! We should be grateful for their persistence.

As Moorhouse rightly argues, his study of the hot rod culture in America is of value precisely because it transgresses traditional boundaries of academic legitimacy, explores new academic territory and thus points up the limitations of past perceptions of academic respectability.

Moorhouse offers us a complex analytical study operating at several levels, dealing as it does with sport and entrepreneurship, industry and the media, with the promotion of ideologies in contemporary capitalism, with 'the car in motion, as a commodity in use, implicated in the activities and structures that are labelled consumption' – another oddly neglected area of sociological analysis – and above all else, as he strongly asserts, 'the importance of enthusiasm in society'.

He has a refreshingly iconoclastic vision, but hopefully it is slightly out of focus in one regard. As this series happily demonstrates, the study of sport in modern society increasingly is less and less 'at odds with the vast bulk of social analysis'.

To Rona Hollywood
for everything

Introduction
Who's interested in hot rods?

As part of a research project, we found that Hot Rod is a magazine read by
reading-deficient high school students. When studying the readability of the
magazine, we found it to be written at upper 12th. to college grade levels. In
light of this, we would like to know if your offices have additional information
regarding the readability/readership of Hot Rod? – Maurice Miller Ph.D.,
Assistant Professor, Department of Special Education, Indiana State
University, Terre Haute, Indiana.
We don't write for any particular age group. Our writers write in their own
styles, after which the stories are edited by our editors for clarity and content.
If we can understand it, we assume everyone else can too. We believe people
will be motivated to read if the subject concerns an area of their interest, like
hot rods. – The Editor.[1]

Why is a middle-aged, middle-class, non-driving Englishman interested
in American hot rods? Which is to pose the question of why he hopes
you will be interested. I stress that 'non-driving' because when I have
given seminar or conference papers on the topic many in the audiences
have assumed I was a hot rodder. They have become puzzled, even
annoyed, when they found that, far from regularly tooling down a drag
strip, I couldn't make a mini move. Enthusiasm masquerading as
scholarship they could understand, after all, everybody is 'really
interested' in something, but here was a numbskull who seemed to be
suggesting that hot rods actually were worthy of serious, dispassionate,
scholarly attention. Of course, the reflex of many an 'intellectual' is to
regard such a topic as intrinsically trivial. One reviewer, considering an
article I had written on the subject in a collection of papers about 'work',
regarded it as 'light-hearted' but I think it was my head he actually
wanted to refer to. This was not stuff of real sociological or historical
significance, unlike the study of the initiation ceremonies of eighteenth-
century French trade artisans or the 'world surveys' on 'attitudes' to
'work' which won his warm approval.[2] Another anonymous idiot, from
the south east of England of course, who heard a paper of mine, thought

1

it very droll that someone might believe they could find something of social importance through reading forty years of hot rod literature. S/he was, naturally, heavily into the totally ideologically sound topic of 'workers' co-ops'.[3]

Readers for publishers took the same line. One admitting to 'uninformed opinions' and that s/he was 'ignorant of the market in publishing' was still bold enough to conclude that a book on this subject shouldn't be published because: 'hot-rodding in its broadest aspects, . . is still, I think, a limited subject'. Another one for a different publisher, my covering letter to whom had made it as clear as crystal that, whatever else, this was not going to be a book about 'leisure', remarked with a broadminded aplomb: '. . . it's not a subject that would appeal to me and I have pretty catholic tastes in studies of leisure'. What closed minds lurk behind the supposedly wide-eyes of some of those who purport to study society. Then there was the one who thought I was going about it all wrong and should try for an 'oral history' . . . the prospect of asking the Economic and Social Research Council for funds to travel to El Verano, California to seek out all the seventy-year-olds who had belonged to the Valley of the Moon Roadmasters was intriguing, but I decided my life was too full already.

I shouldn't pretend that no one took an interest. Several people told me that 'someone' (usually German or French) had already written the chapter that told us all we needed to know about the social impact of cars. I wasted many an hour searching for this mythical piece. The inter-library loans service of Glasgow University did sterling work as odd request followed odd request though the less said about the British Library at Boston Spa the better. The editor of this series, Tony Mangan, took a chance with an unusual topic and shepherded me along past all the missed deadlines and broken promises. Manchester University Press were OK. Frank Bechhofer and Dick Holt occasionally tried to convince me that the world was waiting on my words. The British Academy, The Carnegie Trust for the Universities of Scotland and the British Association for American Studies all allocated me small sums of money which enabled me to take a short research trip to the USA in spring 1987 to read material I simply could not obtain in Britain. To those bodies, backing an arcane and apparently 'non-relevant' project in academically hard times, I have nothing to offer but the deepest of deep thanks. Mind you the libraries of America were quite a different matter. The Library of Congress in Washington DC had lost or mislaid a lot of its catalogued holdings of popular magazines and books pertaining to the

Introduction

early days of hot rodding and didn't seem too bothered about it. When, in frustration, I tried to fill in the gaps by moving on to the New York Reference Library they, ultra-efficient, knew just what had happened to a good part of their supposed stock: 'we threw that out years ago, we knew no one would ever be interested.' I ended up buying thirty- and forty-year-old hot rod magazines in the sleazy bookshops on 42nd Street at a dollar a time. It was worth it to me.

To return to the question I started with, I try to detail why I think the hot rod enthusiasm is a pertinent topic throughout the book but, short and sweet, I think it's interesting because it is an example of the kind of social phenomenon that needs examination if most social analysis is not to go on providing a partial view of people in society and one that has credence only within the narrow confines of the academic world. It is interesting because it involves the study of the automobile *outside* production. Because it deals with people involved in using and consuming commodities and reveals many of the limitations of that ready made, simplistic, 'work'/'leisure' dichotomy which so many intellectuals use to 'explain' the world and quickly denote what are the 'important' and 'unimportant' topics. Because it deals with one example of a whole catalogue of institutions, magazines and activities which are subjectively important to a large number of people but which receive little scholarly attention. It's of interest because the hot rod story is a good yarn and the underlying themes of immense importance in the modern world, rather more important, in fact, than worthy workers' co-operatives for example. So let us begin to consider the hot rod enthusiam of America and, yes, I certainly do hope the heart will be light throughout, why not? But the head will be just as hard as I can make it.

Notes

1 Letter, *Hot Rod Magazine*, 32, April 1979.
2 M. Rose, book review, *Work Employment and Society*, 2, 1989, pp. 549-51.
3 'Work Ethic', *New Society*, 68, 12 April 1984, p. 49.

3

Chapter One
The automobile and social analysis: theoretical perspectives

Someone should write an erudite essay on the moral, physical and aesthetic effects of the Model T Ford on the American nation. Two generations of Americans knew more about the Ford coil than the clitoris, about the planetary system of gears than the solar system of stars. With the Model T, part of the concept of private property disappeared. Pliers ceased to be privately owned and a tyre pump belonged to the last man who had picked it up. Most of the babies of the period were conceived in Model T Fords and not a few were born in them. The theory of the Anglo-Saxon home became so warped that it never quite recovered.[1]

This is a book about an automobile sport and an associated enthusiasm. In part it is a history of drag racing, which originated in various informal automobile activities and rapidly developed into the 'normal' form of major twentieth-century sport with professional circuits, super stadia, paying spectators, rows, business sponsorships, boycotts, multi-million dollar deals, television contracts and so on, all still founded upon some, rather changed, amateur activities and interests. In part it is about the growth of what became the best-selling automotive publication in the world – *Hot Rod* magazine – and about the influences and relationships that special interest literature can have with sports and enthusiasms. In part it is a book about the ways in which, and the degrees to which, activities created in the streets or at 'the grass roots' get incorporated, standardised and provided for by packaged products and stereotyped explanations. In part it is about how a new industry based on the sport and on the enthusiasm found and held a niche between 'Detroit' and 'Washington', between 'monopoly capitalism' and 'the state'. In part this book is about the nature of the ideologies that get promoted in modern capitalism, particularly those regarding the moral under-pinnings of 'fun', 'free time', 'leisure' and spending and how these are rather more complicated than is usually allowed. Above all else this is a book about the car in motion, as a commodity in use, implicated in the activities and structures that are labelled as consumption.

It has, therefore, a set of themes at odds with the vast bulk of social analysis. Sports are seldom studied. Enthusiasms are overlooked. Specialist magazines are ignored in favour of unpacking what is said to be said in the 'mass' media. Incorporation is regarded as a rather straightforward process, easily sketched, the province of big business and mass advertising. Crucially, in most sociology and virtually all Marxism there is a real failure to study or even think much about consumption and its place and weight in modern life and autobiography. This is rapidly changing but it is still the case that consumption remains a step-child compared to the favoured focal concerns of social analysis.

Producing the car, producing social analysis

For nothing is this more true than the automobile. There can be few activities, if any, which have been so thoroughly studied as the production of cars. Detailing its history, its development, its multinationalism, patterns of cross-cultural productivity, distinct stages of manufacturing techniques, etc. is one area where sociology and Marxism can wipe their collective brow and claim the job well done. But while the auto-worker – American, Japanese, French, British, 'old', 'new', black, Mexican, female etc. – is the star of a hundred and more major studies, car drivers await, in the main, their chroniclers and the myriad of ways the car has been used and exhibited, the social relations and institutions it has inspired in the rest of life, what it may have occasioned and connoted *outside* the factory gates, have been quite neglected.

This is no accident. Sociology and Marxism traffic in a world of manufacturing and proceed from this to present accounts of living in capitalism which scarcely ring true. Neither has taken a serious interest in fun and pleasure. Social analysis is permeated with a productionist ethos which lies deep in core assumptions and which, among many other things, helps declare some areas of study as 'most important', as carrying most explanatory weight and as deserving greater professional prestige. Both sociology and Marxism tend to conceptualise people – adults anyway – as labourers. As a result most sociology and virtually all Marxism:

(i) emphasises 'work' as the crucial sphere of being, at least for a male life, with all the rest of life felt to be determined, residual and less worthy of sustained study;

(ii) operationalises this 'work' as equivalent to employment, paid labour;

(iii) utilises a mainly implicit, qualified, but still vital notion that the dominant values of capitalist society do, or at the least once did, stress paid labour as the significant arena of male life, the sphere where men should find identity, meaning, association, achievement and so on;

(iv) uses the categories and institutions of employment to find, define and study its subjects;

(v) contrasts this 'work' and its 'effects' with some other kind of 'work' which is both unspecified and highly romanticised.

Feminist and other gender-based critiques have diagnosed the blinkered scrutiny such a vision ensures but, still, the real force of their objections has not altered the meta-theoretical foundations of the powerful forms of social analysis. Rather these have tended to incorporate the power of the critique by changes in terminology, by insisting on the determined nature of non-paid time and, a point I will return to, through a rather covert decision that the paramount task for students of society is to map out the objective basis of life and not how it is understood, going 'beneath the surface' as it is often grandly put. This latter element involves a debilitating tendency to downplay the importance of 'the level of meaning' in social explanation so that, for example, it is quite routinely assumed that the significance of paid labour to life, identity and conciousness can be easily demonstrated by a quick reference to the amount of time spent in it, whereas I would have thought it was obvious that it is not the *quantity* but the *quality* of time that creates meanings. 'Lived experience', like the working day, is given order and infused with colour by the rare high and low points, by the special events and the magic moments. Analysis cannot mechanically apportion a similar subjective weight to every passing moment. The stopwatch may be able to measure the speed of a line but not, in all truth, the tempo of a life passing.

Not only do the pervasive assumptions I sketch above promote a heirarchy of preferred topics of study and sub-disciplines but they also structure the way the concerns of even the marginalised areas get pursued. For example, within that low status scholarly activity that is the social analysis of sport the automobile very rarely figures. Writing in

1981 about 'neglected sports in American history' Adelman accurately remarked: 'historians have not examined the sport quite possibly most identified with modern technology, automobile racing, even though it is currently the most attended spectator sport.'[2] Even here the focus is on 'real' sports with proper pedigrees, that can hark back to some more authentic, organic age and cars get excluded on the most spurious of grounds. No engines roar in the 'civilising process' and no tyres burn in 'the quest for excitement'.[3] Mandell, in his cultural history of sport, excludes automobile racing from consideration as an: 'activity where the technological apparatus dominates the human performer'[4] and does not stop to clarify what the assertion of 'domination' means precisely or to consider whether the multi-faceted human effort which is involved remains worthy of scrutiny for those supposedly interested in sport and its cultural connections.

Nor does the automobile figure much in those other marginal areas of academic study, 'leisure' or cultural studies. Exponents of 'leisure studies', debilitated by trying to define their key term in reaction to what they accept is the really important activity of 'work', have, in fact, failed to provide many studies about, or make much sense of, what people actually do or feel in museums, gardens, garages and kitchens, or on pitches, package tours, roads or trails.[5] Methodologically, while 'leisure' seems to be a social site where the detailed case study and/or ethnography of particular enviroments, events and enthusiasms is both highly appropriate and relatively easy, very few such studies exist. As a part of this the way that such activities are given meaning or contextualised has been neglected or trivialised. Either it assumed people spontaneously 'know' what they are doing in 'leisure', which is somehow a 'freer' sphere than 'work', or, in the all too common 'radical' grand gesture, 'capitalism' decides. In fact all the throwaway references to: 'leisure industries', 'market provision', 'commodity consumption', 'the commercialization of leisure', 'the commodity form', 'modern consumerism', 'hegemony', 'the pleasure industries' and the like merely indicate where detailed analyses ought to begin and by no means represent analyses in themselves.

This weakness is all the more pronounced since many such studies, especially the 'radical' ones intent on finding some pervasive passivity in the mass culture of advanced capitalism, tend to pluck their examples directly from the 'entertainment industries' and images carried in the mass media to the virtual exclusion of the activities and enthusiasms that people actually engage in. Even in the very new concern with a sociology

7

of consumption, 'entertainment' and 'pleasure' have come to be rather narrowly conceived of as a pre-packed trip down tin-pan alley to the local video shop. Adding to the self-confirming quality of such a methodology has been a growing tendency to provide 'readings' of 'culture' defined as the output of the electronic media. This has led onto an incessant and untestable chattering about 'signs' (usually accompanied by a reference to 'a complex body of theory') set in some functionalist lingo of 'reproduction'. There has now come to be an obsession with an assumed mass obsession with 'images' as the very essence of the post-modern condition, while the actual objects which provide the images or which they serve to sell have rarely been analysed in use or action. Most unfortunately, the emerging sociology of consumption is being aligned with 'post-modernism' as a way of life. The leading British journal here, *Theory Culture and Society*, never managed to carry an article with the car as its subject in its first six volumes.

One body of work which might be thought to provide empirical investigation of such matters, and is often treated as if it has, the analysis of youth subcultures conducted by the Centre for Contemporary Cultural Studies at Birmingham University (CCCS) is, actually, analytically very weak. Because of its Marxist roots it, too, tends to share the assumption of the existence of some promoted, pervasive, persuasive, if past 'work ethic'. This serves as the basis for such phrases as 'traditional working-class puritanism', which make 'the new' all the more shocking and thrilling to portray. This influential body of work also tends to dwell on some 'style' treated as a kind of end in its self. Not only is there a tendency to glorify the 'deviant' at the expense of the study of what the mundane mainstream of the population are up to, but in most of the work of the CCCS there is little sense of what even the youth they do choose to focus on actually *do* as opposed to what they dress like or listen to. The concept of 'subculture' forms the keystone of this approach but is not justified. There is a real neglect of just what the 'subcultural activities' the subjects are said to engage in consist of exactly, what their various levels of commitment to the 'subculture' are and what the concrete institutions of any 'subculture' might be. Overall, the CCCS provide rather little fieldwork and what there is concentrates on images, style and style changes which, just like the post-modernists, the cultural analyst then expertly 'reads', 'decodes' or 'deciphers' to reveal their 'real' meanings which are often enough, apparently, some 'semiotic guerrilla warfare' against some stereotyped 'straight society'. This whole tradition, far too uncritically treated by many sociologists, may provide a useful training ground for the analyst who wants to break into cryptography but offers little real insight into the importance of consumption in modern capitalism, its connections with identity and the various forms it can take among various groups.

Here too, as with so much mainstream work, problems of meaning and the infusion of meaning are trivialised. The underlying assumption is of a 'moment' of 'street innovation' then taken over by 'the market'. There is little interest in the actual processes of 'creation', which are invariably asserted not documented, and, for all the talk of a multi-hued hegmony, the process of incorporation is regarded as uninteresting and simple, as something 'original' and 'genuine' is pulled into 'consensus' and 'market provision'. In short, in the CCCS tradition the investigation of 'subcultures' remains abstract and invoked and does not stoop to the level of sustained investigation or the methodological niceties of investigating the changing forms of any 'subcultures' that might actually have some core activities as opposed to a sound system and a dress sense. The stress is on the 'creativity' of youth, there is much talk of its 'art' and 'culture' and 'authenticity'. Also of 'irony' and 'magical victories' and 'inversions' and even 'double inversions' all deduced by the decoders so that one chief exponent can say (without any irony): 'it is highly unlikely . . . that the members of any of the subcultures described in this book would recognize themselves reflected here.'[6]

Even the CCCS text apparently closest to my concerns, Willis's study of bike boys, shares these general faults. He writes of how the biker's

> mastery of the alienation of the machine, its answerability to the most minute experiential forms of the bike culture, dramatize the widening gap elsewhere between more inturned and nervous sensibilities and the gargantuan, cyclopean forces which are their creation. The capitalist, industrial apotheosis will be the final destruction of human scale. Its most extraordinary achievements will be impossible to live in. The robustness of the bike culture shows us the fragility of the urban sensibility, and the humanized motor-bike shows us the terror of gigantic technologies.[7]

This certainly sounds pretty significant but while there is much talk of 'reverse dialectical moments', 'the concrete transformation of objects' and 'profane creativity' etc., the eager reader infact learns very very little about 'the' bike, the culture of the bike, working on the bike, the institutions of the subculture and so on, and much much more about the interpersonal relations within a small group, about drugs, dress styles and music – 'the rock and roll form' – and why the boys prefer singles to long playing records.

Consuming the car

So far in my review I have made two charges against the bulk of social analysis, charges which I intend will inform this study. The first is that the complex of issues around meanings and the provision of meanings in modern society, especially as they relate to fun, free-time and pleasure, have been assumed or simplified. The second is that while the car in production has achieved iconic status in social analysis the car in use is regarded altogether differently. With very few but very honourable exceptions[8] there has been little attempt to analyse or discuss to any degree of complexity the auto's place in consumption. This is not to say that it has been ignored. Indeed, its presumed significance is often noted. Many acknowledge that it is an important purchase, after a house, probably the most expensive most people will ever make. Then through the twentieth century the car has become swathed in an accretion of symbols and representations which, via pop-psychology and sociology, and their sedimenation into advertising discussion and practice, have become the 'commonsense' understanding of the car's social significance. The automobile as a symbol of modern affluence and its discontents is the level at which most analysis of the car in consumption stops. So almost everybody, let alone all the new experts in cultural 'decoding', can recognise the car, or, at least, some cars, as a 'status symbol' or 'phallic object'. A dreadful example of this kind of 'analysis' can be found in a recent book by Marsh and Collett in which the authors argue: 'The only way to understand the true role of automobiles in society is to look beneath the veneer of rational explanations.'[9] The car is then linked to a variety of innate 'drives' and is said to stand for: the home, the phallus, the womb, aggression, the need for status, a mistress, seduction and almost everything else that any novelist or poet or advertiser, themselves under the influence of paperback Freudianism, has said it represented. Many other academics quickly use the car to represent the 'American Dream' or 'modernity' or, indeed, to fulfil almost any other symbolic function anyone wants to attach to some quite undifferentiated, highly stylised, vision of 'the' car.

Even those profound analysts of the nature of modern popular culture, the Frankfurt School, whose stabs at the quality of life in advanced capitalism sometimes touched on the car, tend to exemplify this shallow approach. Adorno, for example, thoroughly disliked the endemic 'auto-religion' he found in the America of the 1940s. To him contemporary automobiles both contributed to the withering of experience in society and imposed certain types of experience. Dwelling on the 'superiority' of a Cadillac over a Chevrolet as opposed to that contained in 'the old Rolls Royce', he saw modern sales methods as involving a sapping of luxury, part of a general tendency to flatten out tensions in contemporary life and eradicate qualitatively different experiences. Moreover, he insisted that the particular world of objects which surrounded the new human type must have a profound effect. Technology, like cars, which required certain types of movement and gesture, made people jerky and violent in action in a terrible correspondence with fascist forms. Musing, for example, that car doors need to be slammed shut he suggested that this had altered manners, civility and the nature of sociability: 'And which driver is not tempted, merely by the power of his engine, to wipe out the vermin of the street, pedestrians, children and cyclists?'[10] Which at least suggests that the 'urban flâneur' who has become such a hero of post-modernist discourse might need to step lively in the sensory stroll through the city or get run over, rather than overloaded.

Marcuse too used a highly stereotyped version of the car to draw easy analogies with a one-dimensional human condition. When he tried to portray the exact nature of the quality of oppression in advanced capitalism he often used the word 'streamlined', drawing a far from exact parallel between the cars of the Eisenhower era and what he perceived to be a comfortable, frictionless, unfreedom. To Marcuse what was different about control in advanced capitalism was that the bourgeoisie had invaded the private space of the individual and channelled that but, crucially, they disciplined via an apparent liberation and comfort. Deferred gratification as a theme of bourgeois ideology had given way to 'live now pay later'. The main site of this new bourgeois assault was not employment but private life, fun and leisure time. Capitalism had not only delivered the goods for people's material needs but did meet, though in particular ways, some of their human needs, for love, excitement, creativity etc. But what happened in modern capitalism was that these needs were ordered, defined, and, indeed, created in certain ways so as to sell more goods and hold in check the impetus to a much wider and profound liberation. Modern capitalism claimed the whole individual, whittling away at even the rough areas of inner space, once the site of disturbing fantasy and critical opposition. It claimed the whole person by making the individual happy and satisfied and encouraged a positive thinking in which the negative features of life appear to be the essential by-products of progress:

11

I ride in a new automobile. I experience its beauty, shininess, power, convenience – but then I become aware of the fact that in a relatively short time it will deteriorate and need repair; that its beauty and surface are cheap, its power unnecessary, its size idiotic; and that I will not find a parking place. I come to think of my car as a product of one of the Big Three automobile corporations. The latter determine the appearance of my car and make its beauty as well as its cheapness, its power as well as its shakiness, its working as well as its obsolescence. In a way I feel cheated. I believe the car is not what it could be, that better cars could be made for less money. But the other guy has to live, too. Wages and taxes are too high; turnover is necessary; we have it much easier than before. The tension between appearance and reality melts away and both merge in one rather pleasant feeling.

The extent to which such a civilization had transformed the object world into an extension of the individual's mind and body made even the very notion of 'alienation' highly questionable: 'The people recognize themselves in their commodities; they find their soul in their automobile, hi-fi set, split-level home, kitchen equipment. The very mechanism which ties the individual to his society has changed and social control is anchored in the new needs which it has produced.'[11] In fact, for Marcuse, this administered society represented a much more profound condition of alienation where waste and planned obselescence had become part of basic production costs and where indoctrination, preconditioning and the rationalisation of this waste was a crucial part of the society of steered satisfaction.

The trouble with these insights of the Frankfurt School, so much more cutting than similar kinds of high level, rhetorical, analyses of the modern condition that have followed since, is, of course, that they rarely stoop to consider prosaic realities. Assertions of 'harmony', 'uniformity', and 'identical' abound but are not detailed or even likely. The fact that a negro could own a Cadillac was, for Marcuse, a sign of the flattening out of the contrast between the given and the possible, between satisfied and unsatisfied needs yet, of course, 'the' Cadillac was not the same object or an object used in the same way for the black and the manager.[12] Like many other social 'theorists' the Frankfurt School usually only scrutinised society from the highest point and did not deign to sully their hands by scrambling down to investigate, for instance, how people really used or thought about automobiles. Their 'car' was a stereotype, their account of its use a travesty.

Adorno, not a man willing to blink the bleakest of eyes, probably thought he dealt with what I intend to discuss in this book in a rapid dissection of the 'adventurers of psuedo-activity' who sought to break away from the passive status of compulsory consumers and to preserve their own special sphere. One archetype was the radio-ham:

> At twenty he is still at the stage of a boy scout working on complicated knots just to please his parents. This type is held in high esteem in radio matters. He patiently builds sets whose most important parts he must buy ready-made, and scans the air for shortwave secrets, though there are none. As a reader of Indian stories and travel books, he once discovered unknown lands and cleared his path through the forest primeval. As radio ham he becomes the discoverer of just those industrial products which are interested in being discovered by him.[13]

Such people engaged in a lot of purposeless activity in pursuit of their psuedo-individualism and, though they did not realise it, had their interests carefully foisted from above. This is a line of analysis which others have followed to some interest as in Butsch's account of the commodification of the means of production of the hobby of model aircraft construction[14] and there is some truth in it, more truth than many who criticise the Frankfurt School on moral rather than analytic grounds, for their 'elitism', 'gloomy prognostications' or 'intolerable condescension', want to acknowledge, but it certainly isn't the whole truth. There is, in this appeal to 'commodification' as the broad answer to the place of consumption in modern life a neglect of the ambiguities of the activities that remain and, crucially, a stultifying silence on how the activity is *presented* to and how it is *understood* by its practitioners. There is a simple presentation of some original, basic, inherent level of skill and difficulty which gets plainly diluted, not an attention to the precise detail of the alteration in tasks and the changing call to the sense of achievement.

All too often, the basic error here is to treat 'alienation' as true by theoretical fiat so that its nature and extent do not need to be detailed or examined. This is the standpoint of most modern Marxism which can label almost any activity, especially if people are enjoying themselves, as demonstrating 'profound alienation'. A point that should trouble those who cling to such an easy 'explanation' is that modern workers do not just confront technology in paid labour but in all parts of their lives and, whatever the balance in factory or office (and this too is often stereotyped in social analysis), outside the place of employment both the display and experience of it are likely to convince them of its broadly benign and progressive nature, and to locate the modern world in a commonsense vision of the march of science. For a long time the automobile has been 'popular technology' for a lot of people. This was 'hands on' experience with 'state of the art' long before the personal computer and is still a much wider spread encounter. In America, as Steinbeck declares, the automobile was probably many people's most immediate connection with a complex machine and it contained easy lessons, personally related lessons, to the advantages of modern technology. People could use and control its power and relish its idiosyncrasies. In addition, it was and is a technology that is literally used, modified, altered, tested, improved and renewed. Most grand analyses of the quality of 'modern culture' let alone 'the post-modern' would end in ruins before some consideration of the varieties of ways the car is used by individuals. In Lane's neglected study of the ideology of the American common man in the late 1950s, men whose own self-images are purposeful and striving, we are told: 'The men of Eastport believe with all their heart and soul in progress; over and over again they take satisfaction in the technical things they have that their parents did not have, and, with less certainty, the things their children have that they did not.'[15]

It is Lefebvre who provides the best clues to advance here though his basic intention too is to see the automobile as an important part of 'the bureaucratic society of controlled consumption'. Specifically he argues that: 'from the viewpoint of programmed everyday life, nothing can beat the motor car.'[16] He argues that the automobile has an absurd significance in conquering life and imposing 'laws' upon it. It has this prime place in part because it is the epitome of objects, the 'leading-object' directing behaviours in various spheres from economics to speech. Cities, for example, are rebuilt in terms of motoring needs, a lot of everyday life is accompanied by the noise of engines, while its use permits a peculiar quality of human contact in traffic where people meet without mixing and so it contributes to the disintegration of city life and fosters a 'psychosis' peculiar to the motorist. On the other hand: 'the motor car with its retinue of wounded and dead, its trail of blood, is all that remains of adventure in everyday life, its paltry ration of excitement and hazard.'[17]

For Lefebvre too the automobile has the role of all commodities in modern capitalism: that of substitution. It *stands for* eroticism, adventure, contact, comfort, excitement and so on and it is consumed as a sign as much as an object. But, to repeat, I insist that the social analysis of the automobile has to go well beyond this. Conspicuous consumption as a concept should not be narrowed to equate with what is glossy or obvious and status is achieved through action and not just through the display of symbols. In the language of hot rodding 'show' may be important but so is 'go'. In fact, Lefebvre does realize there are other things to be said about the social effects of the use of cars. The automobile fosters visible hierarchies in modern life, an obvious one based on size, power and cost, but also a more complex and subtle one based on performance, and these do not coincide exactly. The gap between generates thought, conversation, discussion and controversy and, indeed, it is possible, through daring and driving skill, to alter one's standing in the second hierarchy and so, perhaps, on the first:

> When I overtake a more powerful car than that which I am driving, I change my place in the first hierarchy by climbing a rung in the second, that concerned with performance and requiring foolhardiness, ability and cunning, therefore freedom; my achievement becomes a topic of conversation with my passengers, later with acquaintances and friends. . . . in these circumstances the hierarchy is no longer oppressive and compulsive, but integrative.[18]

Which, at least suggests that the use of the car, by no means limited to Lefebvre's two hierarchies, might have some quite complex cultural resonances. He goes on to add that one other element in the car's social impact is that it creates its own context:

> the scholar who wishes to complete a thorough semiologic (or sociologic) interpretation of the motor car must include in the basic corpus . . . documents such as legal, journalistic or literary tracts, advertisments etc. The Leading-Object has not only produced a system of communication but also organisms and institutions that use it and that it uses.[19]

The cultural apparatus

What Lefebvre alludes to here, but does not actually even begin, is the scholarly need to investigate cultural work and the producers and promotors of ideologies, especially as these apply to consumption. Meanings always have to be marshalled by somebody: they do not flow inherently from any task. Of course, meaning has not been neglected but more often than not it is asserted. All too often the only 'moral entrepreneurs' that excite interest are those who are trying to reassert an older morality through its old forms, those who seek to declare some activities as 'bad' or 'mad'. The 'new' is assumed to be rather simple, to be read off easily from a few advertisments. Little effort has gone into detailing what the intellectuals of the modern culture industries are doing *precisely*. There is little attempt to rival, say, the studies we have of

15

the way the Victorian 'games ethic' was developed and spread around the world.[20] If modern 'leisure', fun and pleasure are to be understood there has to be much more profound consideration of the ways non-employment activities, including sports and enthusiasms, are actually organised, infused with meanings and linked to the modern sales effort. This is in part what I seek to do in this book.

We find some analytic help here in the work of C. Wright Mills. He pictured Eisenhower's America as 'a set of bureaucracies and a great salesroom'. In such a society the sources of experience and the springs of self-judgement had changed. There had been a shift in emphasis from production to distribution closely related to an individual worry about status as relationships shifted in significance in a changing world. Because of alterations in scale and the reshaping of communities Mills argued for the importance of what he called 'the cultural apparatus'. This comprised 'all those organizations and milieux in which artistic, intellectual, and scientific work goes on and of the means by which such work is made available to smaller circles, wider publics and great masses.' In this apparatus:

> art, science and learning, entertainment, malarkey, and information are pro-duced and distributed. In terms of it these products are distributed and consumed. It contains an elaborate set of institutions: of schools and theaters, newspapers and census bureaux, studios, laboratories, museums, little magazines, radio networks. It contains truly fabulous agencies of exact information and of trivial distraction, exciting objects, lazy escapes, strident advice.[21]

Those who worked in this apparatus formed a new social group whose task was the management and manipulation of symbols and meanings. They observed, analysed, interpreted and re-presented 'human experience'. They shaped aspirations, moods, styles of thought and vocabularies of motivation. The symbols and models they provided formed and constrained the variety of 'experiences' available to their various audiences.

If there is any truth in Mills's brilliant but broad sketch of contemporary capitalism, there has been little filling in of fine detail since he wrote, and what there has been concentrates mainly on the 'trivial distraction'. As part of a more general neglect the savants and entre-preneurs of consumption activities have not been a preferred subject for social analysts. The only members of Mills's apparatus who have received much scholarly attention have been journalists and, even then, mainly those engaged in the sanctified serious business of producing news and current affairs. Yet, as the quotations indicate, Mills conceived of this apparatus as a quite complex and faceted phenomenon, by no means reducible to flip references to 'the power of advertising' or 'the supply of images' or 'the new leisure industries' and so on. I think we can assume that, regardless of the noise in the truly mass media, each sport and enthusiasm will have its own specific intelligentsia, a local cultural apparatus, which is more than likely to comment upon its own field in a very sparse tone and invest it with some wider significance.

For some years I have been trying to think out the complexities of the matters I have sketched so far in this chapter through the study of the ways the automobile has been used as an object and, recently, quite specifically through the investigation of the hot rod enthusiasm of post-war America.[22] The 1940s was the period in which the 'hot rod' became significant in the lives of a large number of (mainly young) Americans. A culture was created around the term with definite values, interests, a special vocabulary and a variety of formal and informal institutions: used-car lots, races, clubs, speedshops, roads, magazines, local and national associations. The term was used for abuse and admiration in the news media of the time, while cinema, radio, television and books drew on the culture for background and for symbolism, refining and spreading its messages. The main theme of the culture was the modification of 'Detriot Iron', the 'lead barges' which were the American production car. There was a technical and aesthetic aspect to such modification. The aura which hung around the culture, and its present-ation in the mass media, was that of 'hot' cars, speedy vehicles engaged in racing, often illegally on public highways. But in fact, engineering and ornamentation, the desire to go faster and the wish to look sharper, were combined or separated in all manner of ways to provide a variety of styles and specialisms. And, of course, like any other activity, there was a continuum of commitment: from simply bolting a few shop-bought accessories onto your car, to creating, through one's own labour over many years, a streamlined special. As we shall see, the activities involved changed through the decades but some things remained con-stant, if nothing else the associated, ubiquitous and illegal sport of racing in the streets.

Hot rodding is an example of what are, usually, dismissively or disparagingly referred to in social analysis as 'hobbies', 'pastimes', 'subcultures', 'leisure activities' etc. As I argued earlier in this chapter, though called by many terms such institutions have provoked little detailed study. Yet through action and activity 'commodities' like the car become the basis for various fields of interests even identities for individuals and, relatedly, become the basis of various enthusiasms and/or sports. I believe that a large amount of personal consumption and, especially, the explanations, ethics, and ideologies which surround consumption, are regulated through involvement in such enthusiasms some of which have sports as their core activity.

The study of consumption

So in large measure this book is about one specific section of Mills's apparatus in post-war America, one which operated to sustain, change and defend a particular sport, enthusiasm and set of economic opportunities which opened up around the automobile being used in a particular way. I want to do this because, so I believe, the developing sociology of consumption requires to be grounded in empirical studies and in the detailed history of the specific forms 'consumption' can take if it is not to simplify the issues involved in the use of commodities. For example, the empirical study of the specific operations of parts of the cultural apparatus would be of some sociological importance because some of the meanings they manoeuvre concern the 'experience' and significance of 'work', matters which lie right at the roots of the productionist preconceptions of most social analysis. The cry that there is some 'decline in the work ethic' or some 'defect in meaning' in labour because of the loss of a moral dimension to the activity of employment is revealed as quite preposterous once we cast half an eye at the ideologies of consumption.

To indicate some of the dangers I perceive as resulting from too generalised an approach to consumption, at least as it concerns personal spending, 'leisure' and identity formation, I want to consider what I regard as about the most important contribution so far to the emerging sociology of consumption, Campbell's *The Romantic Ethic and the Spirit of Modern Consumption*.[23] This book is intended to stand as an extended footnote to Weber's famous essay. Campbell argues that there were other strands in Protestantism – crucially romanticism – which helped to create and justify an ethos conducive to a new form of modern consumption. He locates the spirit of consumerism as 'autonomous self-illusory hedonism' in which pleasure is obtained in large measure through the personal manipulation of stimuli, in fantasising, day-dreaming and longing, for: 'whilst only reality can provide satisfaction, both illusions and delusions can supply pleasure'.[24] He insists that both 'spirits' –

18

production and consumption – need to be grasped together if we are to understand the nature of modern capitalism.

While much appreciating Campbell's effort especially his important 'rejection of the widespread error of treating the Industrial Revolution as if it merely constituted a radical transformation in the means of production',[25] his attempt to explain the nature of modern consumption is flawed largely because it tries to create too neat a mirror image of Weber's thesis and so lapses into a certain formalism and false dualism. In this major work, not withstanding certain qualifications in the text, Campbell tends to:

(i) assume some Protestant Ethic (or spirit of capitalism) did/does operate on most people in capitalist society;

(ii) assume some Protestant Ethic (or spirit of capitalism) did/does not operate to promote and structure consumption;

(iii) remain at a level of 'ethics' and 'ideals' and does not detail the ways through which these might 'enable' or be 'congruent' with action or 'give direction to character confirming conduct' etc. and so, as Campbell recognises, his thesis is likely to replicate the same causal confusions as Weber's original essay;

(iv) concentrate on 'higher' if not 'high' culture and thus be unconcerned with if, why, how, or in what forms this actually 'trickles down', 'reaches' or 'affects' the bulk of the population;

(v) ignore, or regard as secondary, materialist-based explanations for the broad nature and precise forms of consumption such as the development of the modern sales effort, the 'dream work' and 'encoding' of meanings done for consumers, the particular placing of specific commodities and activities within the ideological spaces provided by broad 'ethics' etc.;

(vi) disregard structural changes in society which may have altered the nature of 'communities' or significant reference groups and so may have changed the social locations within which individuals seek and confirm self-regard and personal identity;

(vii) limit the conceptualisation of the nature of modern consumerism to 'autonomous, self-illusory, hedonism', a definition which fits his thesis but which appears to exclude quantitatively and qualitatively important aspects of modern consumption.

I believe that all these assumptions are questionable and that if consumption and its weight in modern life is to be understood, what is required is attention to specific activities and special objects and the precise ways these are organised and legitimated.

Campbell's concentration on 'restless consumption', 'the ceaseless consumption of novelty' with its 'dynamic disacquiring nature' is much more applicable to certain forms of individual, privatised, consumption goods – clothes, drugs, records, etc. – exactly the items which, as I have already indicated, tend to attract the cultural studies school – than to the widespread use of other objects. Campbell specifically excludes the purchase of house and car from his analysis and this shows his unease with goods which are, or which can be, aligned with effort, anxiety, achievement and direct experience. For Campbell actual contact with objects of desire, attempts to realise 'dreams', are doomed because 'reality-pleasure will not live up to the expectations which the experience of dream-pleasure has created'.[26] For:

> The central insight required is the realization that individuals do not so much seek satisfaction from products as pleasure from the self-illusory experiences which they construct from their associated meanings. The essential activity of consumption is thus not the actual selection, purchase or use of products, but the imaginative pleasure-seeking to which the product image lends itself, 'real' consumption being largely a resultant of this 'mentalistic' hedonism.[27]

He does note that there could be what he calls 'traditional hedonism' which is 'another path' to pleasure, though he seems to believe this is an route found mainly in 'traditional' societies:

> This is to pursue pleasure as it manifests itself as an accompaniment of intensive or fateful activity. Action constitutes its own stimulus through its general arousal effect on the body, and if it is associated with events which pose an element of risk, uncertainty or danger, there will be the added element of emotional arousal as well. Hunting is the classic elite activity which can provide pleasure from these sources, but fighting (whether in earnest or play) is another possibility. The overwhelming problem here for the hedonist is the inherent difficulty of concentrating upon the element of pleasure. The exigencies of action demand that the focus of attention is upon the immediate task in hand, especially if real dangers exist (and yet without them, arousal is diminished). Any awareness of pleasure is thus likely to be retrospective or, of course, anticipatory, rather than a concomitant of the experience itself. There is, in addition, the very real disadvantage that pursuing primary pleasure through 'action' of this kind is to seriously endanger one's level of 'satisfaction', exposing oneself to the potential 'pains' of injury, hardship, discomfort or death. Finally, here too, the activity concerned is usually highly significant for the attribution of status and thus the need for prestige works to impose stoicism upon any hedonistic tendencies.[28]

But I believe we can see, if we think of the many uses of cars and the views of Lefebvre, that the complicated nexus of issues around consumption and pleasure in modern society – consider any sporting activity – are being quite simplified here, as with Adorno's radio ham, the better to allow Campbell to concentrate on *an* aspect of modern consumption, the *one* which he finds most interesting. For Campbell: 'It is this highly rationalized form of self-illusory hedonism which characterizes modern pleasure-seeking'[29] which is where pleasure occurs as illusion, by activity in the imagination and not through, in, or around activity with actual projects or commodities. My argument is not that such consumption activities do not exist and are not of significance but this limitation allows Campbell to concentrate on a particular cycle of fantasy–purchase–use–disillusion–renewed desire, and does *not* allow for the working out (or dreaming out) of long-term projects or plans via acting on and with commodities. Such projects and such commodities may well not issue from the bohemian milieux which Campbell, and others, regard as the 'research laboratory' for modern consumption or, at the least, it requires some extension of 'the bohemian' to go well beyond beats and hippies and to include those involved in promoting action, not just the supply of cultural products. So while Campbell's is a most important effort to explain consumption activity I think it is partial and limited as I hope I will indicate throughout this text.

Modelling the enthusiasm

Hot rodding appears to be the type of what Campbell calls 'traditional hedonism' but which he regards (I think he is ambiguous here) as either historically located or as marginal to modern life and so modern consumption. I do not find Campbell's discussion of this type of pleasure seeking at all convincing, nor would Lefebvre, and I do regard such enthusiasms as important elements in modern consumption. However, to trace the connections between, and who makes the connections between, broad cultural imperatives and the varied use of objects and commodities like the car we require some model of what I am calling an enthusiasm.

I use the term enthusiasm[30] to denote a field of interest in people's lives. As I have already suggested I think the issue in modern capitalism I am trying to investigate here has been dealt with before using three main models:

(i) mass society – here a relatively undifferentiated population of individuals are persuaded into activity or consumption by mass advertising or a sales effort which are asserted to operate 'at the centre';

(ii) subcultures – here a quite differentiated group within the general population is asserted to share 'a whole way of life' which they have either created or created from the bric-a-brac passed down in (i). Their 'focal concerns' can be picked up, stripped down, incorporated and spread to others as 'style' or fashion as in (i);

(iii) leisure pioneers – this combines the previous two. A group is the core of a subculture as in (ii), but they act as leisure pioneers for an interested mass who consume the symbols of the subculture but are not involved in its main concerns. The subcultural group create magazines, slang, stickers, styles, etc. which they pass on, or help pass on, to an outward layer of passive consumers who adopt a prepackaged 'popular' culture as style.

This third model, with its focus on core and peripheral layers, is more sociologically adequate than the others, yet requires further development since the structure of most interests is likely to be rather more complex than it assumes and because of the need to take into account a dynamic element of process and interaction between the various layers.

I suggest that it would be better to conceptualise what I will call an enthusiasm in the following way. First, there is a core of professionals and amateur enthusiasts. The professionals will be all those who make a living from the enthusiasm. In this book this group and their interests will referred to as *the hot rod economy*. It includes paid practitioners of the core activities, but also the 'experts' of the enthusiasm of all kinds – administrators, officals, promoters, suppliers, dealers, writers. Those in the economy who own, control or have access to the means of communication of the enthusiasm are the intellectuals of the enthusiasm, the local culture industry, or what I will also refer to as *the hot rod apparatus*. *Amateur enthusiasts* have a great involvement with the focal concerns (and may uphold these against 'mere money-making'). They attend events, have great knowledge about and practise the skills of the enthusiasm. They can constrain and stimulate the professional group in the core. Then there is a layer of *the interested public*, a heterogenous group consisting of dabblers in the focal concerns, mere consumers of symbols, novices and new entrants, state bodies concerned with control, big businessmen seeking opportunities, the mass media looking for stories and so on. To this we must add a notion of process since

22

individuals move in and out of various categories and mere consumers may believe they once were committed to the focal concerns or still are at certain moments. Certainly all the individuals in the interested public will have, or appear to have, more knowledge or involvement, than *the general public* (the true 'mass' in relation to any specific enthusiasm). As we shall see it is likely that one function of the two-step model of communication of media messages is to allow certain groups in the population to gain status and identity by serving local areas or the mass public as 'experts' or 'consultants' in their field and this is well understood by the apparatus of the sales effort. This is the conceptual scheme I will use to try to uncover and discuss the economic, social and cultural ramifications of drag racing and the hot rod enthusiasm.

In this chapter I have argued that the car has been woefully neglected outside the moment of its production and that some of the areas of social analysis that purport to analyse leisure and consumption are far too generalised to encompass some of the important aspects of the activities concerned in the ways cars and other commodities are used. Social analysis has to attend to the empirical examination of particular forms or types of the provision and use of commodities if the actual social weight of consumption is to be measured. Modes of consumption have to be constructed just as modes of production have been, and modes of consumption require as careful a study as modes of production have received. In this text I cannot hope to detail all the ways that automobile sports and enthusiasms not only link into consumption but provide meaning and ideologies. I cannot hope to supply that 'erudite essay' that Steinbeck asked for and it is, of course, far too big a task for one person, but this book is designed to stand with just a few others which try to drive towards an empirically based understanding of the cultural impact of the car on modern life and popular thought. In that spirit of discovery I will begin my investigation by outlining the structures of the early hot rod sports.

Notes

1 J. Steinbeck, *Cannery Row* (New York, 1945), pp. 56–7.
2 M. Adelman, 'Neglected sports in American history: the rise of billiards in New York City', *Canadian Journal of the History of Sport*, 12, 1981, p. 28.
3 N. Elias and E. Dunning, *Quest For Excitement; Sport and Leisure in the Civilizing Process* (Oxford, 1986).
4 R. D. Mandell, *Sport, A Cultural History* (New York, 1984), p. xvii.
5 H. F. Moorhouse, 'Models of work, models of leisure', in C. Rojek (ed.), *Leisure for Leisure: Critical Essays* (London, 1989), pp. 15–35.

6 D. Hebdige, *Subculture: The Meaning of Style* (London, 1979), p. 139.
7 P. Willis, *Profane Culture* (London, 1978), p. 175.
8 The most important for me are A. S. Wolfe, *Vans and Vanners* (Greatlakes Living Press Illinois, 1976). C. G. Dettelbach, *In the Driver's Seat: The Automobile in American Literature and Popular Culture* (London, 1977). W. D. Dannefer, *The Social World of Old Cars*, Ph. D. thesis (Rutgers University, 1977). J. P. Viken, *The Sport of Drag Racing and the Search for Satisfaction Meaning and Self*, Ph. D. thesis (University of Minnesota, 1978). W. J. Belasco, *Americans On the Road: From Autocamp to Motel 1910–1945* (London, 1979). D. L. Lewis, 'The automobile and American culture', Special Issue, *Michigan Quarterly Review*, 19–20, 1981, pp. 434–781.
9 P. Marsh and P. Collett, *Driving Passions: The Psychology of the Car* (London, 1986).
10 T. Adorno, *Minima Moralia: Reflections From Damaged Life* (London, 1974), p. 40 and see pp. 119–20.
11 H. Marcuse, *One Dimensional Man; The Ideology of Industrial Society* (London, 1964), p. 179 and p. 24.
12 D. Dodd, 'Swing low sweet Cadillac', *New Society*, 26, 25 October 1973, pp. 199–202. R. Yoshino, 'The stereotype of the negro and his high-priced car', *Sociology and Social Research* 48, 1959, pp. 112–18.
13 T. Adorno in A. Arato and E. Gebhardt (eds.), *The Essential Frankfurt School Reader* (Oxford, 1978), pp. 291–3.
14 R. Butsch, 'The commodification of leisure: the case of the model airplane hobby and industry' in V. Mosco and J. Wasko (eds.), *Popular Culture and Media Events* (Norwood, New Jersey, 1985).
15 R. Lane, *Political Ideology* (New York, 1962), p. 290.
16 H. Lefebvre, *Everyday Life in the Modern World* (London, 1971), p. 100.
17 Lefebvre, *Everyday Life*, p. 101.
18 Lefebvre, *Everyday Life*, p. 102.
19 Lefebvre, *Everyday Life*, p. 103.
20 J. A. Mangan, *Athleticism in the Victorian and Edwardian Public School; The Emergence and Consolidation of an Educational Ideology* (Cambridge, 1981); J. A. Mangan, *The Games Ethic and Imperialism; Aspects of the Diffusion of an Ideal* (London, 1986).
21 C. Wright Mills, 'The cultural apparatus' in I. L. Horowitz (ed.), *Power, Politics and People; Collected Essays of C. Wright Mills* (New York, 1963), p. 406.
22 H. F. Moorhouse, 'American automobiles and workers' dreams', *Sociological Review*, 31, 1983, pp. 403–26; H. F. Moorhouse, 'Organizing the hot rods', *British Journal of Sports History*, 3, 1986, pp. 81–98; H. F. Moorhouse, 'Racing for a sign: defining the "hot rod" 1945–1960', *Journal of Popular Culture*, 20, 1986, pp. 67–84; H. F. Moorhouse, 'The "work" ethic and "leisure" activity: the case of the hot rod', in P. Joyce (ed.), *The Historical Meanings of Work* (Cambridge, 1987), pp. 237–57.
23 C. Campbell, *The Romantic Ethic and The Spirit of Modern Consumerism* (Oxford, 1987).
24 Campbell, *The Romantic Ethic*, p. 61.
25 Campbell, *The Romantic Ethic*, p. 9.
26 Campbell, *The Romantic Ethic*, p. 246.
27 Campbell, *The Romantic Ethic*, p. 89.
28 Campbell, *The Romantic Ethic*, p. 67–8.

29 Campbell, *The Romantic Ethic*, p. 76.
30 Compare with R. A. Stebbins, *Amateurs: On the Margin Between Work and Leisure* (London, 1979), pp. 19–46.

B

Chapter Two
The early hot rod sports: the lakes and the streets

Come along to a Lakes meet. Out through Newhall, Saugus and Mint Canyon, or Victorville and Barstow; and onto the Mojave, five thousand cars of every description are wooshing by, making the walls of Mint Canyon reverberate like a tom-tom. Most of the cars carry spectators lucky enough to know about the Lakes meet. There have been as many as 20,000 people lining the course, but they are not wanted, and the meets are kept as secret as possible. The night before a Lakes meet, boys begin to gather early. Zero hour is twelve midnight. Racing starts with the first streak of light over the desert, since by noon it will be 120 in the shade . . . in the pitch blackness before dawn, cars are lined up for miles waiting for enough light to signal the start of the test runs.[1]

The lakes

The topography of Southern California includes a number of stretches of arid desert, the dry, dusty beds of long-vanished lakes. People began running automobiles on these from the 1920s. In summer the baked flat tops were ideal for speed contests, while the winter rain covered them in a shallow sheet of water which moved in the wind to refinish the floor and level the surface to billiard table standard. These dry lakes were around a hundred miles from Los Angeles and many miles from any paved road or town but such remoteness commended itself to the early enthusiasts who used these wide open spaces – the favourite, Muroc Dry Lake, was 10 miles wide and 22 miles long – to push their cars to very high speeds.

The earliest meets were spontaneous gatherings so that sometimes few turned up while at others thousands appeared to watch the racers. These were 'run what you brung' contests. A quick question: 'what'll she do?' or a preliminary run measured by rudimentary timing devices served to divide participants up into rough speed classes and then up to twenty cars would line up and, marshalled by a pace car, race for miles over the alkaline surface. It was prudent to be at the front of this mechanical charge for dust ensured that 'It was quite a sensation to sit there knowing there were cars running at high speeds all around you and not being able to see them.'[2] There were no rules, officials, committees or safety regulations. There was little control over cars or spectators. Some 'night tuners' ran across the lakes at high speed in the pitch dark practising or chasing coyotes. There were lots of accidents and some deaths. It appears that the state authorities began to worry about this and/or that such 'anarchy' had an economic cost. For by the 1930s a distinct set of speed shops had developed around the Los Angeles area to supply the demand for special parts. Bulletin boards in these shops spread the word about lake events. The sponsorship of such shops and that of oil companies and the like was offered to the lake meets if participants would agree to basic regulation.

The first meeting held under some kind of central organisation took place in 1931 and these races drew entries in the hundreds and crowds of up to ten thousand. Pictures taken at the lakes in 1933 show crude advertisments painted on some cars for speed shops and accessory dealers.[3] At some point local clubs of enthusiasts were formed: the Road Runners, Velociteers, Gophers, Sidewinders, Albata, Gear Grinders, the all-negro Centuries and the like. Worried by the continuing accidents and lack of firm control, some of these clubs banded together to form a few timing associations. The most influential, the Southern California Timing Association (SCTA), was established in 1937.

This grouping sought to organise activities on the lakes by such actions as:

(i) banning some types of car as dangerous;
(ii) forming technical committees to examine all cars before they raced;
(iii) looking for new and better areas to race on;
(iv) controlling spectators, vehicle parking etc.;
(v) gradually making single car racing against the clock the normal activity as speeds and so dust rose;
(vi) urging its members to co-operate with the police and Highway Patrol and avoid traffic citations.

It also tried to regularise competition by awarding points for places in races which served as the basis for summer-long individual and club rivalries, with prizes and titles awarded at the end of the season. It wrestled with what was to become a perennial problem for the hot rod

27

sports: the definition of appropriate classes for competition. The *SCTA Racing News and Program* for August 1941 indicates that at that time there were four classes based on body types and minimum speeds: roadster (or stock), modified, streamliner and unlimited.[4] Competition classes changed all the time and in the winter months the representatives of the constituent clubs would meet with SCTA officials to discuss the safety rules and changes in the basis for classes. The SCTA preferred roadster (i.e. open topped) bodies and voted to refuse to accept coupes or sedans on the grounds that anyone who wanted to run in their races could buy a roadster body for under $10. The other main pre-war organisation, the Russetta Timing Association (RTA), catered for these other body types.

By 1941 the course involved a three-mile stretch to gain full speed, a timing trap of a quarter of a mile through which the miles per hour was recorded on highly accurate electrical devices perfected by the enthusiasts, and a further three-mile run in which to slow down. Prizes for winning a race or setting a speed record in a class were minimal: a case of oil, a three-dollar merchandise order or similar. After the racing there was the long journey back to Los Angeles where cars were often left covered in the sheet of fine, talcum-powder-like dust which was something of a status symbol amongst the youth of Southern California.

Activities on the lakes ceased with the advent of war. Many racers were drafted, with over 80% of the members of the SCTA joining the armed forces. There was rationing of gasoline. The military took over Muroc Dry Lake. At the end of the war the SCTA consisted of fifteen clubs, eighty-eight active members and $545 in the bank.[5] As the war restrictions ended, enthusiasts returned to the lakes and one association's meet was recorded in a *Life* pictorial in November 1945 which informed it's readers: 'A "hot rod", also called a "hot iron" or a "hop up" or "gow job", is an automobile stripped for speed and pepped-up for power until it can travel from 90 to 125 mph.'[6] For the term 'hot rod' was not well known to the American public and the activity was arcane. In 1947 when *Fortune* magazine surveyed automobile racing in the USA it dwelt on the 'speedway style' of dirt track and Indianapolis-style contests around circular raceways which had become the major American forms of auto-sport in contrast to European-style 'road racing' around irregular courses with sharp turns which had never really caught on in the USA. These were major professional sports and the winners of big events could pick up prizes of several thousands of dollars. The article also mentioned the new midget racing which had quickly become very popular and then made a throwaway reference to the dry lake timing events as a form of competition for the amateur racer.[7] These contests of the lake enthusiasts formed one root of modern drag racing. The other was found in the illegal activity of racing in the streets.

The streets

Illegal contests in automobiles on public highways are one of the subterranean elements in American popular culture and American sport. Such activities have been condemned and hymned over the years in various elements of the mass media but have hardly been recorded, let alone studied, by academic observers. Thus, while many people know 'it happens', its extent, forms and traditions are largely unknown. Yet as I hope to indicate in this book, utilizing the documentation that has been done through the years, this illegal sport was to have a continuous effect on the increasingly organised and official world of hot rodding.

Street racing certainly has a long history. In Los Angeles in 1913 115 juveniles were arrested for what was called 'joy riding',[8] while in his study of boys in the same city in the mid-1920s Bogardus commented ruefully about auto theft: 'The automobile is the undoing of many a boy'.[9] As ownership spread among the population, especially with the ready availability of cheap second-hand cars, it appears that illegal sports associated with driving automobiles increased in extent. In 1941 *Colliers* magazine noted:

Three years ago, in Los Angeles, quiet residential districts were being invaded by wild-eyed kids in hopped-up jalopies. Up and down the streets, stripped cars raced at dizzy breakneck speeds . . . The arrival of the police only added to the hazards. At the first sound of the siren cars darted into side streets in all directions, whipping around blind corners on two wheels. The resulting traffic accidents made the public, the press and the law loudly vocal in condemning the menace.[10]

Like many a similar article that was to follow in the news magazines of middle-America the *Colliers* piece claimed this menace had now disappeared and had been incorporated, in this case, into the regularised activities on the dry lakes discussed earlier. In fact the illegal form of automobile competition lived on and on. Street racing is a sport that will not die.

Moreover, participation in formalised automobile sport, of whatever kind, was never to mean non-participation in the informal activity. Lexicographers investigating speech on the Pasadena drag strip in the early 1950s found a number of terms: 'traffic light grand prix', 'five dollars a gear' etc. which referred to the rituals of the illegal sport.[11] In later decades, when the hot rod economy was quite secure, admitting to being a street racer when young was almost an obligatory aspect of being a star of the world of drag racing and many of these had been office-holders in the various timing associations. Veterans of the dry lakes and early drag strips looked back in nostalgia to give some flavour of the street sport of the 1940s including the 'awesome early mornings along Lincoln Boulevard' where up to five hundred roadsters would show up to race. Lou Baney, ex-President of the RTA, remembered: 'we all did a little street racing on the side. We'd take our lakes machines, after we put the headlights and fenders back on, and gather down at The Picadilly at Washington and Sepulveda in West LA. We'd race either on Culver Boulevard or in the Sepulveda Pass up by the resevoir.'[12]

Mickey Thompson recalled getting 'rumbustious on the streets' as follows:

> During the rainy season there was no racing at the lakes and that was when street racing was at its awful height. I was not one of the wild ones who itched to burn rubber any place, any time. I was careful where I ran and with whom. The place had to be as safe as possible from the standpoints of ourselves, the public and the police. I wouldn't run with the irresponsible squirrels and I wouldn't run with too large a group. Both spelled quick, bad trouble. One of our favourite spots was Fifth Avenue in the settlement of La Puente. In spite of its citified-sounding name it was just a narrow back road way out in remote citrus farming country. It had about a one-mile straightaway and there were only a couple of farmers on that stretch to complain to the police. We'd usually have cleared out of the area before the police arrived. The procedure usually went like this. We would meet a group of other rodders at a drive-in res-taurant and start discussing who could beat who. Guys whose cars were pretty evenly matched would choose each other off and then very quietly – because no one wanted a crowd – would arrange to meet at the usual spot in Puente that night. If I liked the setup I'd include us in at the rendezvous and we'd park someone's car across the road at each end of the straight and the battle was on.[13]

An interview with Dean Moon, veteran of the RTA, recorded:

> After World War II Moon moved his informal sales office to the informal parking lot of the Hula Hut in nearby Whittier . . . The Hut was one of the scores of Southern Californian drive-ins where hot rodders hung out. He sat there each evening in his all conquering '27 T roadster with other members of the Hutters, the car club he was president of, selling parts and waiting for hot cars from another drive-in – any drive-in – to roar in and challenge them. When they did, the rest was simple: race out to Yorba Linda or Placentina, little more than orange groves then, and drag up and down Imperial

Highway. Until the cops chased them away. If the challenge didn't come to them, they took it across town to Hollywood or Santa Monica, to the first drive-in with a collection of roadsters and street rods in the parking lot and they raced on La Cienega or Sunset or anywhere the cops weren't.[14]

Ak. Miller remembered: 'Most of my contemporaries thought street racing was bitchin', the biggest thrill in the world.' They raced for bets of $50 to $100. He claimed that purists carried out timed runs on the wide open streets of California and created a makeshift drag strip on the street of La Puente Boulevard with a marked quarter mile and a battery operated timing machine.[15]

Don Garlits from Florida recalled timing runs on little used roads around Tampa in 1950 and: 'Every night we were on the road, racing at stop lights, hanging around cheap joints until all hours of the night, driving across the Causeway to St. Peterburg to see if we couldn't rouse a little trouble with the guys over there.'[16]

Certainly, from the early 1940s wild teenage drivers became defined as a major social problem in California and, soon, in the rest of the USA. Even private eye Philip Marlowe driving along Ventura Boulevard could not avoid them as one element in general urban alienation:

> There was nothing lonely about the trip. There never is on that road. Fast boys in stripped-down Fords shot in and out of the traffic streams, missing fenders by a sixteenth of an inch, but somehow always missing them. Tired men in dusty coupes and sedans winced and tightened their grip on the wheel and ploughed on north and west towards home and dinner, an evening with the sports page, the blatting of the radio, the whining of their spoiled children and the gabble of their silly wives.[17]

A piece in *Colliers* in 1947 described the situation in war-time thus:

> There were only 'bench races' at first, meetings at drive-in eating places where the kids with hop-ups sat around and argued about speed records and cars, but these settled nothing. And then someone got the idea that it would be alright to stage a race on a wide boulevard, late at night in some out-of-the-way spot, providing all the side streets were blocked off. Somehow the kids managed to get fuel for their hop-ups. It was not always gas. Sometimes it was cleaning fluid, often it was a combination of wood alcohol and cleaning solvent or some other weird mixture with a dash of benzine to prevent burning out valves. There were a number of these meets before the police and public became alarmed. The kids called them 'drags' or 'drag meets'. The time and the place were kept secret by leaders until the very last moment. In the first round-up, traffic officers, police and county deputies managed to nab 75 young culprits. There were many more, but they got away leaving behind only the faint smell of burnt castor oil and benzine. The police could do

nothing about the spectators, though some officials felt that attending an automobile race in the public streets was at least as censurable as watching a cockfight in some dingy underground basement. All through the war these drag meets continued. The police broke them up, but they were never wholly suppressed.[18]

Because of the post-war panic about street racers there were moves in California to introduce state laws to curtail all hot rodding activity and to limit the right to develop the power potential of cars. Veterans reinstituted lake meets, in part, to present a sober alternative to street racing but there were difficulties with this. Muroc had been converted into a major airforce base (space shuttles now land where the earliest rodders ran) and they had to use similar but less suitable spots. El Mirage Dry Lake became the most favoured though it was a good deal smaller than Muroc, higher and so less suitable for the exertions of engines, and quite as remote, lying many miles off the highway along a bumpy desert track, the 'washboard' as it was called, with just one sign stencilled on the side of a water tank to act as direction. Runs prior and post the timing traps had to be cut to one and a half miles. Still, the races were bigger and better than ever with *Colliers* in 1947 reporting five hundred entries for a meet and tens of thousands of spectators. Each entrant in a SCTA meet was given a brass plate engraved with their name and data concerning the time trial. A photograph of the SCTA trophies awarded for the 1946 time trials shows lots of small model roadsters set on pedestals and five big cups to be awarded for points earned throughout the season: 'First place trophies are gold finished, second place silver, third, fourth and fifth place, bronze.'[19]

There was a big boom in lake activities in the post-war period with new timing associations: Bell (1948) and Valley (1949) being formed which combined new clubs and held their own meets. Valley members had to travel around four hundred miles each way to run at El Mirage but by 1951 this timing association consisted of twelve clubs. Russetta was the largest of all, with twenty-three clubs by 1951, with a typical club, the Screwdrivers of Culver City, for example, having twenty nine members who met each Monday night. In each association each club would be allocated various duties at the lakes like setting up the course by laying out cones or clearing up the debris after the runs.[20] Safety committees and technical committees had to adjudicate on arguments about whether a car was running in the correct class or not. War surplus fuel holders for aircraft, 'belly tanks', were pressed into service as new type of chassis for hot rods to provide a primitive form of 'streamlining' and established the basis of a new 'lakester' class. In 1947 the SCTA introduced a new system of competition classes. All cars would now be classified as either roadsters or streamliners and each body type would be divided into four categories according to engine displacement with, for example, category D being 350 cubic inches and over.

There was a brittle tension in this coalescence of activities and, indeed, sports. In post-war America the term 'hot rod' came to be used to refer to a highly visible, relatively affluent, teenage lifestyle which seemed to turn on drive-ins, noise, jalopies held together with chewing gum and dangerous driving on public highways. But 'hot rod' was also a term used to refer to a specialised pursuit of, often, older men (especially the returning ex-servicemen) involved in a much less obtrusive, technical and achievement oriented sport carried out on the dazzling white surfaces of the remote Californian desert. The timing associations had long realised the danger posed to them by traffic offences. They had rules which laid down penalties for any members arrested for dangerous driving on public streets which ranged from a week's suspension from activities for a first offence to dismissal from the association for persistent offenders. This group felt threatened by continuing sensationalised mass media presentations which quickly equated 'hot rodder' and street racing as in this *Time* piece of 26 September 1949:

> The word was relayed through the drive-ins, malt shops and garages speckling the Los Angeles suburbs. 'Tonight Sepulveda and Hawthorne'. By 10.00pm 100 hopped-up jalopies and denuded low slung hot rods had gathered at a mile and a half stretch of straight highway between suburban Torrance and Redondo beach. Lookouts were posted along both sides of the straightaway, flashlights ready to blink at the first sight of the police. The first few cars took off with a roar, sped down the highway at 60, 70, 100 miles an hour. They ripped along two abreast, made oncoming motorists scurry to the side of the road. The boulevard's residents took one frightened look and telephoned the police. Six squad cars sirened into the boulevard. The speedsters roared away in all directions, careering through side streets and bumping across empty fields with crashing gears and wide open throttles. As usual, police caught only a handful.

Or as in *Life* the same year: 'In Los Angeles and Dallas, where hot rodding is at its peak, hundreds of youngsters spend their time in suicidal games on wheels', a story which went on to count the human and the financial costs:

> On the open highways and in the crowded suburbs of the US teenagers and their post-graduate friends have been killing themselves in jalopies with

sickening regularity ever since 1932. But in the past year the problem has suddenly become worse. 'Hot rod' clubs have sprung up everywhere. In the 18–25 age range the number of accidents per capita is twice the normal. Insurance companies, scanning this phenomena, have had to increase rates substantially for any car – including the family sedan – driven by anyone in this age group.

This piece purported to reveal, through a series of staged photographs, six games which American teenagers played on wheels and which could lead to death. Drag racing was one. In 'chicken', a car load of people accelerated up to 70 mph, the driver removed his hand from the wheel and the first to grab it lost status. There was a variant of this in which drivers drove towards each other, front wheels on the white centre line. The first to veer away lost. In 'rotation', at speeds of up to 60 mph, the driver climbed out of his door, round the car and into the back, while those in back seats moved to the front. 'Pedestrian polo' had an objective summed as: 'just brush 'em don't hit 'em', while 'crinkle fender' involved manoeuvring at speed behind another car and just denting it rather than smashing into it. Evidence from other observers, in other areas, at other times, reveals that similar competitive, informal, automobile games were played elsewhere, though the *Life* list by no means exhausted the possibilities of illegal competitive contests in cars.[21]

Across the continent state officials began to link hot rods and a high death rate among youngsters in automobile accidents. In 1947 *Colliers* had summarised the views of the Deputy Chief of the Los Angeles City Traffic Bureau who

> considers hop-ups an out and out tangible nuisance. He feels the situation calls for more stringent legislation. At present there is no big stick the harrasssed authorities can use to put hop-ups out of circulation on city streets. Street racing, Chief Caldwell feels, should be made punishable by arrest and physical custody like drunken driving. Spectators of street racing should be considered partners in the offence. . . . In attempting to solve the problem Chief Caldwell suggests a twofold approach: (i) to find a constructive substitute, and (ii) stricter law enforcement with an emphasis on lack of fenders, mufflers and bumpers.

While in December 1947 a representative of the National Safety Council in Los Angeles announced that his aim was to ban all automobile racing in California. In 1949 on the shore of the other shining sea the Director of the New York State Division of Safety warned parents to increase their vigilance over 'teenage thrill seekers' so as to curb a 'speed epidemic' and declared:

The early hot rod sports

Possession of the 'hot rod' car is presumptive evidence of an intent to speed. Speed is Public Enemy No. 1 of the highways. It is obvious that driver of a 'hot rod' car has an irresistible temptation to 'step on it' and accordingly operate the vehicle in a reckless manner endangering human life. It also shows a deliberate and premeditated idea to violate the law. These vehicles are largely improvised by home mechanics and are capable of high speed and dangerous manoeuverability. They have therefore become a serious menace to the safe movement of traffic. The operators of these cars are confused into believing that driving is a competitive sport. They have a feeling of superiority in recklessly darting in and out of traffic in their attempt to outspeed other cars on the road.[22]

That same year a National Conference on High School Driver Education was told by an official from Nebraska that bumper-bumping games of tag on Midwest highways were a new danger to all drivers: 'Thousands of accidents can be traced to this cause, while there are about as many thousands of miraculous escapes.'[23] At this period a new word – 'teenicide' – was coined to describe a proclivity for automobile deaths among the young.

Young people certainly were involved in far more than their share of accidents. The National Safety Council noted: 'For the year 1949 there were 1, 400 youths under the age of 18 involved in fatal accidents in 28 states, and 450,000 in all types of accidents in 26 states.' While in California itself:

159,500 youths under 18 were licensed to drive
=2.9% of all licence holders
=4.8% of those involved in injury accidents
=4.6% of those involved in fatal accidents
=6.5% of those involved in property damage accidents.[24]

In July 1950 the *New York Times* reported: 'New Rochelle Opens a Campaign Against Teen Age "Hot Rod" Cars' where a Judge, commenting on the death of a youth, said the whole situation was rotten and that investigation of crazy driving in the area had: 'led to the detection of gangs of "hot rod" operators'. His proposed crackdown included enforcing zoning laws about where cars could be garaged, calling gas station proprietors who had helped in modifications to appear before the court and threatening to prosecute the owner of the ice-cream parlour where the boys gathered. In September police in the Westchester area set up a 'dawn patrol' to trap teenagers who had been racing on highways, twisting round trees oblivious of pedestrians or other road users and soon a 'Westchester War on Hot Rod Boys' was announced with the magistrates' association, state youth council, the Westchester Recreation Commission, the New York Automobile Club, the police and others united in 'A campaign to take "hot rod" drivers, "jalopy jerks" and other careless youth off the Westchester highways.' In Los Angeles at the same time some police were equipped with 'souped up patrol cars' capable of doing 90mph in second gear so that they could match the teenagers who had been racing on the highways.[25]

Hot Rod magazine

Given the media furore generated by street sports and the frequent linkage made to 'hot rods', the Californian lake enthusiasts feared that state action against the careless teenagers could curtail their own rather serious and all-American activity. They wanted to offer the lakes as a sober alternative to street racing. They held meetings with the police, civic officials, parent–teachers associations and so on, and a magazine – *Hot Rod* – was set up, in good part, as a voice for respectable rodding. The publication was something of a simple development out of the mimeographed sheets and bulletins that many of the associations had produced for their memberships. It appears that there was hot rod magazine – *Throttle* – in the Los Angeles area before the war but that it had not been very successful.

The first issue of *Hot Rod* in January 1948, with an initial print run of 5,000 copies, contained, among various technical articles, mechanical advice, etc. , an article on the last SCTA meeting of the season (reporting four thousand spectators), a long poem, 'His Car Was Hot' (reprinted in the eighth issue) complaining about the mass media's (mis)use of the term 'hot rod' in their lurid stories of teenicide:

> When the car was really 'junk'
> And the driver just a punk
> Only 17 or 18 summers old.

plus an article boosting the first ever public exhibition of true hot rods which stressed its links with a safety campaign and the general respectability of hot rodding as 'a healthy beneficial avocation for thousands of motor enthusiasts, not a screwball diversion for a lot of reckless kids with more nerve than brain'.

This set the tone of the early issues. There were some articles on other activities which might be called 'hot rodding' – oval track racing and improving a car's appearance – but activity on the lakes was very much to the fore with pages of results, timings and league standings, and features such as the evocative photo-essay 'El Mirage Before Dawn' with its parked vehicles and sleepy drivers out in the high desert waiting for the sunrise.[26] The presentation of the activity was serious but innocent. When a reader in Pasadena wrote to the magazine in October 1948 asking for maps or directions to the areas of the lakes where the SCTA trials took place the reply ran: 'Hot Rod Magazine does not have a map of lake directions but a spectator has only to go to Palmdale between Friday night and Sunday on timing dates and follow the first roadster heading east.' However, as circulation rose sharply, up to 40, 000 copies a month by issue 10, it was clearly selling well beyond the few thousand people who could be regarded as serious hot rodders. Indeed, as its Californian sales points included a number close to the gates of various Los Angeles high schools and as its sales spread across the nation, the magazine was, probably, being read more by those teenagers who wanted to cut a dash and made a noise by fitting cut-out silencers or 'supercharger' pipes and who street raced, than it was by lake enthusiasts. The rapid acceleration in sales carried the magazine well beyond its basic constituency.

This in part created, in part emphasised, several problems incipient in the dry lake sport in the late 1940s. To begin with, this activity and the associated network of commercial interests (of which the magazine soon became one) were threatened by the non-specialist media's presentation of 'hot rodding' and the term's association with street accidents and the consequent constant threat of legal curbs and restrictions. The New Rochelle judge, for example, had ordered all 'hot rod vehicles' to be impounded and sold for junk.[27] Fear of state action against 'hot' cars was to be a constant worry for the hot rod apparatus.

Then the magazine's success highlighted the fact that the dry lakes were a geographically localised phenomenon. In most of the USA it was quite difficult to offer an alternative to street racing. Smart appearance could be promoted, but writing about speeding on the lakes to youth living in New York or Florida was to hold out a dream impossible to fulfil. Even in California the lakes presented difficulties if the numbers in the sport expanded: they were far from large centres of population, were susceptible to adverse wind and weather and were, anyway, unusuable for around half the year. Even in summer they were vulnerable to increased use. The beds which had served a few hundred drivers and a few thousand spectators cracked as the number of clubs increased, as new timing associations formed, as the number of days of racing expanded and as speeds rose. The reports of the various timing associations on their meets began to make constant references to the physical deterioration of the lakes as in, for example, the SCTA and RTA reports of early 1951 which began: 'It's plowing time again'.[28]. The surface of the serious sport could not sustain the increased involvement which the magazine both represented and sought to stimulate.

By March 1949 the periodical was ruminating on just this matter:

> At one time there was a good deal of talk about building a strip somewhere close in, near LA, where a large percentage of the membership lives. However it has come to be realised that the desert and out-of-town atmosphere is as much a part of the lakes meetings as the timings itself . . . A reminder to members and non-members alike: please do not go to the lakes before the meets. Considerable damage can be caused by irresponsible use of the dry lakes.

The lakes' physical decline was accentuated since greater interest led to more commercial sponsorship. Increasingly some cars were closely linked to speed shops and garages.[29] This had two effects. First, increased technical innovation and new fuels meant higher speeds which further disturbed the lake surfaces. In 1939 only twenty nine cars throughout the entire season exceeded 100 mph. By 1948 practically all competitors were able to go over that mark and the average speed was around 130 mph. In early 1952 another hot rod magazine, *Hop Up*, noted that before the war the record roadster speed was 123 mph and that for streamliners 140 mph: 'Now a roadster (even in the small displacement class) has to turn 120 mph or better to make points. Several stock body roadsters have passed the 150 mph mark . . . Three cars (two lakesters, one streamliner) have exceeded 180 mph at El Mirage.'[30] Second, the rapid development of what was, in effect, a group of semi-professionals meant that the amateur who tried to compete on the lakes in the 'old' way was doomed to failure. Lake cars became highly specialised vehicles. Set ups and alignments for gears and steering appropriate for the dry lake racing made for hard going in town traffic. One record-holding car of the early 1950s ran for only 36 minutes all year. It was towed to and from events. In 1947 an average SCTA meeting attracted 235 entries, 90 per cent of which were driven to the lakes and back and used normal petrol. By 1952 such an event had only 68 entries, 95 per cent of which were towed to and fro, and used special fuels. In the same period the number and sales of the speed shops boomed.[31]

These two new factors, which in one sense represented measures of the sport's success, actually fuelled a steady sense of crisis in the hot rod apparatus from the late 1940s. To counter bad publicity and the effects this might have on the sport and the burgeoning economic interests the apparatus aimed at incorporating street racers into the serious activity. In an enviroment of controlled racing young men would be allowed to get the speed bug out of their systems. The new magazines urged readers to go to the lakes. Novices were enticed into a special world of nights spent by bonfires under a skyful of stars, of sleeping out in cars with just a marker cone for a pillow or of all-night 'bench racing' in the motels of Victorville. They were given hints about Rancho El Mirage and mysterious fuel mixtures. They were called to a whole romantic project and this appeal was successful. By 1948 the SCTA had over two thousand active members in thirty one different clubs[32] but increased participation merely served to tear up the lake beds. Parallel to all the stories of serious fun out at El Mirage were increasingly hopeless reports of the steadily worsening conditions. The strategy of incorporating teenagers seemed to be, quite literally, destroying the foundation of the respectable sport. The fear was that the driver who was being urged to take part in the organised sport to 'get it out of his system' would react to the worsening conditions by lapsing into street racing thus tightening the interwoven set of problems for the sport and its associated interests. All this formed the context in which *Hot Rod* began to work so as to safeguard the sport, or at least *a* sport, and thereby to secure and increase the set of relatively small-scale economic opportunities which had become attached to both the sport and the term 'hot rod'.

For a while the solution to this contradiction seemed to lie in achieving a much tighter organisation of action on the lakes. *Hot Rod* soon reported that four timing associations, SCTA, Russetta, Bell and Mojhave, had met to discuss a co-operation programme: 'Hereforeto, a great deal of confusion, misrepresentation, and general uneasiness has been the result of disorganized timing schedules.' Each timing association had different rules as to membership, different competition classes, timed in different ways and did not acknowledge the others' records. The lakes sport was now organised but not standardised. The real problem was, however, that there was just too much racing on the flats. Each association scheduled six or seven meets between April and October (weather permitting) and the surface got loose very early in the season with courses having to be altered regularly in the span of one weekend. Moreover, the meets continued to attract big crowds – the first SCTA meet of 1949 had eight thousand spectators – and the ranchers of the area and the chambers of commerce of the desert towns began to complain about the debris, sanitation problems and cattle rustling. The associations continued to develop El Mirage, constructing staging lanes, starting lights, an officials' stand and powerful public address system, but racing conditions became increasingly poor: 'After the punishment of 17 time trials on its surface El Mirage is about ready to succumb.'[33]

By next July the dry lakes 'have become almost too unsafe to use' and, indeed, in 1950 a driver died at El Mirage, only the second in all SCTA history. One theme of the reports of the associations was a rather desperate search for new places to run as the surfaces already in use became 'miserable' or 'like running on marbles' but additional dry lakes were even more remote, smaller and just as susceptible to crowds and speed, as was discovered in, for example, the attempt by the SCTA to hold a meet at Goldstone Dry Lake.[34]

Thus the hot rod apparatus, orchestrated through *Hot Rod*, had to find new solutions to the set of problems that faced the sport. The magazine, especially with the advent of a new editor, Wally Parks, in late 1949, began to pursue three broad and interconnected strategies for survival which were to shape the nature of the sport of hot rodding and the associated enthusiasm. First, the magazine helped to create and promote a new form of timed racing – drag racing – which became, it asserted, what real 'hot rodders' did and what they wanted to do. The new form both allowed closer control and regulation, and catered for a much more commercialised operation. *Hot Rod* helped create, fund, staff and promote the National Hot Rod Association (NHRA) with which it remained tightly intertwined and which oversaw the new sport. I will deal with this development in detail in Chapter Three. Second, the magazine attempted to improve the behaviour of hot rodders by promoting a puritan ethic which warned against idleness and frivolity, and urged study, labour, artisanship, improvement, patriotism, and the like. One way it did this was to present a monthly supply of upright role models. I will deal with some important examples of this in Chapters Seven and Eight. Third, the writers in the magazine constantly wrestled with the phrases 'hot rod' and 'hot rodding' to try to change their popular connotations, to sever the connection with street racing and traffic accidents, and to allow an ever-increasing readership to see themselves illuminated in an ever-changing light.

In this ideological assault the magazine carried out a continuous attack both on the street racers, who were labelled as 'squirrels' and 'shot rodders' who did not 'burn the midnight oil', and on the ignorant journalists and state officials, 'the headline happy', who constantly presented these idiots as if they were true hot rodders. The respectable rodders hoped to harness the teenagers and control them via rational recreation. The first issue of *Hot Rod* claimed: 'Hot rod racing has given the boys a healthy outlet not only for their speed, but their skill and inventiveness. Street racing is no longer of interest to them', but official fuss around street racing constantly threatened to smash the emerging shape of the whole hot rod world. For example, the magazine's response to the outbreak of street racing in 1949 which provoked, among other things, the pieces in *Time* and *Life* quoted earlier ran: 'In the past Hot Rod Magazine has made it a point to keep on the fence about the controversial issues of the sport. However when a point is reached where the smallest minority can undo the good work of the majority, it is felt that sides must be taken.' It talked of 'the screwball few': 'They met to compare automobile speeds (in gears and at top speed) as well as each other's nerves. Theirs was a selfish purpose with no constructive aim. The effect of these activities on the public was devastating.' Newspaper headlines such as 'Hot Rods Go Wild' were a blot on the reputation of the organised section of the sport: what was to be done? The magazine suggested that the timing associations should make themselves more attractive to prospective members and that the law courts should take a much tougher attitude.[35]

In the next issue the editor mused that 'hot rod' was becoming one of the most misused of words. The SCTA had thought about using a new name but they and the magazine had stuck with it to show its good side. Moreover, despite the headlines, most of the cars in recent events were not true hot rods! 'A real hot rod is a car that is lending itself to experimental development for the betterment of safety, operation or performance, not merely a stripped down or highly decorated car of any make, type or description or one driven by a teenager.' Worrying about the connotations of the phrase became a constant theme in the magazine, in editorials and letters. Then as circulation climbed and climbed – 200, 000 copies each month by 1950 – there was also, as we shall see, an effort to broaden the serious purposes of the 'hot rod endeavour' to encompass almost any interest in car maintenance or performance. The trouble was that the unofficial, illegal street racing aspect of hot rodding went on, attracted adverse media and official attention and was by no means as separate from the respectable facets of hot rodding as the magazine liked to claim.

Editorials of the kind just referred to attracted letters which set out a rational case for street racing:

You seem to point out that unorganized groups of hot rodders should join some sort of club where they will have some place to drag and race. OK that's a good idea, but how do you get in that sort of club? Now for instance, I live in LA. If I were to get in one of these safety rod clubs what would you expect me to do, travel anywhere from 30 to 70 miles and have some legal drags? Why do that when I can go 10 to 20 miles and have illegal drags but in a safe spot? But, then again, why go 10 to 20 miles to drag? Why not go down a couple of blocks to that deserted street. It's a long enough stretch for a drag and it's just as much fun. There ought to be a place for a drag in each city and large town. And if there was one in every city there would be no excuse to drag on the streets.[36]

and other writers came forward to defend the rationality and seriousness of street racing.

The problem remained just what alternative automobile sport could be set before such dissidents? What was legal 'hot rod racing' to be? In the earliest period the preferred alternative was the lake flats. In 1949 the SCTA organised the first National Automotive Speed Trials on the enormous salt flats at Bonneville, Utah to add another, lasting, layer to the dry lakes sport. But, as I have explained, encouraging extra participation on the Californian lakes seemed to be driving quickly into a dangerous dead end. The outbreak of street racing in 1949 added a sharp new edge to the problems caused by the physical decline of the lakes. In March 1950 the editor declared that all organised groups had been asked to a meeting with *Hot Rod* and the Californian Highway Patrol to try to form an Association of Associations: 'this meeting should very well accomplish the highly important feat of establishing a future for the hot rod instead of a fate.' The meeting led to the formation of the American Hot Rod Conference (AHRC), consisting of seven, then eight, timing associations, and whose purpose was to: (i) unify all existing activities; (ii) promote safety; (iii) regularise the recognition of records; (iv) provide new facilities.

The very popularity of the early sports, the cracking of the lakes and the continuation of the streets, seemed to be pushing 'hot rodding' either to extinction or to transformation and rodding was now rather more than an off-beat amateur sporting activity for it involved a whole set of economic interests which displayed considerable potential to spread across the whole of the USA as long as *some* new activities could serve as the very core of the enthusiasm. It was *Hot Rod* magazine that was to lead the way into a totally new form of hot rod sport.

The early hot rod sports

Notes

1 E. Lawrence, 'Gow jobs', *Colliers*, 26 July 1941, p. 56.
2 L. Levine, *Ford: The Dust and the Glory – a Racing History* (London, 1968), p. 143.
3 'Hot rod history', *Hot Rod* Magazine (*HRM*), 1, March and May 1948, p. 20.
4 Reprinted in 'Early lakesters', *Hop Up* (*HU*), April 1952, pp. 9–13.
5 W. Parks, *Drag Racing: Yesterday and Today* (New York, 1966), p. 14.
6 'Hot rods', *Life*, 5 November 1945, pp. 86–8. Also: A. Hamilton, 'Racing the hot rods', *Popular Mechanics*, January 1947.
7 *Fortune*, 36, November 1947.
8 M. Belyea, *The Joyride and the Silver Screen*, Ph.D. thesis (University of Boston, 1983), pp. 182–5.
9 E. Bogardus, *The City Boy and his Problems* (Los Angeles, 1926), p. 69.
10 Lawrence, 'Gow jobs', p. 14.
11 D. Mansell and J. S. Hall, 'Hot rod terms in the Pasadena area', *American Speech*, 29, 1954, pp. 89–104; W. White, 'Problems of a hot rod lexicographer', *American Speech*, 30, 1955, pp. 237–9; L. J. Davidson, 'Hot rodders' jargon again', *American Speech*, 31, 1956, pp. 304–5; and see H. Nye, 'T-bones and cheater slicks: the folkstay of the drag strip', in W. M. Hudson (ed.), *Tire Shrinker to Dragster* (Austin Texas, 1968), pp. 11–35.
12 L. Baney, 'Drag racing: beanfields to big bucks', *HRM*, 26, January 1973, p. 132.
13 M. Thompson and G. Borgeson, *Challenger: Mickey Thompson's Own Story of His Life of Speed* (Englewood Cliffs, New Jersey, 1964).
14 W. Neely, 'The Dean Moon story', *Car and Driver*, 24 April 1979, p. 96.
15 G. Baskerville, 'The hot rod story', *HRM*, 31 January 1978, pp. 33–9.
16 D. Garlits and B. Yates, *King of the Dragsters* (London, 1967), p. 23.
17 R. Chandler, *The Little Sister* (London, 1949), p. 61.
18 W. Smitter, 'Souped-up speed', *Colliers*, 5 April 1947, p. 15.
19 V. Orr, *Hot Rod Pictorial: Featuring Dry Lakes Time Trials* (Los Angeles, 1949), p. 4.
20 E.g. 'To the lakes with the Screwdrivers', *HU*, 1, December 1951, pp. 8–12.
21 'The hot rod problem', *Life*, 7 November 1949, pp. 122–8. For comparison see M. Licht, 'Some automotive play activities of suburban teenagers', *New York Folklore Quarterly*, 30, 1974, pp. 44–65 and W. Chambliss, 'The saints and the roughnecks', *Society*, November/December 1973, pp. 24–31.
22 *New York Times*, 19 June 1949.
23 *New York Times*, 3 October 1949.
24 J. Kenney and D. Pursuit, *Police Work with Juveniles* (Chicago, 1954), pp. 108 and 337.
25 *New York Times*, 22 July, 9 September, 6 October 1950 and 23 May 1951. See also the editorial: 'Curbing hot rod drivers', 31 March 1951.
26 *HRM*, 1, September 1948.
27 *New York Times*, 9 September 1950.
28 *HRM*, 4, July 1951, pp. 9 and 11.
29 E. Jaderquist and G. Borgenson (eds.), *Best Hot Rods* (New York, 1953), pp. 4–13.
30 *HU*, 1, April 1952, p. 12.
31 'Engineering versus chemistry', *HRM*, 5, December 1952 p. 19–21.
32 G. Hill, *Popular Mechanics' Hot Rod Handbook* (Chicago, 1953), p. 70.
33 *HRM*, 2, November 1949, p. 9 and p. 12.

Driving ambitions

34 *HU*, 1, February 1952, p. 10.
35 *HRM*, 2, November 1949, p. 5.
36 *HRM*, 3, January 1950, p. 28.

Chapter Three
Hot Rod magazine
and the creation of drag racing

. . . as a result of constant use, the California dry lakes have become even more unsuited for speed trials. As a result, it now appears that the associations using the lakes may have to abandon their speed trials or seek other locations. Many former devotees of desert trials have shifted their interests to the drag strips, which continue to become more and more popular. It is our sincere hope that the operators of present and future drag strips will exercise as much attention toward safety as the dry lake groups have in the past. At the same time, our hats are off to those dry lake devotees whose foresight has led them to give up their personal likes for the sake of the sport. The dry lakes were glorious – while they lasted. Long live the drag strips – and the hot rod sport![1]

Sports and enthusiasms get shaped in various ways by various institutions. Part of the argument of this book is that in hot rodding (and so, perhaps, in other sports and enthusiasms) it was those who owned and controlled the specialist literature, especially *Hot Rod*, that took the paramount creative role. The hot rod magazines, papers and books both articulated the precise notion of what the sport and enthusiasm should be and took action to try to ensure that this vision had a commensurate reality for the ordinary participant. It is my argument that a neglect of this kind of avenue to the creation of enthusiasms in modern society is one important way in which the study of sport, 'leisure' and 'subcultures' has been deficient.

Hot Rod magazine and the NHRA

In the situation described at the end of the last chapter one thing *Hot Rod* tried to do was to delineate the behaviour and attitudes of those who wanted to be 'true' hot rodders. One of its responses to the street racing of 1949 was to carry a succession of guest editorials and articles by members of the California Highway Patrol. The good intentions of most of the police and the need to work with them became a reiterated point in the magazine. The seventh issue carried the first of what was to become a rather monotonous story featuring a 'good' hot rod club. Its members were solid citizens of their local communities, who co-operated with their local authorities, organised scenic tours when winter stopped timing activities, fined or expelled members who did anything illegal with their cars and helped any stranded motorist they came across. A 1950 article, 'Forming a Hot Rod Club', emphasised this kind of point: 'You are all members of a great big club – your home town.' The Constitution of the United States was pressed upon readers as the model for democratic organisation, and they were advised:' Do not require members to attain a maximum speed as an additional qualification. This usually provides a large amount of very unfavourable publicity.'[2]

Hot Rod also strove to develop a new structure and level of organisation in rodding. It regularly suggested that a national body to represent hot rodders might be 'a good thing'. While it seems to have had a hand in the founding of AHRC it appears that body did not suit the purposes of the magazine for it did not promote the AHRC as heavily as, say, a rival magazine, Hop Up, whose first edition appeared in mid-1951. In March 1951 a letter from a reader to Hot Rod was made into a feature article: 'Why Not a National Hot Rod Association?' The letter argued that any such body would need to be organised through the magazine which was the national focus of the activity. At a minimum an association could issue membership cards and a window decal to, 'signify fraternity and mutual interest' and 'fellowship of purpose with other hot rodders'. Two issues later Hot Rod announced that such an Association had indeed been formed. The publisher and editor had met with 'responsible parties who have demonstrated their loyalty and devotion to the hot rod sport' and had decided that the time was ripe. The magazine was providing a $1,500 interest-free loan for six months to help establish the new body. Its offices were to be at the magazine's address. The magazine's editor Wally Parks (ex-President and other office holder in the SCTA) was to be the President of the NHRA (and remained so for over twenty years). Another ex-office-holder in the SCTA and writer for the magazine was Vice-President, a businessman became Secretary. The statement of purpose of the new association was all about safety, regulation and obtaining more public acceptance. A salaried field director was appointed to travel the country, increase membership and extend organisation. The individual membership fee was $2 but Hot Rod argued that the new body did not aim to compete with the existing organisations in the sport. It aimed to recruit individual members and then help them to form clubs who would then be free to join old or new timing associations. It sought to differentiate the new body from the AHRC by arguing that the other grouping's interest was on West Coast issues while the new Association would have a truly national role.[3]

From this date on another recurrent theme in the magazine was boosting the NHRA and presenting it as the spokesperson for *all* rodders. A couple of pages of *Hot Rod* were soon given over to a 'Bulletin Board' for NHRA messages and information. The NHRA was described as 'the crucible' in which the future shape of the sport was to be forged and the word 'national' in its title was stressed though, as we shall see, others in the sport were to argue that it stayed close, indeed far too close, to its West Coast origins.

By January 1952 the editor was musing that hot rodding was becoming respectable and appreciated all over the USA and a lot of this was due to the efforts of the NHRA. In the next issue the editor argued that as 'old man winter' had stopped the fun in the East and Mid west: 'Now is the opportune time to start making public relations contacts. There can be no better time to stop in and pay a visit to your local police and civic officials.' A plug for the NHRA followed along with a salutary story about a club that had been going along nicely until they 'succumbed to a little unethical speed competition which ended, as it often can, in total disaster . . . let's try living a little more of the safe and sane sport idea which we are trying to sell to the public.'[4] The same issue's Bulletin Board proudly reported that the NHRA had received good publicity in a recent edition of the *FBI Law Enforcement Bulletin*.

The next volume reprinted a pamphlet that had been produced by the NHRA – *The Hot Rod Story*. This text, whose author also wrote for the magazine, had both a historical and a philosophical intent and clearly set out the organisational aims of the new Association and the magazine. Hot rodding was an American creation and young American men were naturally interested in speed. However there had been violations which had played into the hands of sensation seekers mainly because these young men had no organisation to look to which could channel their energies into constructive conduits and direct their activities along well-defined organisational lines. Now, the NHRA provided this and officialdom was happy for:

> What the Golden Gloves have done for boxing by way of transforming street fights and alley brawls into supervised boxing contests in the clean atmosphere of a gymnasium, so the NHRA plan to transform the hot rod movement from a disorganised, sporadic, rudderless activity into an integrated,

regulated and supervised sport.[5]

In short, the creation of the new organising body added extra legitimation to the general exhortations about conduct, behaviour and presentation that were a constant part of the magazine's output. *Hot Rod* used the apparently seperate Association to plea for 'the well being of the whole community' to be a factor in individual and club actions. Far more thought had to be given to public presentation. In May 1952 clubs were told:

> In the formation of a hot rod club the name of the organization is of great importance because of its effect on parents and the general public. Club names that include words such as 'Maniacs', 'Killers', 'Hell', etc. , are not approved by the NHRA. Such titles have a tendency to give a wrong impression of hot rodding and they lend themselves to sensational newspaper stories.[6]

By September 1952 *Hot Rod* claimed the NHRA had fifteen thousand members and in October 1954 that there were over 2, 700 hot rod clubs in the USA. Such signs of interest in driving cars at high speed, revealed too, of course, in the vastly greater circulation of the magazine, could, as I suggested in the previous chapter, have exacerbated the interlock of tensions in the sport as a lakes-based activity. The boys had to be organised and they had to be schooled but they needed somewhere to run other than on the streets of the citys. Where was that to be?

In the late 1940s the hot rod apparatus had expressed a desire for what was called a 'test strip'. At that time this 'dream' took the form of some kind of sturdy replica of a lakes course. The SCTA held discussions with the ranchers around El Mirage in the hope that they would level off and maintain a strip on the Lake that people would be charged to enter. An artists impression in *Hot Rod* in 1949 was of a five-lane, five mile long concreted strip. In July 1951 the first edition of a rival magazine *Hop Up* carried an article 'Wanted . . . One Paved Timing Strip' which began:

> No amount of words can describe conditions at a lakes meet – you have to be there to understand why the almost desperate need for a paved timing strip. While speed-minded Californian youths have been using these dried out lake beds since 1933, the lack of rain in recent years has progressively ruined the once-hard surface. This year it has been necessary to move the course several times during the running of one day's events. The dirt and dust are terrible. For the past several years there has been a growing movement directed towards obtaining a paved timing strip in the Southern California area. Sites proposed are mostly in desert areas, where crowds and noise would bother no one. The greatest benefit a strip would bring is safety. There have been

accidents at these dry lakes meets, but almost all can be blamed on the rough surface throwing a car out of control. A smooth paved surface would eliminate this problem, and would mean faster speeds!

The story added that three organisations in the hot rod world were looking to provide such a strip, the AHRC, the newly formed NHRA and Motorama. This last grouping, as I will detail later, was also closely linked with *Hot Rod*. Other stories in the specialist media in the late 1940s and early 1950s carried a somewhat impoverished version of this 'dream' in which the hope was expressed that state authorities might sometimes close off miles of little used highway to allow for some long timing runs. There was no clear perception of who exactly would provide such a course or why they would do so.

The early drag strips

However, the debris of war in California and around the whole USA included a number of abandoned or little used aerodromes whose artificial surfaces offered the possibility of some kind of speed contests, though for instant acceleration rather than the long runs and top speed competition characteristic of the desert sport. The SCTA had thought about using such airstrips for some kind of competition in the winter when the lakes were unusable but had dropped the idea because insurance costs for possible spectators proved prohibitive. It seems the first quarter-mile timed run 'contest' took place in early 1949 as an impromptu part of a road test of new cars for a sister magazine at which journalists from *Hot Rod* and officials from the SCTA were present.[7] Other improvised and, often, illegal events took place as racers took over an airstrip for an afternoon and in late 1949 the Santa Barbara Acceleration Association organised runs on a back road at a local airport. In December 1949, in what was, it must be remembered, a period of moral panic in Los Angeles and elsewhere about street racing, *Hot Rod* announced the first acceleration meets on paved strips as a 'winter fill-in'. Other references to the use of private roads and airstrips soon followed in the magazine, including a letter detailing how street racers in Illinois had been incorporated into such events which were sponsored by the local police and attracted crowds of 1,500.

In April 1950 *Hot Rod*'s editorial ran: 'Highlighting the interest in a new field of competition is this month's article on Controlled Drag Racing . . . clubs and groups interested in providing activity for their membership, especially in locations where no lengthy straightaways are available are advised to look into the possibilities of developing such supervised events.' This article noted that such events did not require a lot of competitive space and were attracting thousands of spectators and went on: 'drag racing is rapidly becoming an organised endeavour which is providing "off the highway" activity for hot rod enthusiasts and may prove to be the answer to illegal street racing.' Participants were urged to court public opinion. The recommendation was that competition vehicles should be towed to events not driven, proper authority should be obtained to use the venue and rodders should enlist the co-operation of their local police. All in all: 'drag racing really has something but not on public streets or highways.'

From this point on, as lake surfaces deteriorated the magazine increasingly promoted the new form of automobile sport. It provided details and stories of events and merged this new element into its regular feature on 'good' hot rod clubs. In the repetitve 'story' these groups were now presented as either using a local drag strip or as longing for one. Eventually with the help of considerate policemen and concerned citizens, often those who had lost children in unsupervised auto-games, they got one. But *Hot Rod* did not totally ignore the commercial possibilities of the new form. The coverage of these early events often mentioned admission prices and other economic aspects as in the December 1950 story of the use of the Santa Cruz Skypark for dragging which quoted the owner: 'What's in it for us? In the first place, we make about as much in concessions as we do with the airport going full blast. More important we draw hundreds of new visitors to our layout. The publicity is priceless and we know it pays.'

So, the early 1950s were a period of some fluidity as the nascent interests of the hot rod apparatus sought to conceptualise some regularised sporting activity out of the crumble of the lake beds and the ever present dangers of racing in the streets. For a while drag racing represented only one of a number of possibilities. *Hop Up* in December 1951, discussing the rough surface at El Mirage, put it thus:

> Something has to be done for roadster activities . . . It would seem that the next logical step should be reliability runs, hill climbs, maneuverability trials (gymkhanas) and possibly road racing. First they must improve the handling and braking of their cars – two qualities they sadly lack. To start the ball rolling, the American Hot Rod Conference is organizing America's first Roadster Hill Climb. Run on private property, the winding ½ mile asphalt course may prove to be the first of a whole new group of badly needed activities.

In October the same year *Hot Rod* ran a mail questionnaire asking: 'what kind of competition coverage do you prefer?' This listed speed trials, drag races, track racing, reliability runs, gymkhanas, obstacle runs and shows. And there was still talk of creating the miles-long paved strip which would allow a lake-style sport to continue. So 'acceleration trials' were only one of the new forms of competition which were canvassed but the one that had the greatest momentum. *Hop Up*'s second issue had contained an editorial on the topic plus an article on 'Dago Drags' which gives some flavour of the impetus around at the time:

> The San Diego Timing Association is the only organization of its kind to conduct quarter mile sprint races with the internationally recognised standing start . . . the Association's Paradise Valley Sprint Strip, a 0.6 mile, asphalt surfaced ex-AAF. fighter strip . . . The San Diego Timing Association began when a mass meeting of this areas drag enthusiasts was called because the Paradise Valley Airstrip, long the scene of chaotic illegal sprint bashes had been closed by the authorities. The problem of re-opening the Strip for safety-supervised meet crystalised the group.[8]

While its next editorial, on the Saugus Drags, declared: 'now there is no need for such illegal drags. If your car meets the safety requirements, you can prove its merits by going to legal, supervised drags. Lou Baney, President of Russetta Timing Association, is in charge of this wonderful new strip. The timing is by E. C. Huseman, the same fellow who clocks all the Russetta meets.'[9]

As the quote indicates, the timing associations were happy enough to get involved on the drag strips. When the SCTA's first scheduled meet of 1952 was rained off it held a two-day invitational meet on the San Diego Timing Association's strip. Cars would come back from the lakes and go straight onto a Sunday drag meet. For, at first, the meets on asphalt were not seen as a totally new sport but rather one of a number of new ways of running designed to 'take the heat off the streets' and to serve as *adjuncts* to the core activity on the lakes. They were presented as 'proving grounds' on which to work out theories associated with long straight-away competition. Still, as early as January 1951, the editor of *Hot Rod* began to muse that in future the bulk of timing events might have to take place away from the lakes and on these short paved strips. They were safer than Mirage and 'a plan of this type could conceivably bring about a more equalized nationwide appeal for hot rodding and it would definitely help solve the problems that still face hot rodders in many areas.'

With the formation of the NHRA, boosting the new association and boosting drag strips went hand in hand. While drag racing was at first presented as just one *option* for rodders, very quickly organised dragging, and it was, of course, very close in form to illegal street racing, came to be promoted as the very essence of hot rod racing and automobile speed contests. It was the strips that were now to serve as the safety valves for the urges of young men, where, in a serious atmosphere of busy modification and practical experimentation, they would realise that street racing was not only dangerous but dopey. Throughout 1952 *Hot Rod* constantly featured the new form so that: 'A Drag Strip For Your Town' in July was followed by 'Drag Strip Paradise' in August and by 'Northern California Speed Sprints' in September. This last in a set of very similar affirmative articles argued: 'Airstrip drag racing is now highly approved by law enforcement agencies wherever it has been instituted. It has been proven that racing cannot easily be stopped but it can be controlled.' Coverage of the lakes and, indeed, the timing associations began to run down until they were scarcely mentioned. By June 1953 *Hop Up* was reporting that the SCTA season had not got off to a flying start: 'Drag races every Sunday at any one of several strips in this locality, plus the inferior surface of El Mirage dry lake, has turned the contestants away in droves. Inspite of the 4 or 5 new clubs that have joined the association since last year there were only 70 cars entered for the first meet.'

Editorials increasingly celebrated the spread of the new drag form of sport: 'fast becoming the nation's number one hot rod competition activity' and the recognition it gained for rodding everywhere: 'From where we sit it looks as if the drag sport has 'gone national'. More and more communities throughout the US. are begining to see the light and drag strips are being made available where hot rods received little recognition a year ago.'[10] At the end of 1953 there was a valedictory editorial for the lake-based sport which, apart from the once a year big speed trials event at Bonneville, was then ignored for a while though in the late 1950s *Hot Rod* did occasionally provided a nostalgic report from El Mirage where the remnants of the SCTA and RTA still held meets with ninety cars in competition and a couple of dozen spectators.

However, while the development of the drag strips could be loudly hailed, *Hot Rod* perceived two problems that this rapid growth contained, problems that were to preoccupy the magazine, the NHRA and the whole hot rod apparatus through the decade of the 1950s and beyond. These problems concerned: (i) a lack of uniformity in the new form; (ii) the issue of safety and the public perception of hot rodding.

The first of these turned on the explosive rise of the new type of car competition and the varying forms in which 'drag racing' had been invented. A review of the 1952 hot rod year pointed to the increase in the number of strips in Southern California, with five strips operating most Sundays with 200 contestants and a thousand spectators at each, but added:

> It is virtually impossible to compare the results at one strip to the results from another strip because car classifications and rules vary so greatly. As a matter of fact, the same strip may operate under two sets of rules during one year. Serious efforts are being made by several groups to standardize drag strip classes and rules everywhere.[11]

This fragmentation was well appreciated. Indeed, one aspect of the co-ordination the AHRC was designed to achieve was the standardisation of competition classes, recognition of records, etc. for lakes *and* strips[12] but it was *Hot Rod* and the NHRA who actually moved to promote uniformity.

The magazine organised a survey of rules in use at strips and the NHRA supervised experiments with different set-ups using one club, the Pamona Choppers, as guinea pigs. The February 1953 *Hot Rod*, a 'Special Drag Strip Issue', contained an article, 'How To Run a Drag Strip' which sought to create standardisation of operation. The promise was that if this could be achieved it would result in regional, then national, championships for the new sport. The article began:

> For the past year the Editors of HRM in conjunction with the Board of Directors of the National Hot Rod Association have made an extensive study of rules and regulations of the largest and most successful drag strips in the country. The reason for this is that HRM and the NHRA have felt the need for united drag strip rules that are complete, simple and workable allowing them to be used in all parts of the country for all types of competition machines. Of the many and ever-increasing number of drag strips now in operation from coast to coast we have yet to find two strips that use identical rules. Each drag strip operator has apparently seen fit to draw up his own rules to suit the demands made by competitors and spectators at his own individual strip. However in order to be truly National in scope standards must be made made that will be used and recognized throughout the country.

Strips varied in length as did the traps used for timing. Some strips used a rolling rather than a standing start, some strips even used a rolling start off a downhill ramp. Competition classes varied widely with some strips running 'mongrel races' of everything against everything at a rate of one contest a minute. *Hot Rod* argued for the adoption of an exact quarter mile run, with a 132-foot timing trap at the end of the course, with only two vehicles running at any one time.

Then the equipment used to time runs was not standard, which actually reflected some doubt about the new sport's basic purpose. The move on to the strips, their varied lengths and the traditions of hot rodding had led to confusion about exactly which *aspect* of automobile performance was to be measured and/or regarded as 'winning' a contest. Unlike the lakes, quarter of a mile standing start racing was a test of acceleration capability rather than top speed potential. Though for a while the strips were promoted as 'standing in' for the lakes, both the way the cars were set up and driving techniques had to be much modified. The much shorter distance put a premium on the start of the race and so on reflexes and on 'reading' the human or mechanical starter. Unannounced, there had been a fundamental change in the legal sport's basic aim and this created some contradictions. Some strips continued to measure top speed at the end of the run as the criterion of success but a machine could clock the highest finishing speed and yet not be first to cross the line at the end of the short course. *Hop Up* had already argued that an emphasis on top speed was not appropriate for what it often, accurately, dubbed as 'acceleration trials' and *Hot Rod* now put the point plainly:

> It has been proven time and time again that the car clocking the fastest top speed at the end of a quarter mile is not always the quickest to arrive at the end of the course. An elapsed time method, using standing starts would make this fact clear. This system does not have the 'spectator appeal' of the top speed method, yet elapsed time shows a car's acceleration qualities in their true light. The Paradise Mesa drag strip uses both elapsed time and top speed systems but the necessary timing equipment is more intricate and consequently more expensive than the use of the either elapsed time or top speed equipment separately.

The somewhat uncorrelated relation between elapsed time (et.) and top speed was to create issues that ran the whole history of drag racing.

Hot Rod also sought to standardise competition classes, its five main categories – Roadster, Dragster, Coupe–Sedan, Stock and Motorcycle – containing various sub-divisions to yield twenty seven classes in all. But it was not just standardised competition that *Hot Rod* advocated but standardized safety precautions. Infact, it behove the hot rod apparatus to try to *limit* attainable speeds within the confines of a commercially viable strip. A balance had to be struck between speed, and so crowd appeal, and safety. Many of the emerging strips enforced fewer safety precautions than the timing associations had come to apply at the lakes.

To survive official censure any hot rod sport had to avoid accidents. *Hop Up* too urged strip operators to look to safety as in this report on one event: 'One serious accident can be so costly; in injury or worse, in loss of equipment and in loss of public approval that we seriously recomend higher safety rules. Cars were seen running with no shock absorbers, no roll bars, particularly on stripped down jobs, and drivers without crash helmets.[13] *Hot Rod* often made the same kind of points, accidents at any strip hurt other people and the whole sport, now its article 'How To Run A Drag Strip' set out twenty checks that ought to be mandatory on each car by safety inspectors and also gave advice and diagrams on how to separate competitors from specatators as 'rigid spectator control is an essential at any drag strip activity'.

The next month the periodical published a follow-up to this article with a list of extra suggestions mainly stemming from the Highway Patrol and the whole 'How To Run a Drag Strip' article was later reprinted. A similar article appeared in January 1954 as 'Operation Drag Strip' and this was later issued as a fifteen-page NHRA pamphlet available free of charge. This article noted that there were still wide variations in practice between strips. The magazine made its by now regular plea for standardisation and safety and moved on to make detailed suggestions as to how to start a race, record times, label cars, on the provision of enough gatemen and the necessity of a good announcer: 'It is important that a person be selected who can handle any situation without undue excitement or "mike hysteria ˙ since nothing makes a poorer impression on first time visitors to a strip than having wild orders blasted over the public address.' Strips were urged to make an impression of safety consciousness and respectability: 'Most police departments have arrangements whereby off-duty officers can be hired, at reasonable rates, to patrol during spectator sporting events. . . . well compensated by the aura of authority they can lend to such an event.' Good appearance of personnel, vehicles and strip facilities was of the utmost importance in creating a favourable impression of the sport, even the appearance of trash cans was discussed here and:

> As a final word of caution, it might be as well to mention that a drag strip reputation is not solely limited to the success of the meets thereon. The manner in which participants conduct themselves while travelling to and from events, especially with numbers painted on their cars, is an influence on the opinion of the public at large. This also plays an important part in the amount of cooperation that can be obtained from the local police, merchants and others who might be staunch allies to your program.[14]

The free and easy days of the lakes, less than a decade away for some contestants had been left far behind. If drags were to take over as the core hot rod sport a very different aura was going to have to prevail. In early 1954 the NRHA arranged a 'Drag Strip Council' meeting at which representatives from ten top drag strips, all on the West Coast, exchanged information and tried to fashion a set of uniform procedures for the new sport.[15] They agreed to use a standing start and on a basic power to weight method of dividing competition classes. *Hot Rod* characteristically hailed this as worthy self-management: 'As long as the hot rodders themselves continue to govern the sport; we're confident in its future' and many other such meetings were held in the mid-1950s, but, while the magazine talked often in the years to come of councils and conferences, of delegates and self-government by rodders, and liked to insist that 'voting is the backbone of the American way',[16] the crucial directing group here were the closely intertwined personnel around *Hot Rod* and the NHRA.

At this time they effected two other things which developed the sport. In 1954 and 1955 the NHRA and *Hot Rod* (with sponsorship from oil companies, cola firms etc.) organised Drag Safaris – long caravan tours around the USA by NHRA experts carrying the gear to stage 'safe' contests, to spread the word beyond the West Coast, encourage organisation, sell the whole idea of channelling automotive enthusiam to local notables and media, and sanction the proper kind of drag strip. In this way the sport was spread across America and the promise of regional and national championships could be met. Second, the NHRA used the set of uniform rules beaten out in its series of drag strip councils to organise insurance cover for strips adhering to these procedures in all states. *Hot Rod* hailed this as more solid citizens recognising that drag racing was a 'safety program' but what it certainly did do was to remove one financial constraint that had hindered the growth in the number of strips across the USA.

So in the early 1950s *Hot Rod* and the NHRA quickly found a comfortable, if active, new position from which to promote 'hot rodding'. The magazine had always been worried that idleness could lead young men to yield to the temptation of illegal games in automobiles. It had tried to keep hot rodders busy. All the magazines of the enthusiasm suggested new auto-related activities that hot rod clubs should do which would switch the emphasis away from racing and speed towards more public-relations-exploitable tasks such as hill climbs, working on the appearance of rods (and rodders), reliability runs, scenic touring, parking, braking and safety contests.[17] Clubs were urged to hold monthly safety checks where members should sternly examine each other's cars to make sure they complied with legal and other stipulated standards. Points should be given and deducted and trophies awarded. All these would be good for the image as would charitable activities that showed rodders involved in fund-raising tasks for the March of Dimes or leukaemia research. Then local and national Roadeo competitions were promoted for and between high schools in which skill at parking, manoeuvring and knowledge of traffic codes were awarded points. Clearly, however, *some kind* of basic racing activity was necessary to feed the 'boys' interests in speed, competition and measured performance. The drag strips, more numerous, accessible, sturdier and exploitable than the lakes, provided a new and firmer foundation for the whole hot rod enthusiasm. The 'cause' of drag strip provision was championed as harnessing the 'natural' interest of the 'automotive minded youth of America' as the magazine liked to call them: 'In a mechanical age, where youth is instilled with ideas of locomotion, power and speed from an early childhood, there's a natural inclination to go fast. What better place is there to exercise this than on a well-controlled safety proven drag strip, where mechanical accomplishment is acknowledged instead of criticized?'[18]

The NHRA worked closely with the Highway Patrol and other agencies (a Californian policeman was added to the board of directors in 1953). It liked to proclaim that its 'safety program' was 'endorsed by law enforcement agencies' and the good cop, the hot rodding cop, became a regular feature of hot rod magazines and in hot rod novels in which the hero was weaned away from wild street racing, usually after the death of many teenage friends, to a steadier world of roadeos, reliability runs and organised drag strips. *Hot Rod* sought to enthuse citizens more senior than teenagers about dragging:

> The key to the solution of most so-called 'hot rod driver' problems is recognition. By helping a club in your community obtain a drag strip upon which they can conduct organized events, you'll win their confidence, earn their loyalty, and gain enthusiastic cooperation. That's why we're all out for the drag strips. Thy're a way to show that we believe in the hot rodder, a perfectly normal citizen whose hobby is as American as baseball, horseback riding . . . or even golf.[19]

The magazine thought up more and more ways the strips could be regarded as socially beneficial. It argued that the strips not only gave 'the boys' a place to let off steam but also attracted thousands of car owning

C

spectators to races on the day the truly dangerous 'Sunday motorist' was loose on the highway. This was especially significant for the ordinary American production car was beginning to have considerable speed potential. The magazine also argued that well run strips were making a big contribution to general maintenance standards. They insisted that participants had to pass a strict safety inspection for mechanical condition before they raced. In many states all that was needed to drive on the public highway was a licence, there was absolutely no compulsory safety requirement. Police policies went along with this view. The gist of a number of guest editorials and features by members of the Highway Patrol and other police officials was that 'working on cars' was a natural and an American thing for young men to do but it could lead into traffic situations hazardous to others. They had to be educated and controlled.

The partnership between the hot rod apparatus and the law had its clearest expression in an article by the Police Chief of Pamona, 'Harnessing the Hot Rods', in which he explained how his department had stopped trying to chastise the rodders and had tried to understand them instead: 'When we looked at their crimes in the light of what we had done in our teen-age years, we had a guilty conscience. Society and congestion had grown up around the kids, but society had not learned how to harness the devilment, exuberance, and tack their boisterous sails along orderly lines.' Through a liaison officer, provision of a meeting place, and Operation Drag Strip the rodders were pulled into a club:

> An extensive safety program was initiated into the club's curriculum and added life was given to the club's activities through the medium of supervised 'poker runs', time runs, secret destination runs, and planned group tours. To stimulate interests further, an activity chart was set up to bring out the spirit of competition. A point system was established wherein the club members could gain or lose points according to their degree of participation in the program.

In these and other ways the police chief could assert, rather chillingly: 'The hot rodder is no longer a problem in Pamona – he is part of a program.'[20]

Problems for the new sport

However, the reiterated claim that the new sport conveniently combined a safety program, solid citizenship, public service and speed contests threatened to get undermined by problems which started to plague this form of hot rodding from its inception. These were:

(i) the issue of competition classes and a related issue of cheating at the strips;

(ii) the role of commercialism and professionalism in the new sport;

(iii) official doubts about the validity of the argument that organised drag racing promoted safety on the streets.

I will consider each of these in turn. They were of different orders of significance but interconnected, and all served to darken the bright picture of the new sport that *Hot Rod* and the NHRA were seeking to promote to hot rodders and to a wider public.

By 1955 *Hot Rod* was openly worrying about cheating in drag racing. The Stock classes were the ones supposedly for the classic 'little guy' rodder who slightly modified his own standard machine and drove it on the streets as well as the strips. However, some contestants had been found using specially modified machines which they had declared to be stock. To *Hot Rod* this not only indicated a lack of that sportsmanship, sincerity and fellowship it was promoting as hot rodding's selling points to the world outside the enthusiasm, but also suggested that some people were beginning to take the activity far too seriously: 'the hot rod sport, including drag strip contests was developed for recreational enjoyment. Prize money has been kept out of the picture in order that it may remain an amateur sport wherein each participant runs primarily for the fun of it. Classes and rules have been established to promote equality; a man's honor being trusted to determine his true place.'[21] In 1955 at the NHRA's First National Championships some competitors had been taken aback by the thoroughness of the safety standards applied. This not only revealed the laxness that still occurred in enforcing accepted standards at several strips but, even more significant, when after the races the technical committee had further inspected winners to see whether cars had been running in their true classes, many had been disqualified from the Stock classes. In one class, the first, second and third had all been found to be cheating, while overall in the Stock classes, as another magazine detailed:

> Out of four classes, two would be winners were disqualified and another was found to be 'legal' by the rarest of accidents which made him as guilty as the others by intent. Only one car of the four was completely legal. Second place cars that would normally be declared winners under such circumstances, were also found to be illegal, so in two classes there were no winners. This is a pretty sorry reward that borders on disgrace.[22]

Yet another magazine, *Rod Builder and Customizer*, recorded in December

1957 how the abuse of classifications was causing a lot of arguments at the strips. Such cheating was particularly worrying as the NHRA and *Hot Rod*'s ethos for this new form of sport stressed fun and amateur ideals. Cheating seemed to smack of a win at all costs mentality with a disturbing whiff of professionalism. As I will detail in a later chapter, through the whole history of drag racing, in different ways and degrees, *Hot Rod* and the NHRA fought against the development of a professional group of drag racers and tried to regulate the level of prize and appearance money they could earn.

During 1956 a new problem arose in the same category. The Detroit companies had begun making special speed equipment which was dolled out to a fortunate few and were even producing 'factory hot rods' straight off the assembly lines but in limited quantities thus posing a difficult question about what exactly 'stock' was to mean. By allowing these vehicles into the Stock classes 'we are granting them favors that are not made available to the average car owner who buys a stocker and then adds his own power equipment.'[23] The answer to this, as it was to many a similar problem that was to arise in the future, was to amend the nature of competition classes so as to make them even more complex: 'The outcome is a newly developed system wherein any factory production car having a power-to-weight ratio of less than 15 lbs per bhp (shipping weight divided by advertised brake horsepower) is automatically advanced into the Gas Coupe/Sedan section of competition, which is the section for power equipped, gasoline burning street machines.'

The over-riding worry here was that cheating or factory specials might turn the ordinary guy away from the strips and back to the streets to get more honest competition. However, a paradox lay in the NHRA response, for some readers wrote to the magazine to argue it was just all the complexities of rules, regulations, inspections and classes at the strips which was pushing people back to the streets for a little straight up, simple automobile racing. This paradox, between the constant re-jigging of rules to make competition 'honest' and the off-putting effects of all the complications, was one which would effect the very nature of the drag racing sport in years to come.

The issue of what the underlying ethos of the sport was to be was intertwined with another problem about the role of commercialism at the strips. There were profitable possibilities here. Baney recalled regular crowds of well over a thousand at one of the earliest locations, the Saugus strip, with an entrance fee of 99 cents (a price designed to avoid tax). The strip offered prizes of War Bonds at $25 or $100 for big

Hot Rod magazine

meets or rather less in hard cash. However, in the early 1950s *Hot Rod*, through and with the NHRA, strove to set the new automobile sport in a context of serious fun, enjoyable endeavour, amateur enthusiasm, public service and charitable work. As it put it in May 1956: 'Proceeds from organized drag strips are normally diverted into qualified benefit programs . . . Crippled children's hospitals, the March of Dimes and many other notable projects have received thousands of dollars from non-profit making hot rod organizations who operate drag strips through out the country.' The magazine's preferred solution for the provision of drag strips urged a social project with the emphasis on welfare and charitable work: dragging for cancer funds, giving half the receipts towards the purchase of police reserve uniforms, donating blood and the like. It wanted strips to be police sponsored, community built and club operated. This, of course, neatly complemented the other, necessary, stress that drag racing was, as the NHRA logo had it, 'Dedicated to Safety'. *Hot Rod* was insistent that new drag strips promoted automobile safety but lax strips and or those that paid too much attention to commercial pressures, and at this time *Hot Rod* basically equated the two, might well thwart this. *Hot Rod*'s vision of drag strips as a community provision tended to get undermined because anyone could open a strip and overtly operate for profit not social policy. The magazine was far from keen on this kind of development: 'In the case of the promoter sponsored drag strips the guys in the T-shirts and levis, who are the basis of the sport, seldom have a voice in the operation.'[24]

At least some of the lack of standardisation that abounded in the early 1950s reflected the desire of commercial operators to make their strips as welcoming as possible to whoever wanted to run and to be able to claim 'record times' for their courses. Some strips became notorious for their 'easy clocks' and 'fast times'. *Hot Rod* argued that at such strips the desire for quick revenue would mean high entrance fees for spectators and a sacrifice of safety to the promotor's desire to have a full race card: 'The fact that operators of this type are placing the entire hot rod organization program in constant jeopardy appears to be a matter of no concern to the promotors of these off-beat strips.'[25]

The magazine urged readers only to patronise good strips. From 1952 the NHRA, registered under Californian law as a non-profit making organisation, began to sanction certain strips which met its criteria for standard procedure and precautions. Its first approved drag meet at Pamona attracted an unexpected fifteen thousand-plus crowd on its second day.[26] By now the magazine's parent company, Petersen Publications, had swept up *Hot Rod*'s first rival, *Hop Up*, and repositioned it in a different place in the market for auto-magazines under the new name of *Motor Life*. The well-being of the magazines and that of many other economic interests which hung around the sport, particularly the equipment makers and speed shops, did not depend on commercially oriented strips. They could all thrive if the kids had somewhere respectable to run and as long as the hot rod apparatus could stave off the constant threat of legislation to limit *all* hot rod activities and the modification of engines and cars. Thus *Hot Rod* tried to isolate the sport from dangerous contamination by overt commercialism. By October 1954 the editor was warning rodders: 'Look Before You Leap'. *Hot Rod* and the NHRA were organisations 'Whose aims and purposes are based solely on the development and protection of a wholesome amateur sport'. What they were seeking was organisation, association and participation at the grass roots but now: 'Concurrent with the hot rods sport's widespread acceptance by the public it also becomes especially attractive to venal interests, who are less concerned with the ultimate future of the sport than they are with its immediate commercial prospects. Along with the 'do-ers' there'll naturally appear some "ballyhooers".' While in November the editorial stressed the NHRA's proud history of organisation building and finished: 'We shall carry on our diligent crusade to protect the sport from those who would seek to exploit it for commercial gain (there are a few such groups in existence today) with a determination that it shall remain the truly recreational amateur activity that it started out to be – coordinated by, and for, the hot-rodders themselves.'

These, and other warnings about the dangers of 'creeping commercialism' actually heralded the formation of a new body seeking to organise and represent hot rodders and drag racing which *Hot Rod*, characteristically, never deemed to name. The Automobile Timing Association of America (ATAA) was linked with the development of a overt group of professional racers – Drag Racers Incorporated – who demanded money for appearing at tracks where their fame, spread through the hot rod literature, guaranteed promoters a large crowd. The net of relations between *Hot Rod* and the NHRA, the ATAA and the professional racers will be dealt with in detail in Chapter Five but a simple example will indicate what was at issue. When the NHRA organised the first 'Nationals' championship in 1955 the rewards for winning were merchandise prizes donated by speed equipment manufacturers and 'beautiful trophies' but no cash.

The point I am making here is that *Hot Rod* sought to protect its own place and that of the hot rod economy in the developing sport through a rhetoric of amateurism, social service and by shunning overt commercialism in various forms as inappropriate, foreign to the true ethos of rodding and as, potentially, highly dangerous to the sport's health. In May 1958 it was still warning of the dangers of 'opportunists' and 'the threat of overcommercialism' and 'get-rich-quick schemes'. It turned its fire on a recent symposium held in the Mid-West which had concentrated its attention on ways to exploit every possible dollar from the drag racing sport, even proposing 'volume sales of pit admissions as a means of gaining additional revenue. No amount of attention was given to the sport's community benefit nature as the business proceded towards its intent of forming a promoter's association for drag racing. We readily agree that the sport must be profitable to succeed, but the sum profit isn't necessarily counted in mere dollars and cents.'

However, *Hot Rod* had already been forced to note some problems involved in taking an implaccable stance against 'commercialisation' for, as the sport mushroomed, a stress on amateurism did not fit too easily with its other emphasis on the necessity for close bureaucratic regulation of safety standards and competition classes. The article 'Operation Drag Strip', one of those in which it had sought to set out a blueprint for drag racing, noted:

> Of equal importance to the basic material facilities is manpower. Here is where most strips stumble, whether they are operated by clubs or by private parties. Dependable personnel is the keynote to success in any such venture and should never be taken lightly. Some strips have found that it is necessary to hire all their officials and crew members in order to keep them on the ball, while others have been able to handle the details through assignments to members of sponsoring organizations – some such members are eager to contribute their time and effort just for the sake of their *sport* but since so much of this work is a thankless chore, the attractiveness often wears off after a few months and crews must be reassigned.[27]

In effect, the bigger drag racing grew as a sport and spectator sport the more difficult it became for the NHRA to hold on to the 'community program' type of presentation but this, as we shall see, was a vital part of *Hot Rod*'s stress that drag racing was as wholesome as apple pie.

Through the 1950s *Hot Rod* gloried in events and testimonials which suggested as much. In September 1953 the Secretary of the Interior was enrolled as the fifteen thousandth member of the NHRA: 'the Secretary hastened to point out that true hot rodders are not menaces, as the public often brands them, but are a safety conscious segment of everyday life with mutual interests in things mechanical.' In the journal of the National Safety Council police chiefs attested to the fact, repeated by the hot rod magazines, that if you gave a hot rodder a break there was nothing wrong with him. The Chief of Detectives of Kansas City, Missouri revealed how they had got up to 1,300 local kids into thirty two clubs organised around a safety programme, formed a new Kansas City Timing Association as a non-profit making organisation and isolated hot rod racing onto a new drag strip, the first day of sport on which had involved 200 racers and 18,000 paying spectators, and how, the summer season of 1955 had involved ten meets and a profit of $21,800 which had helped pay off the debts involved in creating the strip. Future surpluses would go to local high schools to fund driver instruction scholarships for teachers so that they could give correct lessons in driver training and the like.[28]

The difficulty was that the informal and not so respectable aspects of hot rodding would not disappear. The editor became increasingly curt to readers whose letters suggested there was a rational case for street racing. In December 1952 Bob Kirchner of Los Angeles wrote:

> The Tuesday night drags have been going on for countless months on streets that are just outside of the city limits. The streets are rarely used at nights and spectators as well as draggers keep a sharp lookout for cars. When one does come it can be seen a long ways off, and racing quits until the car passes. No accidents have occurred and I doubt if any will. Most of the participants can be seen at numerous drag strips – Santa Ana etc. on Sunday afternoons. A couple hold records there and at San Diego. Why can't these strips of highway be blocked off for night dragging legally? Time clocks aren't neccesary as the guys just want competition!

To which the editor replied: 'Apparently, you haven't seen the light. The squirrel tactics in which you and your few fellow drive-in Barney Oldfields are indulging yourselves in are precisely the kind of thing which will kill legitimate hot rodding for thousands of others of us who are interested in actual performance data . . . You're more out of date than the horse!' And such irritatation is not difficult to understand for whenever, every two years or so, the magazine patted itself and NHRA on the back for the 'good publicity' hot rodding was getting and for the elimination of street dragging, soon enough there would be another 'outbreak' of the illegal sport and/or a media-inspired moral panic often via fiction or a film which led on to threats of bans in various states on all hot rodding activity or on all hot rod cars. In the early 1950s *Hot Rod* was to attack, among others, *Esquire, The Saturday Evening Post, Life,* record companies and Hollywood for putting out stories which promoted street racing or dangerous games on wheels. The prelude to the *Esquire* short story gives the flavour: 'it's a chicken town, but if your rod's running smooth you can still get your kicks on the road'.[29] The *Saturday Evening Post's* story of 1956 tells it all in the title – '52 Miles of Terror'. *Hot Rod* complained bitterly.

A further irritation was that every so often figures in authority would crack *Hot Rod's* virtuous circuit by claiming that, far from promoting safety, drag racing was either irrelevant to traffic accidents or actually served to promote speeding on the public highways. Thus *Hot Rod's* ire was aroused in 1953 when the National Automobile Dealer's Association, in a move praised by the *New York Times,* resolved at its convention not to sell parts to hot rodders.[30] Then in 1954 the Californian police department which had pioneered cooperation with hot rodders began to withdraw from such contact 'lest there be public criticism'.[31] In early 1955 a big street race in metropolitan Los Angeles received wide publicity, in which the press claimed that 125 people were arrested though *Hot Rod* insisted that police reports revealed only seventy four arrests only one of whom was a member of the NHRA. The magazine drew the moral that such behaviour might be expected when the nearest drag strip to the area was over thirty miles distant but also averred that such behaviour 'neutralized the effects of at least three years progress in the field of gaining universal respect for the very worthy hot rod sport'.[32] A letter in the next issue from an officer in the Traffic Education department of the Los Angeles police department argued that of the seventy two actually arrested (forty three juveniles and twenty nine adults) only four had beeen engaged in street racing: 'This program of assigning men to work with the hot rodders has paid off in Los Angeles, and we are proud to say that hot rodders are among our most enthusiastic boosters. We want to assure the hundreds of hot rodders in the Los Angeles area that the L. A. police department will continue to assist them in the future as we have done in the past.'

However, the situation never remained too cosy for too long. The next year there was a well-publicised 'hot rod riot' in Daytona, Florida at the time of the National Association for Stock Car Automobile Racing (NASCAR) Speedweek.[33] NASCAR, established in 1948, was, basically, the family-controlled organisation which developed and controlled another form of American autosport which grew into a multi-million-dollar business – stock car racing.[34] Each year it held a big meeting at Daytona. This time it and a rival organisation to the NHRA, the Automobile Timing Association of America, had announced the festival would include a week of drag racing too. This, *Hot Rod* indignantly asserted, had been untrue, such drag racing as had been arranged was spasmodic and ill-organised. The town had been packed with auto-enthusiasts with nowhere to run. One young driver had clashed with a policeman and his treatment had sparked off 'the riot'. Still, the National Guard had moved in with loaded carbines to disperse a ten thousand strong crowd and newspapers across the nation carried headlines like: 'Tear Gas ends Hot Rod Riot: Troops Jail 85'. For the rest of 1956 *Hot Rod* fought a defensive action against official condemnation not just of this incident but of organised drag racing too.

In June the editor reported:

> Recently a representative of one of the nation's many Safety organizations (not the National Safety Council) took the sport of drag racing to task, branding it 'detrimental' without having either fact or figure to warrant his attack. Not only were his prejudiced opinions distributed among other Safety organizations but they were reprinted by newspapers in several areas, with the result that the organized hot rod sport's reputation felt an undeserved sting.

Hot Rod went on to make its usual claims about safety checks, self-discipline, charitable works, the need to harness the inherent speed urge into an active programme of applied safety rather than distributing 'don't do this' 'fancy worded' posters and:

> As to the statistical safety factor of organized drag racing, fewer injuries are encountered throughout the entire country in a whole year's drag racing than occur during a single season of football at most any college. Records kept by one of America's leading insurance companies, which regularly insures drag races throughout the US, substantiates this statement.

In August the editor reviewed the sport's close relation with the California Highway Patrol and pointed to recent articles by policemen in the publication of the National Safety Council which attested to the benefits of organised drag racing especially when organised in the public benefit way. But in the very next month the editor reported a blow to the sport's solar plexus. Newspaper stories around the country were repeating a controversy among top policemen 'as to whether drag racing was a merit or a menace':

> An interesting coincidence was noted in the three locales which produced the

most violent objections against the acceptance of organized drag facilities: not one of them had as much as given the program a trial. Like ostriches with their heads buried deep in the sand, civic and/or law enforcement officials had vehemently refused to consider the commonly known fact that wherever properly run drag strips have been provided they have proven to be community benefits![35]

However, the International Association of Chiefs of Police (IACP) meeting in convention in Chicago did soon pass a resolution assailing the safety effects of organised dragstrips or, as headlined in the *New York Times*: 'End 'Drag' Racing Police Chiefs Ask: Group says Legalized Speed Contests for Teen-Agers Threaten Road Safety'. The police chiefs argued that the element of competition encouraged through racing was inconsistent with co-operation, the basic quality of good driving on the road.

> It was argued that if time, money and effort expended in supervised 'drag' competition were applied to driver training among the young, a sounder approach to the problem of speeding and reckless driving would be assured. The committee declared that speed was the leading contributory cause of major accidents and 'drag' racing placed prime emphasis on speed. Drag racers compete from a standing start to maximum acceleration within a given distance. The group's resolution declared that this tended to inspire participants to carry the practice to the public streets.[36]

In November *Hot Rod* claimed that the matter had come up unexpectedly at a sub committee meeting at the convention. There had been little debate and few of those present had any first-hand familiarity with well run drag strips. So a few ignorant individuals had produced a damaging opinion. The committee had called on police forces to 'outlaw' drag strips. *Hot Rod* scoffed: how could this be done? But the next month the magazine had to concede that it was the new Commissioner of an old ally – the California Highway Patrol – who had not only headed the committee of the IACP which had produced the anti-drag strip resolution but was going to pull the Patrol away from any involvement with sanctioning strips: 'because there was considerable evidence they did nothing except encourage speed competition'. The editor demurred and cited the views of an Assistant Commissioner who said there was a decline in accidents among hot rods and a decline in complaints about them.

Another blow fell in 1957 when the National Safety Council issued a statement opposing drag racing in the cause of traffic safety.[37] *Hot Rod* fought back, but the early years of the attempt to define and create a new

Driving ambitions

automobile sport revealed that the way ahead was not likely to be clear and easy. Despite a decade of great effort the hot rod apparatus had not suceeded in convincing authority that hot rodding really was quite respectable and socially beneficial. In various combinations, the issues of road safety, commercialism, Detroit and state regulation were to cause the hot rod apparatus many more problems in the years to come, especially as the automobile itself, icon of the post-war American way of life, came to be regarded with more and more scepticism.

Notes

1 *Hot Rod* Magazine (*HRM*), 6, December 1953, p. 5.
2 *HRM*, 3, December 1950, p. 28–31.
3 'National hot rod association formed', *HRM*, 4, May 1951, p. 24 and editorial, June 1951.
4 *HRM*, 5, February 1952, p. 5.
5 L. Ryan, 'The hot rod story', *HRM*, 5, March 1952, pp. 30–2, 62–3.
6 Similar advice was carried in *Hop Up* (*HU*) and in e.g. *Rod Builder and Customizer*, 2, August 1957.
7 W. Parks, *Drag Racing: Yesterday and Today* (New York, 1966), p. 27–32.
8 *HU*, 1, September 1951, p. 38.
9 *HU*, 1, October 1951, p. 13.
10 *HRM*, 6, January 1953, p. 5.
11 E. Jaderquist and G. Borgeson (eds.), *Best Hot Rods* (New York, 1953), p. 21.
12 *HU*, 1, March 1952, p. 3.
13 *HU*, 2, August 1952, p. 34.
14 W. Parks, 'Operation drag strip', *HRM*, 7, January 1954, pp. 56–60.
15 *HRM*, 7, July 1954, p. 5.
16 'Forming a hot rod club', *HRM*, 3, December 1950, p. 28–31.
17 E.g. 'Indianapolis hot rod derby', *HRM*, 9, June 1956, pp. 52–3.
18 *HRM*, 7, May 1954, p. 39.
19 *HRM*, 7, September 1954, p. 5.
20 'Harnessing the hot rods', *HRM*, 8, June 1955, pp. 44–5.
21 *HRM*, 8, October 1955, p. 5.
22 *Car Craft*, 3, March 1956, p. 4.
23 *HRM*, 9, June 1956, p. 5.
24 *HRM*, 5, August 1952, p. 5.
25 *HRM*, 6, January 1953, p. 5.
26 'Southern California championship drags', *HRM*, 6, June 1953, pp. 24–7.
27 *HRM*, 7, January 1954, p. 57.
28 Major E. Pond, 'Give the hot rodders a break', *Public Safety*, May 1956, pp. 4–6.
29 K. Kolb, 'Sunday drive', *Esquire*, May 1953, p. 95.
30 *New York Times*, 1 March 1953.
31 *HRM*, 7, April 1954, p. 5.
32 *HRM*, 8, February 1955, p. 5.
33 E.g. *New York Times*, 26 and 27 February 1956.
34 Like all auto enthusiasms stock car racing and NASCAR lack documentation

but see J. Ingram, 'Battle of the independents', *Southern Exposure*, 7, 1979, pp. 92–9 for some very interesting details of the way this sport was organised. Also R. Pillsbury, 'A mythology at the brink: stock car racing in the American South', *Sports Place*, 3, Fall 1989, pp. 2–12.

35 *HRM*, 9, September 1956, p. 5.
36 *New York Times*, 14 September 1956.
37 *New York Times*, 12 February 1957.

Chapter Four
The development of drag racing and the early hot rod economy

Thoughts pertaining to youth, hot rodders and Chevrolet

The Hot Rod movement and interest in things connected with hop-up and speed is still growing. As an indication: the publications devoted to hot rodding and hop-upping, of which some half dozen have a very large circulation and are distributed nationally, did not exist some six years ago. From cover to cover they are full of Fords. It is not surprising that the majority of hot rodders are eating, sleeping and dreaming modified Fords. They know Ford parts from stem to stern better than the Ford people themselves. A young man buying a magazine for the first time immediately becomes introduced to Ford. It is reasonable to assume that when hot rodders or hot rod-influenced persons buy transportation, they buy Fords. As they progress in age and income, they graduate from jalopies to second-hand Fords, then to new Fords. Should we consider that it would be desirable to make these youths Chevrolet-minded? I think that we are in a position to carry out a successful attempt. However, there are many factors against us:

1. Loyalty and experience with Ford.
2. Hop-up industry is geared to Ford.
3. Law of numbers – thousands are and will be working on Fords for active competition
4. Appearance of Ford's overhead V8, now one year ahead of us.

. . . The slide-rule potential of our RPO V8 engine is extremely high, but to let things run their natural course will put us one year behind – and then not too many hot rodders will pick Chevrolet for development. One factor which can largely overcome this handicap would be the availability of ready-engineered parts for higher output. . . . (Internal Chevrolet memo 1953)[1]

Most sports and enthusiasms are involved in a particular set of economic opportunities and enterprises, and these change through time though not always in the simple way that broad references to 'capitalism' or 'commodity provision' or 'big business' or 'professionalisation' etc. might lead us to believe. *Hot Rod*'s, the NHRA's and other magazines' and organisations' worries about official condemnation of drag racing

The development of drag racing

gained in force through the 1950s and the early 1960s as the economic possibilities which surrounded the sport or, at least, the term 'hot rod', increased and expanded. It is necessary to sketch the scope of the early hot rod economy here since it had important effects on the way drag racing developed.

The auto magazines

In 1947 the business magazine *Fortune* published an issue: 'Dedicated to American Selling' which estimated that while real incomes had risen by 40% in the period 1940–7, the amount available for discretionary spending was up 160%.[2] This figure, and the rise and shifts in population, caused *Fortune* to speak of 'portentous changes' in the American market, and this was soon to be proved a correct assessment. The automobile was the exact symbol of these changes. During the 1950s general consumer indebtedness rose three times as fast as personal incomes, while in the decade which ended in 1957 credit for the purchase of automobiles rose by 800%.[3] Between 1947 and 1955 forty-five million new cars were registered in the USA.[4] By 1955 around one-third of spending units in the *lowest* quintile of incomes owned a car, and by 1958 five million teenagers held a licence to drive and around one and a half million teenagers owned cars.[5] Advertisments sought to convince the better-off of the horrors of 'one car capitivity' and Americans began to travel a billion miles a day on tyres. The eccentricities of the annual model change became a prime news story, car parking space in some New York garages shrank by 15% in four years as cars grew bigger, and, in a real flavour of the times, Moscow, Idaho boasted it had more service stations than Moscow, Russia.[6] In short, in America the years directly after the war were that period of 'affluence' when most people became comfortable and well-off compared to their parents or pre-war standards and the car seemed to be the perfect expression of this. Such analysis as there is of this cultural change dwells on *new* cars: making some none too clear connection, for example, between tail fins and some unspecified 'American Dream', but at this period the automobile in *all* its forms came a new peak as commodity, as an object in use and as cultural icon.

One result of this was a new spate of magazine appealing to motorists of all kinds including those interested in various kinds of auto sport.[7] The first – *Speed Age* – appeared in 1947 devoted to oval track racing, followed in the same year by *Road and Track* then *Hot Rod* and several others in the 1950s. Basically these magazines split into two groups, those that dealt with hot rods and those that favoured the, mainly European, sports cars. I will discuss this element more in Chapter Eight. I have already noted that *Hot Rod* was set up as a voice for respectable rodding. The magazine was first published in January 1948 with a print run of five thousand: by 1950 two hundred thousand copies were produced each issue, while by 1956 it was the world's top-selling automobile magazine with half a million copies sold each month and a claimed readership of well over a million. It had become the flagship of a thriving publications group established by one of the founders of *Hot Rod* R. E. Petersen. In short, this magazine was a great commercial success. The embarrassment regularly caused by media commentary on 'outbreaks' of street racing and high rates of automobile accidents among the young seemed to suggest that the title was a liability, and the new magazines which were soon developed by the owner of *Hot Rod* to serve other automobile interests had much more circumspect titles – *Motor Trend, Car Craft, Auto Sportsman,* etc. However, the title's sharply rising sales curve seemed to indicate that the term was also an prize asset to be guarded. 'Hot Rod' was registered as a trade mark in 1950, and other magazines or organisations that started to enter drag racing or use the phrase 'hot-rod' were derided for having missed the hard times and for seeking to cash-in.

There was a very close relation between the specialist magazines and the administrative organisations of the enthusiasm. *Hot Rod*'s link to the National Hot Rod Association (NHRA) tended to ensure that other organisations in the sport were 'represented' by other magazines drawn in because of the evident success of *Hot Rod*. They tended to present the same kind of stories and ideologies as *Hot Rod* but allowed views dissident to the NHRA to find an airing and some clearly favoured other associations and their stories. So, for example, *Rod Builder and Customizer* tended to push the Automobile Timing Association of America (ATAA) and dwell on its World Series championship rather than the NHRA and its major races. As we shall see, the development of competing associations interlinked with competing magazines combined with some other problems of developing sport, in ways that were to pose quite a problem for *Hot Rod*, the NHRA and their control of the nature of drag racing. My point here is that the plethora of enthusiasts' magazines represented one element in the early hot rod economy.

For those who owned and controlled, the magazines, especially *Hot Rod*, caught the tide of post-war affluence and specifically that wave which lapped around the automobile, automobile sport and associated do-it-yourself activities. This was observable in the change in form of the magazine: a swift transformation from twenty-four pages with a few small advertisments up to seventy-six pages with a rotagravure section, twelve full page adverts and plenty of smaller ones. And *Hot Rod* was only the first of many ventures by its publisher, soon to be called Trend (later Petersen) Publications which, at this time, shared the same address as the magazine and the NHRA. It swallowed *Hot Rod*'s first competitor, *Hop Up*, in 1954, renamed it and repositioned it in the market for auto-enthusiasms. Trend had set up its own 'rival' to *Hot Rod*, *Honk*, in 1953, which was quickly renamed *Car Craft* (sub-head 'The show-how magazine') and was aimed at a slightly different market though, in the 1960s, it was to become Petersen's main publication concerned directly with drag racing. Petersen also established *Rod and Custom* in 1952 as its offering in the market for pocket-size automotive magazines. By early 1953 an advertisment claimed a combined readership of half a million for *Hot Rod* and its sister monthlies *Custom Cars* and *How to Buy a Car* magazines. In mid-1949 *Motor Trend* was launched and by 1955 was referred to as: 'Motor Trend – The Car Owner's Magazine, the largest selling automotive magazine in the world' with a registered 431,101 sales monthly though it was overtaken by *Hot Rod* itself in 1956. Various other car-related periodicals were added to the stable: *Cycle and Auto*, *Auto Sportsman*, *Motor Life* and so on, as the publishers discerned or tried to create new fragments in areas related to the auto as an object in use.

By 1957 the Petersen Automobile Group claimed all its automobile magazines had a combined circulation of over 1.1 million and a readership of 4 million each month. *Hot Rod* started to carry a series of advertisments aimed at potential advertisers as in:

The Petersen Reader is Influential

The Petersen Automotive Group's 4 million readers are recognized authorities on things automotive. Friends and neighbours follow their lead. Reach them with your sales message. Sell them, and you'll also sell the additional millions who are directly influenced by P. A. G. readers.[8]

revealing that it is not just sociologists who are aware of the two-step channel of the communication of media messages. The publisher went into books too: about hot rods (which got favourable reviews in the magazine), about cars and then about sports and DIY. more generally. A 1956 Trend Books advertisement in *Hot Rod* listed these auto-associated titles: *Sports Cars, Plastic Cars, The World's Fastest Cars, Custom Cars, Hot Rod Annual, Classic Cars and Antiques, Automotive Yearbook*, while other titles included: *Pleasure Boating, Spin Tackle Fishing, Underwater: The Skin Divers' Manual, Archery Adventure, Home Music Systems, High Fidelity*, and so on.

From the initial venture with *Hot Rod* a group was built up which claimed to be the largest automotive publishing house in the world by 1962 and one that was to appear many times in the business magazines and financial pages of corporate America. The first of these was when *Hot Rod*'s owner and publisher appeared on the front page of *The Wall Street Journal* in 1960 as one of a series about 'new millionaires and how they made their fortune', which told the story of how a barely solvent press agent of 1948 had become sole owner of a business with sales of $10 million a year and a personal fortune of $3.5 million and whose interests now included share dealings and real estate. Of course, there were rivals in the automotive publishing field. *The Wall Street Journal* article noted how competition from other publishers in the early 1950s had turned a group profit of $65,000 in 1952 into a $102,000 loss in 1953.[9]

Not surprisingly given *Hot Rod*'s success, other magazines and other publishers were attracted into the field of opportunities around rodding and drag racing in the mid-1950s. Pocket sized magazines were: *Rodding and Restyling* (1954) and *Rod Builder and Customizer* (1956) published in the East; and *Custom Rodder* (1957), which became *Speed and Custom*, and *Car: Speed and Style* (1957) which both had the same Ohio publisher. Most of these rival publications tended to take digs at the very powerful economic position *Hot Rod* and the NHRA had established and which they sought to convert into a moral pulpit to speak for *all* enthusiasts. Several smaller pulp magazines concerned with drag racing and the hot rod enthusiasm also entered the market, relying on press handouts and stories ghost written in Detroit and by other auto industry press agents, and trying to get a cut of the lucrative advertising which was attracted to the hot rod world. For, as I have suggested in noting *Hot Rod*'s changing format, the magazines of the enthusiasm soon attracted a deal of advertising, much of it auto-related but a good slice concerned with general expenditure: cigarettes, clothes, soft drinks, spot removal cream etc.

Other direct economic opportunities

As early as February 1953 *Hot Rod* ran an article called 'How Much Did It Cost?' which was, infact, a response to a piece about the enthusiasm which had appeared in *Business Week* in March 1952 – 'Hot Rodding Roars into Big Business'. *Hot Rod* began: 'One of the country's top business publications last year estimated that hot rodders would spend approximately $50 million dollars on hot rod parts alone.' The article went on to say that the staff of the magazine had been sceptical at first but when they started figuring it out they weren't so sure. Then followed a fairly obviously advertisement-related questionnaire in which readers were asked to answer questions like: 'What have you purchased recently?', 'Have you bought an automobile this year?', 'Check your income bracket' and the like. Attracting big advertisers became another economic opportunity the enthusiasm provided.

One set of regular advertisers, the manufacturers of special equipment, bolt-on speed items and the like, formed another set of economic interests who depended on the activity and its central core of drag racing, along with the owners of speed shops which, at this time, were the main outlet for equipment, associated clothing and paraphenalia, magazines and so on. As I will indicate in Chapter Six, many of the equipment manufacturers and shop owners had been racers, vetrans of the dry lakes, as were the writers for many of the magazines. The major sponsor of the ATAA was the Maremont Corporation, a maker of automobile parts and oil companies became involved in various aspects of sponsorship. The strips too became part of the economy for the NHRA and *Hot Rod* had to accept the dominance of commercial tracks from the late 1950s. While the magazine went on boosting club activities, urging them to hold Christmas parties for mentally retarded children etc. it soon had to accept that its civic ideal would not hold as clubs generally relinquished the management of drag strips to professional promotors especially as strips became more specialised facilities as the rise in airport traffic no longer allowed clubs to use spare runways. Then, as the internal Chevrolet memo published at the head of this chapter suggests, a memo that was acted on and led to the 'muscle car' era of the mid-1950s and on, hot rodding did attract the interest of Detroit and, as I will sketch later, not simply, as is sometimes suggested, as a source of styling ideas. The way enthusiasms can vibrate into mainstream consumption is rather more complicated than is often allowed.

While 'hot rod' was a term of abuse in the 1950s, the magazines' success and the boom in the sales of components in the speed shops seemed to indicate that the term had connected to some mood in post-war America which existed in a much wider audience than that which raced on streets or strips. The first-ever issue stated: 'Hot Rod is published to inform and entertain those interested in automobiles whose bodies and engines have been rebuilt in the quest for better performance and appearance' and the journal was quick to distinguish between hot rodders, who experimented, studied, and laboured over their vehicles, and a 'fringe element' of 'shot rodders', whose 'trim jobs' had only the surface appearance of a genuine hot rod. The real hot rod project was a serious one and those who engaged in it had put too much time and money in their machines to risk them in street races and dangerous driving. The magazine sought to draw its younger readers into this serious project by sympathetic leadership, organisation and a distinct 'show-how with know-how' approach. But some dangers lurked in this strategy. The magazine's title had been chosen precisely because it overlapped two activities. The redeemable portion of the frivolous teenagers were to be attracted and lured into the graver sub-culture of effort and sacrifice. However, adopting this name might mean that the magazine and its offshoots would be marked by any brush trying to tar street racers and delinquents, and this might well endanger its future commercial success and growth to a market well beyond teenagers. A decade and more of struggle about a sign – what *exactly* was a 'hot rod' – ensued out of the initial choice of title. The magazine constantly worked with the meanings of the term, redefining it, seeking to extend its frontiers to enclose more and more people, and to convince the swelling readership that they really did all belong in 'the hot rod movement'.

In May 1953 a new permanent subtitle was placed across the front page: 'The Automotive How-To-Do-It Magazine' and by the beginning of 1954 the editor was in an expansive mood: 'Little by little the boundaries that used to define a hot rod are being stretched further and further. As they are the category takes on a much more extensive meaning, embracing most types of automotive vehicles that are developed for the purpose of providing more than just transportation for their owners.' At one time the term had applied only to 'stripped down, souped-up cars of the vintage roadster type but now applied to custom cars, closed cars, even sports cars.' The common desire was 'to do something different and outstanding for the improvement (in their own eyes at least) of their automobile'.

This attempt to broaden the meaning of the term so that almost any home-tinkering or maintenance could qualify continued throughout 1954 and 1955. In June 1955 the editor asked readers to write in saying whether they wanted more features on cars other than '32 roadsters:

> The hot rod term may have been applied only to stripped down cars of rather dubious ancestry at one time and certainly there was no token of respect in the

early use of the title, but today the term has expanded its meaning to a point where it doesn't actually represent a particular type of car but rather an endeavour, an interest, a desire to create a car that is different.

And the message was repeated in December:

> Where the so-called hot rod craze once concerned itself with the mere stripping down and souping up of early model autos for little other than all out top speed performance, the current interest lies not only in boosting the car's potential speed but also in improving its appearance, comfort, handling and road-holding qualities, efficiency, economy, endurance and all-over safety. Add these all together and you're bound to produce a better automobile – which hot rodders do regularly.

This enlargement of what a 'hot rod' could be, and what hot rodders did, was reflected in some of the feature stories and advertisements which the ever-expanding magazine carried. Even the letters selected for the 'Shop Talk' technical help section began to concern modern family cars not vintage Fords, and at the end of 1955 another boundary moved with the first 'Rod Test' of a new Detroit model, a change not unconnected, presumably, with the increase in mainstream auto-advertising being carried. This 'break with long standing precedent' was rather nervously explained in the next editorial of January 1956. The editor argued that the magazine had become dissatisfied with tests done by other magazines, that many refinements developed by rodders were now stock items, that 'rod tests' would specialise in basic mechanics and inherent performance, not the fripperies of styling or meaningless 'performance statistics' and went on: 'the learned mechanical world recognizes the amateur auto enthusiast has much to offer. As a result we've undertaken the responsibility for passing along the new car appraisals of our crew of experienced hot rodders, they're people who know, love and live engines and automobiles.'

In the ensuing months this innovation produced shoals of letters complaining about the way the magazine was developing. In the March 1956 issue the author of the 'Rod Test' prefaced his article with a column justifying such reports, repeating the editor's arguments and adding that rod tests would suggest do-it-yourself changes which could improve performance. While in May a reply to critical letters argued, disarmingly: 'the current eight page increase makes it possible to include the rod test as a bonus rather than minimize the typical hot rod coverage' and the 'Rod Test' that month could be titled 'Dodge D500: A Production Line Hot Rod', a claim to be repeated in months to come as in, for example: 'a lightly disguised factory hot rod' which continued on: 'It was a happy day for motorists in general when the big wheels who design the autos most of us drive got the "go" fever not so long ago and borrowed some of the hot rodders' sacred devices to make them stock equipment on their formerly dull machines.'[10] By January 1957 the editor was confident this change in direction had been successfully achieved. Noting that 'we have found that our habitual readers represent all avenues of automotive interest' he went on that the magazine hadn't been sure that readers would accept new model tests in *Hot Rod* but enough letters of acclamation had accumulated 'to more than justify the slight departure from our previous restricted path.' And the magazine now regularly referred to hot rodders, or rather 'the vast ranks of the hot rod world', in the broadest of terms as 'automotive enthusiasts'.

In July 1958 the editor mused: 'One of the questions most often asked hot rodders is, "Why don't you get away from that term hot rod?" ' He noted that the origin of the term was unknown and argued that the brevity of the phrase made it very adaptable for use by publicity seekers and in sensational headlines, yet:

> The true hot rodder is a person blessed with an extraordinary interest in, and understanding of, automobiles – nothing more, nothing less. He is by nature an experimentalist, one who enjoys doing things the hard way. His ability to improvise makes him a handy man to have around in a pinch. Not content with normal production standards, he likes to exercise his own originality and ingenuity through means of making experiments and testing their worth. The term hot rod identifies this interest. Good or bad, it pinpoints the automotive experimentalist and his realm.

It had been a long uphill fight to create acceptance and respect for the 'hot rod crusade' but the magazine had 'refused to hide behind more flowery titles accepting instead the challenge that went with the hot rod handle'.

Soon another shift took place. The 'Automotive How-To-Do-It' subtitle was dropped from the cover to be replaced by 'Everybody's Automotive Magazine'. This change was explained in January 1958 when, dwelling on its position as the world's best-selling automotive magazine, the editorial ran: 'All this success hasn't come easily. Due to the controversial nature of the magazine's title Hot Rod has had to sell itself, literally converting public opinion and building acceptance for the field of activity it proudly represents. The past ten years have been filled with suggestions that we "get away from that hot rod name and the stigma that goes with it".' Instead the magazine had campaigned and organised. It had stressed safety and expertise:

> In order to convey the hot rod message to more people, we've made Hot Rod 'Everybody's Automotive Magazine'. It is no longer limited to features about stripped down, hopped-up, early model cars – you'll find a cross section of the diversified automotive interests that attract people to cars. However we'll still maintain a goodly portion of top quality coverage on competition and custom cars – they're the real backbone of our magazine and our main stock in trade.

But such changes, and the increasing number of general interest automotive articles, created reader dissent and in April 1958 the editorial replied to these criticisms in somewhat conspiratorial tones. It argued that much of the merit of the sport remained hidden within the ranks of rodders and seldom reached the general public:

> This is also one of the prime reasons for making Hot Rod 'Everybody's Automotive Magazine' – to get the word around. The best way to introduce Mr. Average Citizen to hot rodding's accomplishments is to bait him with something that's of particular interest to him. Hence our Detroit products coverage, our Quarter Midgets, Go Karts, etc. A continued increase in circulation figures supports this theory. So if you're one of those dyed-in-the-wool hot rodders who tends to resent the intrusion of these sideline subjects into your magazine, bear in mind that HRM is seeking more genuine recognition for *your* sport and getting it.

Still letters continued to appear arguing for a purer, more restricted, definition as in May 1958 complaining about an article on pick-up trucks: 'The type of article is crowding out those good old technical features that HRM was famous for. They are useless to the average hot rodder and only serve to disgust him with the magazine.' Or as when an article on small economy cars provoked a letter in October 1958: 'I scarcely miss an issue of Hot Rod. Now some people have different definitions of hot rodding, some good and some bad, but I'll lay odds that nobody considers a 90 hp Rambler or an 85 hp Volvo as being in the realms of hot rodding.'

Again and again the magazine tried to justify its tactics. Its overall stress, albeit defensively, was now on general mechanical automotive interests and technical participation. For example, in December 1958, and in marked contrast to the messages of 1948, the editor wrote:

> In spite of frequent criticisms, Hot Rod has clung to its title, accepting the challenge its name may have implied, and dedicating its contents to the combined subjects of automotive appreciation and safety. Today's picture looks bright . . . the term hot rod has become a definition for mechanical

know-how. The hot rodder's dedication to safety and driving courtesy has helped make our highways safer, and his contributions to automotive development have added many useful and beneficial improvements to today's family car. Aware that others, too, not necessarily hot rodders, were interested in automotive experimentation and fact-finding we've developed Hot Rod into what is termed 'Everybody's Automotive Magazine' adding variety to the scope of its coverage.

It argued that a lot of the original dry lakes enthusiasts had moved into new fields like go-karts: 'those diminutive hot rods that are sweeping the country', or as in May 1959 when introducing a new section in the magazine: 'Maybe you're one of our long time readers who remembers the days when we featured roadsters, roadsters and more roadsters, almost exclusively. If so, you may be lamenting the fact that ol'HR's coverage has been expanded into many phases of automotive interest and you'll probably snap when you see our newest addition, Boat Roddin'?'

In the pages of this very successful specialist magazine the phrase 'hot rod' was generalised, stretched and exploited so as to be applied to almost any activity related to mechanical propulsion. So boats were referred to as 'drag craft', while articles like 'Hot Rods in the Sand' insisted that dune buggies were the latest expression of the true hot rod spirit. An article 'Draggin' at the Lakes' in March 1960 had nothing to do with late night journeys to the high desert or with skidding across the dust of El Mirage, those days had long passed: it was about power boating on an artificial stretch of water. Adverse letters always appeared, and reappeared again and again in the following decades as *Hot Rod* made some rather sharp changes in focus such as this example of March 1962:

> Would you please define the term hot rod? In your magazine you have called the following at one time or another a hot rod: competition sports cars, dragsters, customized passenger cars, track roadsters, Indianapolis cars, land speed record cars, motorcycles. There may be others which I have missed. If the word hot rod is so all inclusive then it has lost its value as a use for identifying a certain type of vehicle . . . over the years the term has lost its meaning.

One thing the hot rod experience revealed was the way *other* enthusiasms could be spotted, nutured, shaped and profitably sustained through an active, educational, even political, approach and this was a route the Petersen Group, and others, were to follow many times. The magazine's role was now to stand at the centre of a major publishing group and to act as a test bed in which the market in new interests could be explored. That said, it is most important to appreciate, as I will detail later, that while the magazine coverage did sometimes veer away from a direct contact with drag racing and even difficult automobile modification through the years, it never broke the basic bond, and time and again a new editor would announce that it had strayed too far, lost its way and declare that *Hot Rod*'s real purpose was to cater for those who wanted to re-build cars to increase performance, it was not for mere 'parts exchangers' and that he was going to move its articles back on to the classic course. Oscillation there was but the magazine never got too far from a 'show-how with know-how' line.

In addition to publishing with its associated advertising revenues, the originators of the magazine, as I mentioned earlier, had also been prominent in arranging the first exposition of lake racers and street rods in Los Angeles in January 1948, designed as part of the campaign to indicate how serious respectable rodders were. This venture transmuted into an annual Motorama starting in 1950 and later the Motor Review: full-blown motor shows which drew large crowds, displays by the Detroit companies, extensive media coverage and so on, and where hot rods appeared as but one of a number of elements in displays of all facets of 'the' automobile or as prizes in newspaper competitions. Among the officers of the companies which organised these shows were the publisher of *Hot Rod*, writers for the magazine and for the NHRA. The companies all shared the same address for a while until the NHRA moved to a new one in 1956.

Petersen tried to explore other economic avenues. *Hot Rod* brought out toy hot rods for children for Christmas 1949 and even tried to get into hot rod records and established its own label in the early 1950s, another move explained as an attempt to get good publicity for rodding. It issued at least two 'platters' by 'hot rodder's favourite band': Joe 'Leadfoot' Darensbourg and his Flat-Out-Five. The magazine plugged these in April 1952 in a rather untypical 'jive' talk: 'Drag Race opens with a realistic, drag start rap that should really fracture the fiends.' But 'Hot Rod Harry'/'Hot Rod Cowboy' and 'Saturday Night Drag Race Parts I and II' do not appear to have been successful. In July 1955 the magazine told how the staff of *Hot Rod* acted as automotive consultants for Key Records on Jack Benny's Sportsmen Quartet's record 'Hot Rod Hop' which included authentic hot rod garage sounds – a fender grinder, a mallet hitting a tyre beading, etc. – presented in dance rhythm. *Hot Rod* described the result as 'a real garter snapper' which integrated two top hobbies of the younger set – hot rodding and interpretive bop. In some of the dances suggested: 'each couple embellishes the dance with automotive motions such as steering, hand signalling, fixin' the flat', etc. Windshield wiper was made 'by each dancer representing separate hot rods each with twin blades arcing in separate directions'. Readers were urged to 'dig these dipstick doodles!'

While *Hot Rod*'s own excursions into the pop aspect of youth culture do not seem to have been successful there certainly was a market in post-war America for rod-related records though often ones that highlighted aspects of rodding the magazine frowned on. 'Hot Rod Race', a talking blues number of 1950 sold two-hundred thousand copies with verses that ran:

> Yes, he was all revved up and rarin' to go,
> Wanted to match wheels for a mile or so.
> So we made grease spots of many good towns,
> Left the cops runnin' round and round.

Another disc, 'Transfusion', with the key line: 'slip the blood to me bud', sold almost a million. An article in *Life* in 1960, 'Blasting Off to the Races', on America's fastest growing spectator sport, auto-racing in all its forms, revealed how Riverside Records had found a niche in the market for selling records of auto-racing sounds.

> A real racing fan can listen to the sound of a car's engine and tell you how many cylinders there are. He listens for other sounds, too – engines idling or revving up or just passing by. And the true aficionado likes perhaps best of all to hear the sound of gearshifts. Particularly in stereo. . . The only thing missing from the picture is the smell of burning Castrol, which is a special oil used in high speed engines. We have often considered including with our records a little packet of Castrol. I am positive that we could get anyone who buys our records to put a bit of Castrol on their frying pan in the kitchen and let it burn a bit while they're playing the record. Castrol incense – it would be easy to do.[11]

So certain aspects of the exploitation of the hot rod term and enthusiasm did drift away from the direct grip of the hot rod apparatus. Still if we add together all the elements I have sketched so far in this chapter the extent and variety of elements in the economy of the enthusiasm can begin to be appreciated. We can see a whole network of business opportunities which were settling around the term and the sport. However, three dangers lurked round the edges of this hot rod economy: the efforts of other organizations to 'horn into' drag racing, mass media sensationalism and the continuing official concern with dangerous driving on highways.

Dangers to the direct hot rod economy

One problem for the original hot rod apparatus was to repulse attempts by other organisations to challenge it's position at the centre of the sport. Drag racing was looked down on by other American automobile sports and organisations, who represented the European tradition of Grand Prix and sports car contests, and they took not the slightest interest in drag racing for some time, but, as it blossomed, other organisations did try to take a hand. The National Association for Stock Car Automobile Racing (NASCAR) dominated another, different, indigenous automobile sport but in 1957 it announced it was now prepared to sanction drag races because such things were: 'no longer regarded as a hot rod or chicken sport'. *Hot Rod* scoffed that this was the very organisation whose incompetence had engineered a damaging 'riot' and who had then blamed 'hot rodders' and provided some background explanation:

> This year a private sponsor asked the National Hot Rod Association to assist in the presentation of a series of night drag events at Daytona planned as a program to help occupy idle hours when the beach activities were not in progress. NHRA's response was an offer to send its national Field Director and a trained crew of specialists to set up and supervise the operation of first class drag racing events. Then a top NASCAR official stepped into the picture announcing that there wouldn't be any drags around Daytona during Speed week and promptly demonstrating the fact that he controlled the area's available airports. Furthermore he added that he wanted no part of the NHRA in evidence at Daytona, nor any association whatsoever with the 'hot rod' term.

But, the editor went on, there *had* been drags at Daytona, and with NASCAR bigwigs collecting the receipts and NASCAR was trying to get into what it called 'acceleration programs' on what it called 'testing areas' as part of a 'spark' to a nationwide programme to improve driving standards. *Hot Rod* commented sourly:

> NASCAR didn't offer any of that 'spark' during the years when the going was really tough, in the days when hot rodders were struggling to gain the high status of recognition and popularity the drag strips now enjoy – but that was before an AMA ruling compelled the Automobile Manufacturers to withdraw their lucrative support from Stock Car Racing wasn't it?[12]

As this example suggests in the early history of drag racing various supervising associations stepped forward to organise the sport. In turn these associations were supported by various magazines and newspapers that portrayed events to the average enthusiast and these struggles related to certain economic interests, including, but by no means limited to the direct takings from the sport and the media of the enthusiasm. In June 1956 *Speed Age* surveyed the structure of control in the sport in an article headed, 'Are Hot Rod Associations a Racket?' which posed the question: 'are these organizations really serving their members – or are they captive associations, organized to serve some hidden sponsor? Many enthusiasts sneer at them.'

Hot Rod and the NHRA had soon been followed into the enthusiasm and into drag racing by others keen to provide for and sell to the hot rodder. The ATAA was set up in 1953 based in Chicago, sponsored mainly by the Maremont Automotive Products Company. It offered the same kind of services to its thirty thousand members as the NHRA to its forty thousand and had more or less the same safety rules etc. It sanctioned another network of strips and set up its own 'World Series' of drag racing to compete as a major championship. *Hot Rod* did not mention the first of these in 1955, and *The Dragster*, the ATAA house organ, had, in turn, managed to overlook the NHRA's Nationals that same year. *Speed Age* tried to assess the differences in approach of the two sanctioning bodies and its charge against the NHRA was that it was quite undemocratic: 'Many experts claim NHRA wants to be absolute dictator of the sport. As proof they cite the fact that NHRA hasn't held an election since the day it was founded. They wonder, suspiciously, whether all of NHRA's interest in hot rodding isn't really just a smokescreen to sell more Hot Rod magazines.' Since 1951 the original board had done a good deal of work for the sport:

> But what irks a lot of fans is that they won't give up. They are still at it. They haven't held an election since the original meeting, Besides not allowing themselves to be replaced, they've kept a tight rein all over the country. They appoint all of their local representatives and have ignored all pleas for holding any kind of local elections for their representatives.

In the article the NHRA's Vice-President reply to this charge was couched in terms of effeciency. He asked rhetorically: 'how the hell can you get anything done?' and added: 'It's swell to be democractic but anytime you try and run a business on the basis of a popularity contest, you're in for trouble. We pick representatives we feel will do the best job, not just the guy who wins the most trophies.' In *Hot Rod*, the editor was much more angry about this attack by an unnamed but 'lesser-known magazine' and its 'masterpiece in mixed-up insinuations' obtained from 'unqualified disgruntled individuals': 'Grasping at straws, the article branded the National Hot Rod Association as 'undemocratic', yet this organization's governmental system is patterned after ones used successfully by the Boy Scouts of America, the YMCA, Little League baseball, National Safety Council, the AMA, USAC, NASCAR and countless other membership organizations.'[13]

When the *Speed Age* review considered the ATAA it found that it did contain some semblance of democracy. It held elections among its members for regional representatives but it still looked remarkably like a front through which to advertise and sell the auto-related products of its commercial sponsors, especially Maremont who admitted providing the association with $40,000 a year to defray running expenses. The article hinted that there would soon be another rival to the NHRA, and the American Hot Rod Association (AHRA) was indeed established in 1956. Its pitch was that it was run by hot rodders for hot rodders and had some semblance of democracy with elections to offices and so on. *Hot Rod*'s strategy was to ignore any other institutions and rarely referred to them by name while constantly promoting the NHRA as 'the sport's sole sanctioning body' or for providing: 'the "glue" necessary to hold a sporting group together in a coordinated body, one that can move with purpose and get things done'.[14] Still, as we shall see, the original hot rod apparatus was never to have its claims to centrality go unchallenged.

The second danger for the hot rod economy was that *other* economic institutions sought to exploit the term 'hot rodding' in different ways. I have already suggested that when *Hot Rod* and the NHRA insisted on the public service aspect of rodding and its socially beneficial nature it was not just a sport that was at issue but consumer dollars and, as my comments on records earlier in the chapter indicate, while the hot rod apparatus wanted to pursue economic advantage through themes of safety and respectability others sought to cash in by exploiting the street racing and unsavoury aspects which *Hot Rod* deplored. The theme that games on wheels were a major source of accident and death and part of the teenage problem became fixed in the entertainment mass media in the 1950s. 'Drag Race: A Teenage Play in One Act' of 1958 is summarised thus:

> After the biggest dance of the year – the Senior Prom – the high school crowd takes to the highways for further celebrations. Ken, who promised to drive carefully in his father's car, is arrested for drag racing and is brought to the police station in the small hours of the morning. Ginny is frightened and Enid is in tears. Martin jeers and Ken blames everyone but himself. All of them envy the driver of the other car who got away. Concerned by their attitude,

the policemen try to make them face the seriousness of what they have done. But even when distraught parents arrive, the young people show no signs of understanding. It is only when the other car is found that sudden realization comes at last.[15]

For Spike has wrapped both car and himself round a tree.

Probably the most famous and commercially successful depiction of dangerous hot rodding, based on a story previously published in the *Saturday Evening Post*, was the film *Rebel Without A Cause* of 1955, in which James Dean and others played yet another variant of 'chicken'. Less ambivalent offerings were to be found in the material aimed directly at teenagers as suggested in the production company's synopsis of the B picture *Dragstrip Riot* of 1958:

> This is the story of teen-age youths who live as fast as their hot rods will carry them. Gary Clark, as the newcomer to the gang is running away from his past, his flight being hampered by a gang of motorcyclists who throw a reign of terror over his very existence. Courage is measured as drag races are performed on railroad tracks, the climax building up to a free-for-all between the two gangs. All this is accompanied by rock 'n' roll numbers and actual flat races at Santa Barbara, California.[16]

What appears to have been similar material was served up in e.g. *Dragstrip Girl* (1957), *Hot Rod Rumble* (1957), *Hot Car Girl* (1958), *High School Confidential* (1958), *The Ghost of Dragstrip Hollow* (1960) and so on.

Hot Rod had cautiously praised early Hollywood offering like *The Big Wheel* of 1949 and *Hot Rod* of 1950 which used street racing to attract an audience but indicated that it was not a righteous path for young people to travel. In the period of legal threats to the future of hot rodding the NHRA became increasingly active in its relation to the truly mass media. A number of books were written for teenagers which ran the NHRA line in that while they featured street racing, accidents and deaths, ultimately, the redemption through temptation of the hero was obligatory. The earliest and most commercially successful of these was *Hot Rod* of 1950 (into its twentieth edition by 1967) in which the town of Avondale sees 'half its teenagers lowered in coffins'.[17] The NHRA seems to have been instrumental in presenting its view of the relationship between undisciplined racing and 'true' hot rodding:' if you don't offer them a supervised outlet they're bound to . . .' as the storyline of a number of low budget films and in quite a number of popular radio and TV shows of the 1950s and early 1960s – *Dragnet, Life With Riley, Public Defender, The Bob Cummings Show, The Real McCoys, Dobie Gillis* and the like. In some of these the NHRA offices, indeed, NHRA officers, were portrayed. Oil companies sponsored short films, promoted for club showing in the magazine, which dwelt on the serious and safe side of organised rodding. Still the hot rod economy was always going to be ideologically vunerable to, though perhaps paradoxically its sales were stimulated by, those who wanted to milk rodding or drag racing for sensational fare for the truly mass market.

This hooked up with the third problem for the hot rod economy. For all the hot rod apparatus's protestations of respectability lost force if state bodies questioned the 'safety program' ideology for the spread of the drag strips within which *Hot Rod* and the NHRA had enveloped the sport. This is what made the dissent of the International Association of Chiefs of Police (IACP) in 1956 troubling and in 1957 a particularly wounding blow came when the National Safety Council (NSC), the state agency concerned with traffic safety, appeared to turn against the sport. A Subcommittee on Hot Rodding of the NSC's Traffic and Transportation Conference issued a statement: 'The National Safety Council opposes speed contests. Since speed violations are so often involved in traffic accidents, the National Safety Council cannot condone speeding even in the name of competition.' The council had polled 1,500 city and state traffic officials, school authorities and local safety councils: 'While the poll revealed that many hot rod clubs promoted traffic safety and good citizenship, it showed that more than 80% were primarily interested in racing.' The council recommended authorities not to endorse, support or participate in drag racing or any other speed competition. Even though hot rod associations had put their view of the situation to the Council it went on to recommend economy runs, driver clinics and the like instead of drag racing.

The essence of the argument was whether drag racing's concern with speed served to encourage drivers to race and speed on public highways. In vain did the hot rod apparatus refer to the few accidents on sanctioned strips as compared to the carnage – one hundred thousand dead and a million injured in the years 1953–56 – on the public highways. In vain did they allude to the extra power Detroit was now building into its 'muscle cars' available to the most unskillful to drive right out of the showrooms. In vain did they argue that competition was part of everyday living and the American ethos, and that drag racing was a regulated outlet for the urge for speed which would otherwise take more dangerous forms. In vain did they stress that less than 20% of highway fatalities occurred where cars were moving at 60 mph or over. In vain did they insist that these officials were mistaking shot rodders for hot rodders. In vain did they point out that no relation had ever been produced between auto racing and highway accidents. Official condemnation continued threatening the sport. In pique *Hot Rod* wondered whether the Safety Council wanted: 'a return to the bygone days of uncontrolled, rampant street racing?'[18] but the Council went on to pass and publicise an anti-drag strip resolution.

In May 1957 *Hot Rod* mused whether there would ever be another Drag Safari to spread the safety programme, for attacks like those of the IACP and NSC had caused the sponsors to pull out, still it could see a silver lining in the gloom of adversity: 'Bad breaks are not new to the dedicated automotive enthusiasts who constitute the vast ranks of the hot rod world. Infact, their sport has grown stronger as a result of having so many obstacles to overcome for acceptance.'[19] And the sport was growing, for the NHRA's Bulletin Board in the same issue stated that the NHRA alone had sanctioned 659 events in 38 states in 1956 with over a one million spectators and more than 65,000 cars in competition plus some 4,000 motor cycles.

Emphasising safety became a preoccupation. Good hot rod clubs were now not only presented as law abiding in their own behaviour, they even informed the police where illegal racing was to be held.[20] The necessity of imparting a safety image was instrumental in leading the NHRA to a momentous decision in 1957 to ban the use of special fuels, which, as I will show in Chapter Five, not only had economic costs but threatened its position in the sport. A concern with safety also led to some rather odd suggestions about the form of the sport. In September 1959 the editor announced: 'Eighth-mile drags are the coming thing, take our word for it.' He went on that say that tests had been carried on around the country using such a distance which had gained approval all round:

> Reduction of high terminal speeds and the handling problems they incur was the prime motivation behind the switch from 1320 to 660 feet for acceleration. But other advantages and benefits soon became apparent. One of the foremost was the fact that the short-distance events require much less area in which to operate. Whereas a full mile is essential to safely run quarter-mile drags, the new eighth-milers easily get by on 2,500 feet.

This meant it was easier to develop strips on non-premium land and that 'spacious parking lots now become suitable as sites for first-class eighth-mile drag events' and led to a desirable equalisation in go between large and small engine cars.

Such advocacy was rapidly qualified and the buoyant tone deflated, for the editor soon had to note: 'One or two loud piercing screams were heard following our last issue's endorsement of eighth-mile drags for locales in which no adequate facility is available for full quarter-mile drag events.' Some of these had come from the owners of big, expensive, new strips which they feared would now be obsolete: 'No such thing. Knowing hot rodders as we do we can't visualize any mass migration to the 660 foot clutch-off, – at least, not immediately . . . Until there is more glory in conquering the eighth than there is in the quarter it's hardly feasible that contestants will forsake the full length strips.'[21] Still, this editorial went on, there was merit in the smaller strip and in three years it believed there would be a lot of them, bigger strips could run both: 'but most of all, keep safety foremost.'

But authority would not be convinced. The Commissioner of Traffic Safety for Pennsylvania wrote in the *Saturday Evening Post* in 1962 about 'drag addicts', 'the failure of the legal drag strip' and asked: 'Why do we tolerate drag strips? They teach people to drive like maniacs on wheels.' Mr. Shipley argued that, in fact, drag strips were the schools of instruction for irresponsible drivers:

> Some years ago, when hot rods and drag races on the open highways first became a menace a number of officials did go to the trouble of setting up off-highway drag strips in the hope that youngsters could race safely and learn, with adult supervision, something about safe driving and the rules of the road. It was a happy thought, but it didn't solve the problem. A minority of hot rod drivers – those belonging to the more responsible national organizations – have never been a real problem; they have for the most part raced on special tracks, observed strict safety precautions, had a healthy respect for the dangers of speed driving and regarded those who raced on public highways as 'shot-rodders' and 'squirrels'. But for the shot-rod majority, a night or two of drag racing every week, under the eyes of police officers or community volunteers, proved pretty tame. They kept right on racing on the highways, using the 'approved' drag strip to practice their lethal art. Law-enforcement officials were reluctant to admit they'd been wrong, but the majority have now soured on the plan, and most of the 'approved' strips have been closed down. But the commercial drag strip hasn't. This, to my mind, is a horrible example of making money out of one of mankind's most unpleasant instincts.

Drag racing strip operators were lax about safety and spectators were looking for blood and: 'I am convinced that drag strips teach the worst possible type of driving to both participants and spectators, and that the lessons learned at drag strips are daily – or nightly – put in practice on the nation's streets and highways.' They adopted the drag strip form on public highways, killed themselves and innocent passersby and attacked the police if they tried to stop them, the most spectacular recent instance of this being a 'hot rod riot' in San Diego in 1960 when 116 had been arrested.[22]

Hot Rod responded doggedly as it did to all threats and attacks. These were muddleheaded, misinformed or after cheap publicity. The NHRA asked the *Saturday Evening Post* for space to reply but it did not get it so it was *Hot Rod* that printed the endorsements from various sherrifs and police chiefs as well as indignant protests from rodders.[23] One writer insisted that in the sport: 'about the only blood that is seen is when your wrench slips off your chrome plated supercharger and leaves you with a skinned knucle.' Still, official disapproval showed that rodding and drag racing were never going to have an easy existence. A range of economic opportunities had been opened up around the new enthusiasm and its core activity of drag racing but their exploitation required constant defence against encroachment. *Hot Rod* was the enthusiasm's champion, but, the magazine did not have complete freedom of action either within the sport, as the gaffe over eighth of a mile drags indicated, or without, where worries about street racing and traffic accidents were only the first of a number of social problems which came to be attached to hot rodding, the proposed solutions to which constantly threatened the very existence of the enthusiasm and it's economy. It is to a more detailed exploration of these matters of sporting politics – internal and external – that I turn in the next two chapters.

Notes

1 Memo from automobile engineer Zora Arkus-Duntov to his boss in the Chevrolet Division of General Motors in 1953 reprinted in *Hot Rod* Magazine (*HRM*) on many occasions. See e.g. January 1987, p. 21.
2 *Fortune*, 36, November 1947.
3 M. Dubofsky et al., *The United States in the Twentieth Century* (London, 1978), p. 427.
4 R. P. Smith, *Consumer Demand for Cars in the USA* (Cambridge, 1975), appendix A, table 1.
5 J. Barnard, 'Teen age culture: an overview', *Annals of the American Academy of Political and Social Science*, 338, 1961, p. 4, and Smith, *op. cit.*, appendix A, table 3. J. Jerome, *The Death of the Automobile* (New York, 1972) gives the flavour of the time.
6 V. Packard, *The Waste Makers* (London, 1961), p. 37; K. Schneider, *Autokind versus Mankind* (New York, 1971), p. 108.
7 B. Yates, 'Road testing the road testers', *Car and Driver*, June 1969, pp. 37–40, 93, provides a useful survey of the early development of car magazines.
8 *HRM*, 10, July 1957, p. 13.
9 'Road to riches', *The Wall Street Journal*, 22 July 1960, p. 1. See also, 'Driving

down a new road', *Business Week*, 10 October 1964.
10 *HRM*, 10, February 1957, p. 24.
11 'Blasting off to the races', *Life*, 13 June 1960, p. 25.
12 *HRM*, 10, September 1957, p. 5.
13 *HRM*, 9, July 1956, p. 5.
14 E.g. *HRM*, 12, October 1959, p. 92.
15 A. Martens, 'Drag race: a teenage play in one act', *Baker's Plays for Amateurs* (Boston, 1958), p. 1.
16 R. Staehling, 'From rock around the clock to the trip: the truth about teen movies', reprinted from *Rolling Stone* in T. McCarthy and C. Flynn (eds.), *Kings of the Bs: Working Within the Hollywood System* (New York, 1969), p. 245.
17 H. G. Felsen, *Hot Rod* (New York, 1950). The book was dedicated to the Des Moines Safety Council. It was a commercially successful text and was followed by a number of other novels with similar story lines, e.g. R. S. Bowen, *Hot Rod Angels* (Philadelphia, 1960) and A. Johnson, *Hot Rod Reporter* (New York, 1961).
18 *HRM*, 10, April 1957, p. 5.
19 *HRM*, 10, May 1957, p. 5.
20 *HRM*, 12, July 1959, p. 80.
21 *HRM*, 12, October 1959, p. 5.
22 O. D. Shipley, 'Maniacs on wheels', *Saturday Evening Post*, 235, 12 May 1962, pp. 10–11. See also the letters in the issue of 16 June, p. 5. The *Saturday Evening Post* had published other articles which sought to dispel the wilder image of hot rodding: see F. Pierce, 'I've got a thunderbolt in my backyard', 18 November 1950, pp. 28–9, 108–11.
23 *HRM*, 15, July 1962, pp. 5, 8–10, 84 and August, pp. 5 and 86.

Chapter Five
Sporting politics:
fuel, professionalism and associations

PHONY TIMES ARE HERE AGAIN!!
204 . . .?

When 204 was again recorded by a car, this time in a match race, and the other car was the winner, pulling away at the finish, dual lane clocks gave the losing car 204; something was wrong!!!

People interested in knowing the facts checked the clocks and found a BLOWN FUSE. When this FUSE in timing circuit is blown, the clocks register 204. It's as SIMPLE as that. This PHONY time should stop right there, but NO, the FRANTIC, HUNGRY, PANIC STRICKEN MANUFACTURERS pick it up, kick it around and even have GALL enough to advertise it as a record and make the fellow that turned the PHONY time the 'PATSY' The fellows that can turn 180–185 are 'Joe Laboobs' in the eyes of the fans who are gullible enough to believe anything that is printed.

FORGET these PHONY TIMES, and when the day comes that someone turns a true 200, he will receive the credit justly due regardless of make of cams he is running. (Advertisment, Giovannoni Racing Cams)[1]

The economic exploitation of a sport or an enthusiasm is rarely a simple matter. The tendency in social analysis is to flatten out tensions and avoid complexities in the way consumpion is provided and exploitation is organised. Terms as diverse as 'subculture', 'hobby' or 'commodification' slide over the conflicts and factions within the institutions supposedly being discussed. Yet the history and social relations of all sports and all enthusiasms involve struggles for power about control and, often, about the exact forms through which they can be marketed commercially. Some of these struggles concern defending the external frontiers of the social space the enthusiasm inhabits and warding off threats to them. I will try to examine these in the next chapter. But there are always internal conflicts about what the exact 'mission' of the sport is to be, who is to make money from it and in precisely what ways. These provide, often in a mediated form, some of the event and strife that is part of the excitement of sport, part of the 'experience' it provides and which feeds talk, debate and division among its followers. Certainly, the hot rod economy was not a stable or totally united entity and the way that *Hot Rod* and the NHRA had come to present, control and exploit rodding was not the only way money could be made from it and so, periodically, was challenged by other groups within the hot rod apparatus. This is my subject in this chapter.

Fuel

I have already suggested that disused airfields were an important catalyst for changes in the hot rod sports but one other product of the Second World War had a major impact as well and that was the development of a host of new fuels. After 1946 some drivers at the lakes began experimenting with these, basically with mixtures of alcohol and nitrohydrocarbons, most commonly, in the vernacular, with methanol and nitro. Methanol had a property which allowed the engine to run cooler at higher revs. The greater charge of fuel drawn in gave the engine more power. Nitro was an igniter fuel which speeded up combustion and raised the flame temperature, bringing more oxygen and nitrogen into the combustion chamber. The exact mixture was a matter for experiment and some danger. Details were scarce, for rodders proceeded on an individual trial and error basis, but, occasionally, reports from the lakes began to supplement their long passages of the details of mechanical modifications with rather mysterious sentences about what was being poured into the tanks: 'There is some evidence to indicate that Waite burned an ethyl alcohol mixture in his 286 cubic engine.'[2] Fuel mixtures soon gained a place in the whole mystique of 'craft secrets' that served to put certain performers at the top. However it quickly became clear that it was not simply a matter of amateur chemistry as the speed equipment industry soon became involved.

The use of special fuels rather than ordinary gasoline posed three dangers to the early hot rod sports. To begin with such fuels were one of the main reasons for the dramatic rise in speeds at the lakes with all that entailed both in terms of accidents and so dents in the respectable image and damage to the surfaces of the lakes. Then the chemistry involved in producing these 'brews' seemed to offend the whole ethos of hot rodding which revolved around higher speeds being achieved through mechanical improvement and engineering innovations. While the use of fuel entailed subsequent mechanical alterations they appeared, to many, to be an illegitimate route to automotive power and far too 'easy'.

In effect the special fuels, like the use of drugs in many another sport, raised a question about the whole basic purpose of hot rodding. Of course, the aim was to go faster but through mechanical development not the manipulation of test tubes. For some years the hot rod apparatus struggled with this dilemma and tried to resolve it. In March 1950 *Hot Rod* ran an article on the 'Pros and Cons of Super Fuels' which argued: 'A decision should be made concerning the relation of chemistry to our hereforeto mechanical sport.' One of the pitches of respectable rodding was that it was involved in engineering research on autos which would, when it filtered through to Detroit, benefit *all* motorists. The use of 'witches' brews' offended against this and so cut away one of the basic tenets of what hot rodding was about as a socially responsible activity. In December 1951 *Hop Up* ran an article, 'More Horses Thru Chemistry', which argued that what was going on was 'an impractical use of chemistry'. Mechanical advances had been passed on but knowledge of fuel additives would never be used to improve the performance of the family car. Cost – nitro-methane retailed at $4 a gallon – and consumption at three miles to the gallon meant, quite apart from the danger, that fuel would never be pumped into Detroit's family machines. So while the hot rod magazines found it difficult to declare that the speeds and racing success which the fuels produced were a 'bad thing', and, for example, *Hot Rod* ran a number of articles in 1951 informing its readers about the makeup and use of nitro, many rodders simply could not afford the ingredients.

So both the *Hot Rod* and the *Hop Up* articles just referred to alluded to the third problem fuel posed for the hot rod sport which was its link with the growth of professionalism. Fuels were expensive and were likely to be the prerogative of well-heeled racers or those whose costs were met by others. Thus they accentuated a general drift towards the creation of a professional caste of hot rodders. As the *Hop Up* article put it:

> A large number of the Dry Lake record holders are sponsored by speed equipment manufacturers who bear part of the expense involved. These same record holders also benefit by the manufacturer's research, so they have a two-fold advantage over independent competition. Those who lack the right 'connections' thereby lack the speed to compete with the lucky minority. Many entrants are discouraged from competition because of the obvious impossibility of ever attaining the speeds of the 'chosen few'.

As always the immediate worry was that such an unequal contest might drive the boys back on to the streets to get fair competition but it also put a question mark against the very spirit of the sport. What was the point in stressing backyard experimentation if 'cost was no object'?

> If the right brains and money are concentrated on a maximum horsepower project, years of dry lake trial-and-error fuel experimentation can be crowded into a few days in an engine laboratory. The damage already done to the speed sport promises to be much worse if fuel isn't regulated . . . unless fuels are regulated, auto racing and speed trials will become such frauds that they will cease to be sports.[3]

But a total ban seemed impractical since, after all, the basic object of the exercise at lakes or strips *was* to make cars go as fast as possible. So when *Hop Up* asked some lake competitors what they thought of the above article some spoke for a ban in terms of cost and increased participation but for others, as Jack Stecker put it:

> If a guy is going to travel this distance to run his car he might as well go all out, I know for myself I want to go fast and if a mixture will make me go fast then that's for me! If a guy wants to run gas let him go to a drag race! A guy goes thru a lot of trouble and expense just to see how far his car will go. We don't get money for running up here. All we get is trophies and on my trophies I want the fastest time my roadster can do. I don't want to have to say . . . 'and that was on gas,'[4]

While Stecker upheld one basic goal of rodding – speed – over another – mechanical innovation – he was rather mistaken about the position at the strips as fuel was starting to be used on those too. In the same article some lake competitors argued that perhaps the answer was to have seperate classes of competition as they had heard certain drag strips were beginning to do. This division, rather than an all-out ban, was *Hot Rod*'s preferred answer to the problem.

The issue would not go away in the 1952 season, as *Hop Up* put it in a November editorial, 'Amateur or Pro?':

> Disgruntled mumblings are rising and rumbling across the dry lakes and drag strips of the country. They concern the sponsorship and/or building of competition engines by professionals. The little guy, as the amateur calls himself, says, 'I can't hope to compete with cars running engines built or sponsored by the manufacturers. They have more equipment with which to work. More basic knowledge of the problems involved. More experience both theoretical and practical. And they have the money necessary to the development of their new ideas or theories. They are actually professionals competing against us amateurs.'

The editorial went on to argue that this was a reasonable point but that there was another side. Manufacturers needed to test and develop products that would be sold across the counter to the amateur and those rodders who did benefit from sponsors had already proved their ability in truly amateur racing:

> Out of this discussion of the pros and cons arises this question; Do we want to continue progressing rapidly as in the last few years? Or do we want to keep the sport on an absolutely amateur basis which might result in much fairer competition, but might also slow progress to a minimum? Hop Up suggests one logical solution – fair to both sides. Leave the lakester and streamliner classes wide open to any and all comers with no holds barred – amateur or professional builders; any engine; any fuel. In all other classes limit the fuel to pump gas and the engines to product block assembly.

This kind of discussion was repeated in a text which surveyed the 1952 season which argued that hot rodding was going semi-professional because, in Southern California at least, hot rods were a sizeable business: 'the average rod had been so far outclassed by the semi-professionals machines that there was little reason for it to bother to come to the starting line. The day of the amateur rodder had passed . . . but in his place has come something far more important – the serious record car owner.'[5] Not everyone took this view, indeed, later in this book the editors noted that the RTA was indeed going to alter its rules to try and attract the average street rodder back into organised competition by creating competition classes which seperated cars by the fuels they used and other restrictions on the engines used. This article argued that those driving specially built competition cars were hammering the men who tried to compete in rods capable of being driven on the streets, not least because they were able to spend more than $30 on special fuels alone for the weekend meet. Moreover, there were rumours of a new powerful purple 'bug juice' that would produce a prodigious increase in power output involving special engines that would take the elite even further away from the normal stock engine most rodders had to use and which, so the hot rod apparatus told them, they were improving for the good of the general public. 'One thing most observers agree on is that some way should be devised to allow amateur to compete against amateur, semi-pro against semi-pro. To paraphrase the old fight maxim: A good rich hot rodder can always beat a good poor hot rodder. An equalizer is necessary.'

Hot Rod addressed the same problems in December 1952 in an article: 'Engineering Versus Chemistry: Are the Superfuels Drugging the Hot Rod Sport to Death?' Written by a lakes vetran, member of the SCTA and RTA and partner in a speed shop business, it argued that the superfuels were like a drug that apparently stimulated the sport while having an overall weakening effect. The answer was to seperate the two categories into different classes: 'The return to gasoline as a competition fuel would turn hundreds of mechanically minded young men back to working on engines that have been so sadly neglected since the introduction of chemical horsepower.' This would lead rodding back to serving the general American public. The article produced a number of letters in subsequent editions commending its tone. One correspondent, who had been running on the lakes since 1932, added a plea for a general move to simplicity:

> There is less and less place for the poor fellow with a stock bodied coupe at the lakes these days . . . Lets start running again on gas and leave the hot fuels to the lakesters, tanks and modified jobs. Give the poor fellow with the stock body street job a chance. It is good to have things regulated and under control but there comes a time when the rules are so many and so strict that it takes all the fun out of racing against time.

He argued that this would send people back to race in the streets, just as he had in his youth. Another correspondent argued: 'Let's rely more on "know how" and less on "drug store brew". If we can't buy it at the gas station it isn't exactly in the true spirit of automotive achievement which we look for in hot rods.'[6]

The inter-related issues of special fuels and nascent professionalism which were affecting both the declining lakes and the booming strips were handled, as many commentators suggested, by framing rules to set out categories which, in effect, seperated the amateur from those with the wherewithal to go as fast as possible. RTA rules for 1953 contained classes competitors in which had to run on gas to be issued at the start line. The NHRA soon framed recommended rules for drag strips which not only included type of fuel as one of the criteria used to create classes and insisted that cars in a number of categories should be street legal, but also stated that the Stock category must use a stock engine as in rule five: 'Optional equipment other than that produced by the car manufacturer will not be allowed. Non-standard production equipment, export kits, superchargers etc. automatically advance an entry to the Gas Coupe/ Sedan section.'[7] This, though the ability of local technical commitees was always being tested, seemed to have dealt with the matter but the issues of fuel and professionalism were to return again and again in the years to come in explosive combinations which were to threaten not only the structures of control in the sport but its very existence.

Amateur or pro?

From its outset *Hot Rod* had argued that hot rodding, in all its forms, should be an essentially amateur activity. This fitted with the public oriented, community service, safety conscious, ideology which it promoted for its readers, the NHRA and the drag racing sport. It had found the semi-professionalism of the lakes an uneasy topic to discuss and the same was true of the annual trip to the Bonneville which became a landmark event in the hot rod sport. In 1949 the SCTA organised the first set of speed trials on the huge salt flats in Utah. In 1950 an editorial responded to those who asked why the top speeds recorded there were not being registered as world records:

> The answer to this question, which is often asked, is relatively simple. The SCTA and the other timing associations now specializing in hot rod speed timing, value their activities as a strictly amateur sport and they intend to keep it that way. As long as the boys are running for the *fun of it* rather than for the almighty \$, the sport will remain a hobby and recreation. Main objective in entering any sport is for relaxation and the attainment of self satisfaction.[8]

But Bonneville was a spot and had associations – world speed records – which attracted a great deal of publicity in all sections of the specialist and mass media. The week of trials was sponsored and manufacturers and oil companies began to subsidise a lot of the competitors too and *Hot Rod*'s position, just outlined, became hard to sustain in its pure form as the editor mused in November 1952: 'That participation at Bonneville is an expensive proposition is not to be denied and there were many cars running which were financed entirely or in part by sponsors who are well aware of the sport's continual growth and what this growth can do for their own particular businesses.' The products of some sponsors had no direct connection to hot rodding but this only revealed how respectable the sport had become, still an issue about the sport was posed here:

> Without these sponsorships many a fine car would be left grazing in the garage because individual owners and builders would not be able to stand the financial strain of the long distance haul and a week's participation away from their daily jobs. This also proves that sponsorships *are* available if the plea is properly made. Some say that such sponsorships smack of professionalism, and in a few instances such remarks might be justified. However in the majority of cases the sponsors advance money, or time, or materials, or a combination of these to defray the expenses incurred during the event, thereby salvaging the individual's pocketbook from complete collapse, allowing him to experiment in any way he sees fit.

In July 1953 *Hot Rod* discussed how the amateurs Hill and Davis had refused to allow their names to be used in an advertisement by a manufacturer of speed equipment who would not pay for the privilege. This sounded mercenary but they had received a sponsorship of $2,100 to get their car to the flats and why should another company benefit?

However, if *Hot Rod* was willing to take a relaxed attitude to the springs of participation in the special circumstances of the Salt Lake, it remained quite rigid about any overt professionalism invading the booming drag strips. It wanted to maintain the aura of 'running for fun'. In effect, *Hot Rod* and the NHRA wanted a kind of shamateurism to continue, whereby top drivers derived income *indirectly* from the sport via subsidies from commercial interests or their own rod-related businesses rather than directly. As I have already noted, editorials warned against the dangers attendant on 'commercialism' and promotors more interested in quick revenues than the good of the sport. It wanted prizes for winning at the strips to remain as cheap trophies, low value war bonds or small items of merchandise. This enabled drag racing to be presented as a public service programme dedicated to safety, the province of selfless civic groups. The commercial ramifications, like the magazine itself, would then seem incidental and be unobtrusive.

However, in the early 1950s a group of top drivers began to rebel against this arrangement of the sport. They argued that they should get a share of the money being made at the strips. *Hot Rod*'s editorial in March 1954 warned of the pitfalls which could lie in hot rodding's path if there was too much attention to the $ sign and a 'dog eat dog' atmosphere crept in:

> Currently a few of the West's consistent winners of drag strip events have banded together in a collective attempt to demand 'appearance money' from the strips at which they compete. The newness has worn off their being recognized as the top-notchers, and their trophy shelves are loaded with awards which have lost some of their luster. Now, they're out for something real big – they think . . . We've seen as much excitement among the crews of cars in the slower classes as in those of the all-out 'thing' divisions . . . aren't the 'also rans' the ones who pay the freight at any strip? We're in favor of keeping things as they are – no appearance money, no cash prizes. If some of the 'big boys' have lost their sense of perspective of the hot rods sport's intent, let them try some other sport and see how they make out. There are plenty of others standing by to take their places and keep running their cars for the *fun* of it.

The argument continued two months later against 'members of one group that has lumped some of the hot dog car owners together into a combine that runs for money or else'. This editorial related how they had linked up with a car club's monthly drag meet with the proviso that they took 60% of the proceeds. According to *Hot Rod*:

> The whole thing developed into somewhat of a Frankenstein monster of an event – one which a comparatively inexperienced sponsoring group found itself incapable of handling. Nobody seemed to know who was running in what division, and the entire operation was completely foreign to most participants. As a result most of the 'visitors' vowed they'd never return to the strip. On the other hand the strip operators weren't too sure they wanted them back. The end result of this sudden rise to anticipated fame was that the entire drag racing sport suffered a black eye in that area – one that will take quite a lot of organized activity to overcome.[9]

Through the next decade the editor was to warn again and again of the interlocking dangers of commercialism and professionalism while insistently stressing a counter-theme of community service and safety first:

> As long as we remain cognizant of the constructive purposes for which this activity has been developed, drag strips should continue to be successful. Hot rodding as an amateur sport has always been concentrated on *fun* – it is a recreational hobby based upon safety and accomplishment. Diligence of the sport's devotees, who compete for *enjoyment* rather than for monetary rewards, has kept the sport wholesome, respected and successful. It is on this premise that civic, service, business and educational groups have lent their support. The guy to watch out for is the conniver who would exploit your sport by dangling prize money inducements before the eyes of unwary contestants, selling your sport's 'tomorrow' down the chute in an instant, just to get *his* end of the take 'today'. Most drag strips have been acquired on the basis of their public-benefit, amateur recreational status, they could be withdrawn much more easily than they were attained.[10]

This blast was associated with a renewal of concern about fuel. The various hot rod magazines still discussed the pros and cons of the 'poor man's supercharger', the difference between isopropanol and acetone etc. The fuel classes had gone on using nitro and speeds were rising sharply and beginning to outpace the abilities of some drivers and the contours of some strips which simply did not possess the space to allow drivers to 'shut down' safely after the traps. There was a growing threat to the lives and limbs of drivers and crowds with engine blow-ups, fires and driver gassings and so by extension, of course, to the whole safety pitch of the sport. After a year of articles speculating about the issue and what was likely to happen, the NHRA banned the use of fuel at its sanctioned strips from March 1957.

The fuel ban 1957–63

The decision was presented as being accepted by the NHRA at the behest of some of its major Californian strips but other magazines closer to other sanctioning associations doubted this. *Rod Builder and Customizer*, which tended to promote the ATAA and often carried articles on the types of fuel and how to use them, argued in September 1957 that the whole thing had been brought to a head by the National Safety Council recommendation opposing any speed contest discussed in Chapter Four. It thought the ban was little more than a peace offering to the Safety Council. It agreed that there was lack of 'cool off' pavement on some strips for ultra-high speeds but outside California this was not really a problem; moreover if fuel was banned the East-coast drivers would never get a chance to catch up on all the experimentation the West-coast elite had been doing through the years and would remain subordinate for ever. Fuel was expensive but no one was forced to use it and a seperation into fuel and gas classes would allow people to run what they wanted: 'A third point presented is that fuel and its high cost is chasing away the very people for whom drag racing was originated, namely the teen-ager or young adult interested in cars who, except for the drag strips, might do their testing on public streets. While something may be keeping some of these people away from the strips, I do not believe it's fuel.' The answer was to refine the competition class system to give the kid with basic equipment a chance to run. Strip safety could be improved by keeping spectators back and the sanctioning bodies being more vigilant and the article made a telling point: 'It is well known that most of the competitors are against cancelling fuel. This was recently brought out in a poll taken by the ATAA among a number of clubs through out the country. The clubs were overwhelmingly in favor of the continuation of fuel.'[11]

As all this suggests, the NHRA ban on fuel was also, in part, a ploy in the struggle against the group of professional or neo-professional racers who were, in the main, the people reaching very high speeds. *Hot Rod* did not approve of 'the boys who uncork their speed from a can' and who had strayed so far from the mechanical ideals of rodding that they were profligate with parts and getting downright dangerous. Throughout the ban the magazine virtually ignored those who still used fuel and published sceptical articles about it's efficacy by, for example, a doctoral candidate in chemistry at Michigan State University, a piece which ended:

Fuels are a very expensive way to power at best, and there are many times when mechanical perfection doesn't seem to count for much, if only the engine will hold together. (One dragster went through more than 30 DeSoto and several Chrysler engines in approximately 3 years. The machine cost right on $14,000 for maintenance alone, which shows dramatically why fuel is an expensive proposition. – Ed.)[12]

We can more fully appreciate the factors involved in the imposition of this ban by approaching it from the other direction, through the career of the biggest star in the history of drag racing, Don Garlits. He had the classic start as a motor-literate street racer in Florida in the early 1950s. As regular drag racing got established he ran on the strips and won a local reputation and opened a garage to support his racing. He was the winner of a regional NHRA Drag Safari championship in darkest Florida in 1955. Encouraged, he travelled to the NHRA's first Nationals where he learnt a lot about the competition he was up against in building and tuning dragsters. He started to look around for more big-time competition just at the time when the NHRA banned fuel: 'The racing newspapers were ballyhooing the Automobile Timing Association of America's fourth annual "World Series" of drag racing . . . and I decided that would be a good place to try my luck against the stars.'[13] There he gained more advice on 'tipping the can', for neither the ATAA nor the newly formed AHRA followed the NHRA in banning fuel on the strips they sanctioned or in their championships, and offered prizes for top speed at the meet and lowest elapsed times. Garlits began running, very successfully, on other circuits than the NHRA's. He had a win at the World Series meet that gained him a good deal of publicity and then he ran a very high top speed. Suddenly equipment manufacturers were ringing him up asking: 'anything you need?' He had become a star of drag racing.

> The response to my record was immediate from coast to coast. Weiand, Iskenderian, and Bruce's tires all featured my car in advertisements that proclaimed the role of their products in the record run. The drag racing periodicals ran the story on page one and many newspapers mentioned it on their sports pages. Even better than the publicity, the record caused a tremendous boost for our speed shop business.

However:

> By the time I returned to Tampa the word was coming back from California that I was some kind of a big phony – running against bad clocks with a second rate car. Some well-known people in drag racing circles were saying, in print and otherwise, that my record was set on a hick strip with inaccurate timers.

And besides, they said, even if the timing had been on the mark, the concrete surface made the top speed meaningless.[14]

Thus was set up one huge element in Garlits's star persona and in drag racing politics. He was an Easterner out to beat the Californian establishment of drag racing who either scoffed at 'Don Garbage' or maligned the outsider or, in the case of the NHRA, simply ignored him since he was running on fuel. Thus, in another magazine, *Rodding and Restyling*, we find:

FROM THE WORLD'S CHAMP

Dear Sir,

Recently I read that letter in your April issue by Jack W. Harnsberger praising Hot Rod Magazine and the NHRA, and knocking you. Well, I have another version on what Mr. Harnsberger calls the hot rodder's 'bible'.

Anyone inspecting the last few issues would think it was concentrating on 'go carts', 'kiddy cars' and the like rather than rods. Also it has lost sight of its original aim to serve hot rodders throughout the country in its attempt to become dictatorial in the hot rod world and is most certainly partial to its own little clique.

This is entirely my own personal belief, but I feel I don't stand alone. I speak from experience, as in their treatment of my recent world's record. Hot Rod and the NHRA seem to refuse to accept the fact that an Easterner has the intelligence to build a record-breaking car even though all possible proof in the form of affidavits and such has been submitted.

As to Mr. Harnsberger's statement that R&R readers were a minority group, maybe so. But in Florida, at least, you will find R&R selling out in a day or two while Hot Rod clutters the stands. R&R readers' only regret is that it is not a full-size magazine such as Hot Rod – for if it were, I feel confident that it would soon enjoy first place in the field, especially in the East. – Don Garlits, 12828, Nebraska Ave., Tampa 4, Florida.[15]

In response the editor noted that, like many others, he was surprised that there was any hesitancy about Garlits's high speed run.

For years, because of the NHRA fuel ban *Hot Rod* ignored the non-NHRA stars or, in coded language, impuned their motives. It reported and enthused about a sporting world that raced parallel to the fastest drag racing in the USA. Rarely did it even acknowledge the existence of the other plane running on fuel for other associations. This had some odd consequences for the less sophisticated reader. In March and April 1958 the editor predicted, then praised two dragsters who had broken a twenty-year-old record for the standing start kilometer in an attempt organised by *Hot Rod*. The magazine was seeking world recognition via such international marks, to convey evidence of the whole sport's achievements to a wider audience.

> To say that we're proud of the achievements of our 2 dragster crews is a gross understatement. And we're sure there are numerous other hot rods in the US. that might have done equally well had they been given the opportunity. But our boys represented the entire hot rod sport . . . they both got the job done neatly, simply, without fanfare or pre-publicity; and on the first attempt.

A rather different view was set out in the next issue as part of the regular full page advertisement for Iskenderian Cams, which was associated with one of the record breakers:

> On February 2 a secret and closed meet was held to make an assault on the 20 year old 2-way kilometer world record . . . While the showing of the 2 cars was creditable it's not clear why the top performing cars like Don Garlits, Cook-Bedwell and others were by-passed. Garlits's time for the 1/4 mile 176. 40 mph. (official) is actually better than Rice did in the 5/8 mile run, 2½ times as far. These cars, undoubtedly would have passed well over the 200 mph. mark in this distance. In the American tradition drag racing is a competitive sport. The laurels belong to, and should be rewarded to, only those who have earned it. Let's keep it that way.[16]

The editor was stung enough to respond to 'an advertizer who chooses to editorialize'. The drivers and machines involved had been picked for their sincerity and stability at high speeds:

> Last but not least came the matter of car sponsorship and integrity. This was where the real screening came in. Since the basis for the entire project was the establishment of *genuine* records, no one could risk having irresponsible advertising or mis-leading claims jeopardize the end results . . . the runs were *safe*, they were *successful*, and the people who did participate were respectful in the references to records set under conditions that warranted them being official, not imaginary or one-time flukes.[17]

As we shall see, varying claims of 'records' and arguing through advertisments was to become quite a feature of the sport during the ban.

The fuel ban took on more moment since at just this time the NHRA swallowed one of its rival associations, the ATAA. Most magazines greeted this with rather muted voice. There had been arguments that it would be a good thing if all rodders were united. The existence of three 'national' championships seemed odd. Some magazines ran articles proposing more co-operation between the sanctioning bodies and one in *Custom Rodder* was greeted enthusiastically by one official in the sport:

> Dear Larry,
> Bravo for your February editorial, It's the first time I've seen in print a

proposal that all the major hot rod sanctioning bodies cooperate for the good of the sport . . . How about a 'United States Hot Rod Council' composed of representatives from all qualified associations that could present a united front to the critics of our sport while still allowing room for differences in opinion as to the specific details in the operation of drag strips and governmental procedures?

Don Elliot, AHRA 2nd. Vice-President, Buckner, Missouri.[18]

However, there was a danger that the NHRA, which anyway claimed it already was 'the national body', might become a monopoly and its Californian connections might stop it fairly representing all rodders across the country. The East versus West was becoming a fulcrum of events and action in the sport and a sales pitch for both professional drivers and magazines:

Custom Rodder is an Eastern magazine, in the sense that it is edited and published in the East. The editors are extremely proud of the gains that Eastern rodders and customizers have made in the past few years. We think the East deserves more recognition than it has had in the national press and we'll do all we can to see that it gets as much publicity as possible.[19]

Moreover there was a disquiet about the style in which the merger had been arranged, as *Rod Builder and Customizer* indicated:

What makes us feel like hollering 'Tilt', is that the deal came about without any attempt to find out whether ATAA members and clubs wanted to join with the NHRA. Nobody sent out a questionnaire and nobody took a vote . . . We feel that Democracy has its place in US. rodding just as in government and it would have been much better if the 'big wheels' had checked with the 'little wheels' before they got rolling.[20]

This edition also carried an article about the merger by Jim Lamona who had been a top official in the ATAA but who had not been consulted about the deal which had been worked out by Parks and Maremont. He asked why the NHRA had been bothered:

I think the answer to that question becomes pretty obvious when you look at the history of the ATAA and NHRA during the last two years. In 1956, NHRA was definitely the biggest gun in hot rodding, sanctioning 659 meets, while in the same period ATAA only began a sanctioning program holding a little over 70 sanctioned meets. However, 1957 was different again. The NHRA combine showed signs of slowing, adding only 21 meets to the 1956 total to make it 680 for 1957. At the same time ATAA more than tripled its sanctions for a total of nearly 250 meets . . . From the number of strips that had requested ATAA sanction by March 10th. , the ATAA would have conservatively sanctioned more than 500 meets in 1958, double that of 1957, while at the same time it appears the NHRA would have lost some of its strips to bring its total sanctions below the 1957 level.[21]

In short, the fuel ban and consequent, but undeclared, ban on a lot of the top stars, was having a big effect on the NHRA's position in the fast growing sport, and their swallowing of ATAA was a defensive manoeuvre. Lamona found Maremont's horse-trading harder to understand since the rise of the ATAA to prominence was supplying his products with a lot of publicity while removing the need for heavy financial aid. Other commentators simply assumed that Maremont had swapped the ATAA to ensure more publicity for his products in the top selling Hot Rod.

Lamona argued that competition to the NHRA would continue and predicted the formation of a new Association. Infact, though it was the fledgling AHRA which moved in to become the NHRA's main rival and to run circuit which allowed the use of fuel and so on which most of the stars of the drag racing world could run. Garlits, for example, began to run on 'outlaw' tracks under the juristiction of no sanctioning body but mostly in AHRA events. Indeed, he was elected President of the organization in 1958 but records that it turned out to be only an honorary title and he heard very little from the national headquarters in Missouri. In 1958 Garlits was offered appearance money for the first time, $450 to appear at a Texas strip, and at the end of that year he got calls from track operators, manufacturers, promotors and magazine people all trying to set up his first encounter with the Californian elite on their own strips: 'The Smokers Hot Rod Club which was sponsoring the Bakersfield meet, agreed to pay me $2000 to appear, with $1500 to be paid following the race and $500 to be held by Ed. Iskenderian prior to my arrival. The appearance money guaranteed by the Kingdon and Chandler tracks jumped the total purse to $5000.'[22] And this was the start of his career as a travelling pro.

It was the fuellers who were attracting the crowds at the strips but Hot Rod did not mention the professionals or the fuel matches or championships editorially. Instead all through 1959, for example, the editorials warned that a few bad strips had forgotten the 'sports public service aim' and that: 'Today the sport stands on the verge of getting out of hand . . . a few non-conformists continue to openly invite disaster. Drag racing was originated as a combination recreation and public safety program. Why let a handful of glory hunters and money grabbers spell its doom?'[23] It went on and on about 'mercenary strip operators' and that: 'A few unscrupulous promotors still capitalize on the sport by presenting fictitious championships, making false claims and taking unearned gate receipts'[24] all, typically coded, references to the AHRA and the fuellers.

But while *Hot Rod* billed the NHRA's Nationals as 'The Championship Money Can't Buy', one which had got rid of 'the bugaboo of $5 per gallon fuel' and gave the 'have-nots their chance', Garlits and others and their deeds did start to appear in the magazine in advertisments for speed equipment manufactures. The regular full page Iskenderian advertisement in May 1959 headlined: 'Drag Racing Now Rates As a Major Sport' hailed the US Fuel-Gas meets held recently which, with little publicity, had attracted thirty thousand spectators and argued: 'No doubt spurred by the interest of cross country rivalry, plus the appearance of national titleholder Don Garlits, these events nonetheless proved that forward and positive thinking by strip operators can make such attendance figures almost commonplace.' This advertisement went on to connect Garlits with its products but it wasn't the only one to stake a claim, as a letter in July 1959 complained:

We'll guess with you

Gentlemen,
I'm confused. In your May issue of HRM on pages 19 and 107, two seperate firms credit Don Garlits as 'world champion drag racer' and 'world's fastest dragster'. Both give different speeds and ets. On page 88 another ad. states that Chrisman and Cannon's dragster is '. . . world's fastest.' Then on page 91 the 'Cagle and Herbert dragster is the fastest in America' ad. hits you between the eyes. Yet this ad. boasts speeds less than the 'world's fastest' which is back on page 88. Maybe if you could find a little 2in. x 2in. corner someplace in your great mag. for the latest in top speed and low et. runs so we, the confused readers, might become enlightened as to who's turning what and on what. It would help if we knew which boys were tearing the asphalt apart with fuel and which were doing likewise with ethyl. As a regular feature, this article would give us all wanted info.
Charles Pedersen, La Grange Park, Illinois.

To which the editor responded:

You think you're confused? – we've long ago given up trying to keep pace with all the miscellaneous claims of world domination in drag racing. New speeds and super-low elapsed times are being attained almost weekly, most of them authentic, and some questionable. No attempt is made by HR. Magazine to establish any of them as 'world records' – we leave that complicated and precise detail to the auspices of FIA. , international certifying body, which has yet to approve the quarter-mile as an official distance for world records.

The contradiction between editorial comment and features which continued to boost the amateur endeavour and the advertisements which spoke of a completely different structure of the sport featuring fuel stars, new 'records' and all the rest, continued through 1960. Iskenderian's page in January contained a section on 'The Second West Coast Tour' which declared that Garlits and two other Easterners were coming back to California, interested strip operators were asked to contact the drivers or Iskenderian. In February the editor announced that the NHRA was setting up certification teams to monitor 'Official national records for drag racing' on page 5 while on page 17 Garlits was pictured as world record holder under a 'Dragster zooms to new world record using Pennzoil Motor Oil' headline. In March a letter complained that the advertisements were claiming 'Too Many Champions' while another in May wondered why the magazine was giving so much prominence to go-carts, boats etc.: 'Why not cover in detail some of the actual fuels used by the top dogs?' In that issue *Hot Rod* announced plans for 'Drag Racing's World Champion', a new NHRA system of competition that was to operate over a twenty-six-week season, with points to be won at regional, divisional and at the National meet, with special bonus events etc.

In July the editor fulminated again about 'spurious world records':

> Promiscuous claims of world supremacy in the quarter mile are once again on the march, happy clocks again telling of fabulous isolated, one way runs topping the double century mark . . . Few magazines are more eager to see legitimate world acclaim given our sport than HRM – we worked hard to help gain it on several occasions – but repeated month by month claims without official cognizance make it extremely difficult to work with the national and international bodies when the real thing does come along. NHRA, USAC and FIA, in that order, are the parties concerned.

While in response to a letter asking what the NHRA rules were for championship runs as, in Illinois, the writers had seen a fantastic run timed at 204. 5 mph and they wanted to know why this would not be a world record, the editor replied that the NHRA's rules were that runs had to occur at a regional, divisional or national event with the following conditions:

(i) a certified survey of the strip to show there was not very much down ward slope.

(ii) two sets of et. and top speed clocks to time each run with at least one a Chrondek with a current certificate from proper authorities stating the clocks were accurate to within one hundredth of a second.

(iii) a NHRA certification crew had to be present to ensure all provisons of a record run were in effect:

Some rather fantastic times have been recorded at drag strips. Strip officials and concerned drivers, however, have elected to maintain a 'maybe' attitude to avoid ridicule and degradation.[25]

Despite all this doubt, despite the claim that the NHRA was 'the national governing body', despite proclamations of NHRA's 'World Champion' and that a 'national drag records system', had been established there was little doubt of the impact that Garlits and some of the other professionals were having nor of the related interest in fuel. But these found a somewhat anarchic expression. The advertisements of the camshaft manufacturers in particular began to bicker about claims for 'records' and about what equipment the 'holders' had actually been using as in the advert set out at the head of this chapter or in:

False and Misleading Advertising

We could shout in headlines about 200 MPH. The 'Big G' equipped Garlits– Malone dragster was credited with this time at the strip giving out those phony times but it was found that the traps were 6" to 1' short and that the clocks were not functioning properly and were giving increased false times as much as 25 MPH. We are not so desperate for records that we have to go along with another cam grinder who stated in his ads that Garlits and Malone ran his equipment at Bakersfield and Fremont when only the IDLER PULLEY was made by his company. We have no time for misleading statements, false claims, or making IDLER PULLEYS, Aluminium Rods and other Mickey Mouse accessories,[26]

Some of the adverts featuring Garlits claimed his record runs had been done 'with NHRA officials in attendance' and even *Hot Rod*'s editorial pages occasionally had to acknowledge his position and the interest in fuel as when a reader wrote into 'Shop Talk' saying that he owned an Chevy dragster and what fuel combination did they recommend for all-out performance?

I'm sure the old standby, nitro-methane, Benzol, and for the less stout hearted, alcohol, will do the job. Fuel user Don Garlits recommends 25% nitro, 2% Bennie and 73% alky for the sissies. To get into the 'Boys' class, he believes 75% nitro, 2% Bennie and 23% alky will do. But to be a real 'blood and guts' man you've got to give 98% nitro and 2% Bennie a try. Be careful and good luck![27]

The answer, printed round a motor exploding into a mushroom cloud, rather belied the primness of the NHRA's and *Hot Rod*'s stated position. While the magazine continued to devote pages to detailing the NHRA's gas based 'National' and to uphold the amateur ideal as in these comments on the race for the NHRA's points based 'world champion':

> One of the reasons why the competition has been so keen is that no awards were posted in advance – the contestants were running for the pure satisfaction of seeing who'd come out on top at the seasons end as drag racings first official World Champion. Very few inquiries were ever made as to what the chap would win proving that recognition still rates as high as money, bonds and big awards.[28]

it was clear that the sport of drag racing was moving fast in other directions than those being portrayed in the main magazine of hot rodding.

Professionalism accepted?

In 1963 fuelers were allowed back into NHRA competition. Re-entry was not that easy. *Hot Rod* was always ready to argue that the sports image was threatened by just this group. Crowds at NHRA strips boomed in 1963 with over two and a half million paying to attend but the magazine also indicated that accidents were up too. 76% of the year's major accidents had occured among a mere 3% of competitors – the all-out dragsters – and 65% of these were attributable to the fuel-burners who made up a fraction of 1% of total participation.[29] New fuels and additives, e.g. hydrazine, were constantly being developed and just as constantly *Hot Rod* warned of the dangers.[30] At major meets there were lots of accusations that the NHRA were discriminating in favour of the professionals who had stayed with the association through the ban and a decade and a half later a professional wrote into *Hot Rod* in response to a claim they had made about these years remarking: 'As you know, I was one of the racers who spoke out and fought NHRA about the fuel ban. From that point on, my name was never uttered in print in Hot Rod, as far as I know, though I was one of the top racers in the US for over ten years. I am used to being ignored and treated as though I do not exist by NHRA and Hot Rod.'[31]

Hot Rod and the NHRA tended to explain the return to the use and reporting of fuel as a consequence of the development of new safety devices, better chassis construction, surface conditons, aluminised fire suits, etc. , so that nitro-machines could now be accepted into the 'proper' programme of drag racing. There was some truth to this. The speeds being achieved by the fuelers and then by, especially, professionals who stayed with the NHRA circuit and found ways (superchargers, multi-engines, etc.) of developing more power from gas driven engines, were straining the contours of many strips. Presumably this was one of the reasons *Hot Rod* advocated eighth of a mile racing in 1958 as mentioned in Chapter Four, and a few operators at this time did shorten the racing strip: 'cutting it down from the 1320 foot 1/4 miles to 1000 foot and in some cases to 660 feet (1/8 mile). While they should be commended for recognizing the safety values of such a move, we must also recognize the fact that such a move certainly does not contribute to the future progress of the sport.'[32] One top driver told the writer of the above article that there were only three strips on the West Coast where he could stop safely. Another, who had appeared that year on twenty strips said that his runs would have been unsafe on fourteen of them without the use of a chute. The development of a parachute which opened at the end of the run to slow the cars down rapidly was one of the developments that could allow the NHRA to declare fuel machines 'safe'.

But there were a number of other reasons most of which had to do with the rhythms of the hot rod business. The fuel ban had not allowed the magazine to cover the main developments in the sport. Letters had been printed asking questions like 'what ever happened to the big boys?' Paying spectators at drag racing events increased from one million to three million between 1961 and 1963 but crowds at NHRA events had been falling. Some touring professionals had now become well institutionalised stars at the apex of the sport. When Garlits wanted to get out of driving for a time he had to contact drag strip operators to check whether they were agreeable to having his machine driven by another man. Pros raced for money prizes but made most of their income from appearance money – $1,000 a time in the early 1960s for the very top names – and the handful of big national meets were important not so much for the prize money or awards they offered but as opportunities for publicity to provoke promotors to put up the cash to appear at smaller events. At regional championships or local meets on sanctioned or outlaw tracks and in invitation meets sponsored by strip promotors or the drag press, the pros. raced against the local hot shots or against each other in travelling match races and increasingly in 'grudge races', 'feuds' and 'challenges' announced through the drag publications. Major championships and high-speed runs served to encourage promotors to put up appearance money for these match races which were the main source of the professional's direct income from the sport.

Press agentry and hype became part of the pros' world and every big star was soon allocated a nick-name so that Tom 'the Mongoose' McEwen could joust with Don 'the Snake' Prudhomme and Connie 'The Bounty Hunter' Kalitta could start marking off the big names that had fallen to him. At non-championship meets the stars might attempt top speed 'records' and the like. Garlits notes that big build-ups by the track announcer, booing and heckling fans and big money wagers that racers wouldn't hit certain speeds or elapsed times all became features of the sport at this time. The look and sound of the professional's machine also became important rather than simply how fast it was. Garlits suggests that the acceptance of fuel by the NHRA was: 'largely due to the pressure of the big NHRA stars, who complained that the strip promotors simply weren't willing to pay appearance money for gas cars, while the faster, noisier, more spectacular fuelers were available.' The cars of the professionals now had to be for 'show' as well as 'go' and this began to effect the very design of the top dragsters. Garlits notes:

> The racing business is probably more fad-conscious than any other in the world. If somebody does something that appears to make a car go faster or look better, everybody jumps on the bandwagon without a second thought . . . The fall of 1963 introduced a big fad for streamlined bodies and tail sections. The experienced racers soon discovered that fully enclosed streamliners caused too many areodynamic problems and discarded the concept, but everybody suddenly had to have exotic, swooping tail sections for their dragsters and Ed and I knew we'd have to redesign our old 'squareback' chassis to keep up with the times.[33]

While jet-powered dragsters were never recognised as an official class by any sanctioning body and had an existence only as exhibiton cars, the *style* of speed as well as just speed became an important aspect of the role of professional racers in the hot rod economy.

Of course, publicity in the big meets and in all the drag papers, especially the still dominant *Hot Rod*, was also important to professionals to increase other inputs to their incomes. There was a symbiotic relationship between the specialist press and the professionals. Garlits remarks about 1961: 'These Californian races were particularly important to me because successes there inevitably got into the drag racing press and led to contracts for summer appearances. Many of the East coast strip promotors came west for Bakersfield and signed up pros like myself right on the spot – provided we did well.'[34] In 1964 when Garlits was confident that he had a new machine that could record an 'official' 200 mph. he contacted the editor of *Hot Rod* who came to the East coast to check the validity of the car in a 'tear-down' which took place in a corner of a factory lent by a tycoon in the speed equipment business and to supervise, and photograph, the record run. The story: 'Don Garlits Tells All His Speed Secrets' was featured on the cover of a ensuing *Hot Rod* and Garlits records how after his run was officially sanctioned his phone did not stop ringing with strip operators across the country wanting him to appear: 'I was the only man with an officially sanctioned 200 mph clocking and I was doing my best to exploit it before the Nationals.'[35]

Of course, wide publicity in the specialist press was the corollary of another source of income, sponsorship. Don Prudhomme records just some of his sponsors in the early 1970s as: Carefree Gum, Coca Cola, Wynn's Oil, Cragar, Pennzoil, Lenco-Racing Transmissions, Lee Batteries, Bell Helmets, Simpson Safety Equipment and so on. In return sponsors were concerned about all details of the car, even what it should be painted to show up best in colour photographs. Another source of income was from the professionals' own motor-related businesses. One new aspect of this was that some of the elite, Garlits among them, began manufacturing 'production-line dragsters' for enthusiasts who lacked either the knowledge or the equipment to make their own. One firm sold nearly eight-hundred such machines in 1959 and obviously a replica of a winning and well-publicised machine sold well. This, new source of machinery however, seemed to represent another sign that rodding was changing for such standardisation and guaranteed performance seemed to cut across the basic ethos of the sport.

All in all, the economic interests of both sides pushed the NHRA towards incorporating the fuel-using pros. For an additional factor was that drag racing and its professional group had begun gaining the direct interest of Detroit who began funding certain drivers and machines and producing their own 'stock' cars to be introduced into competition. John Z. DeLorean, a young manager with the Pontiac division of General Motors, sought a racing image to appeal to the youth market and Garlits, who had been feuding with the NHRA, notes:

> During this period I was beginning to establish a working agreement with the Dodge Division of Chrysler Corporation. That group's Public Relations chief and driving force in their racing program, Frank Wylie, felt it was important that I return to the big NHRA meets . . . Frank Wylie was involved in trying to beef up Dodge's performance image and we worked out a deal whereby I would campaign the dragster under the Dodge banner and also maintain and

race a new 1962 Dodge sedan in the expanding 'Super Stock' class for high-powered Detroit cars.[36]

Wylie smoothed the way for Garlits to return to the big NHRA events, with Garlits, for a while, running both fuel and gas machines until the NHRA accepted fuel.

The sport and Detroit became much more intertwined at this period. The Detroit companies had been much more involved in other aspects of automobile racing, but the growth of drag racing as a spectator sport and a ban by the AMA on the big auto companies' involvement in other forms of auto sport (because of worries about traffic accidents) led to a rather more overt intervention on to the drag strips. Levine outlines the new interest of Ford in the early 1960s:

> From a manufacturer's angle, and especially from the viewpoint of a corporation trying to re-establish a reputation in drag racing, the program must be twofold: On one hand the brand name must be carried by exotic type equipment (such as supercharged rails) to build the image, to be the headliners at the various strips and to be interesting enough for the enthusiast magazines to publish stories on the car. The second part of the activity is to make sure the basic product, the one the kids will buy and drive from the showroom to the drag strip, can be purchased in a competitive configuration.

Competitive success in auto-sports was usually held to benefit the company indirectly through contributing to its image for engineering expertise and adding lustre to its romantic aura but: 'in drag racing it is different. The car strongest at the strip on Sunday will show a measurable sales increase in the surrounding dealerships on Monday.'[37] Thus local dealerships also sponsored drag racers (some dry lake vetrans had become car dealers) or gave them help with equipment. The travelling pro sponsored by a big company would be expected to show up with his machine at local dealers near to big championships and so on. Of course, many purchasers never intended to go drag racing but, the youth market was thought to be responsive to the performance image and, in the early 1960s Detroit went all out, stressing 'performance' and 'muscle'. So the major companies began to produce lightweight, ultra fast specials which looked something like a stock model for distribution through dealers.

This intervention by the mainstream manufacturers caused something of a turmoil in the competition classes of drag racing. Generally, the developments in the gas-powered cars had meant that changes had to be made to equalise out competition. A broad division of dragsters, altered and street machines had to be constantly reworked to keep

competition between technically similar machines. The altered class
carried restrictions as to the type and degree of modification allowed but
the complexities of development often defeated the intentions of the rule
books. In the early 1960s Tom Nancy had to give up competing in the
classic modified roadster he loved because many of his opponents were
actually dragsters merely clothed as roadsters. In any case:

> The class structure of drag racing poses some problems as well as as offering
> some advantages, and my modified roadster came to be competing against
> gas dragsters more and more in the final eliminations. Running 'out of class'
> made winning that much harder. I had three alternatives, as I viewed it: quit
> racing, continue in the so-so racer category, or build a dragster and get
> involved on a professional level.[38]

The NHRA and other associations constantly had to refine classes so
as to allow the car that was driven out to work each day a space in which
it could compete seperate from machines which had been modified
beyond recall. Changes were also necessary in the professional ranks
from the early 1960s. A new Super Stock class had to be introduced at
major meets for Detroit specials to run in when at least fifty of a type had
been produced and, soon after, a 'Factory Experimental' category was
introduced to cater for even more exotic Detroit output. Similar
pressures to those noted above drove most top professionals, including
Nancy, into the classes spectators wanted to see and those the big
manufacturers gave most help to:

> Top Gas as a drag racing class enjoyed a number of years of popularity among
> fans and competitors alike, but by the end of the 1960s, Top Gas competition
> had become almost an intermission show between the 'big' attractions; fans
> jammed the hot dog stands when the call for Top Gas was made. Those of us
> making up this class of racing naturally began feeling resentment. It didn't
> really seem fair, considering the fact that the only difference between the two
> categories was mechanical and, in reality, the speeds and elapsed times for
> Top Gas dragsters were far beyond those of stock competitors. To an outsider
> these 'slower' dragsters might lack the glamour and excitement of Top Fuel
> rails and Funny Cars . . . I guess I identified with the Top Gas category of drag
> racing; when it lost spectator acceptance and entered the oblivion of
> 'sportsmen' racing (as opposed to 'professional' competition), I felt I'd been
> rejected along with it.[39]

Eventually the greatest rewards for the professional drivers were to be
found in the 'Big Three' classes: Top Fuel, Funny Car and Pro Stock. This
last category developed from the Factory Experimental and consisted of
stock bodied cars which had to use engines and bodies from the same

manufacturers, meet minimum weight requirements and use pump gas. The intervention of Detroit to make at least the apex of the sport an advertising and marketing effort also effected the 'honesty' of some racing. Some of the feuds and match races which criss-crossed the country between big names, who were in any event partners in business and split their winnings, were fixed so as to create spectator interest, and now more systematic rule-bending entered:

> Drag strip operators throughout the country were willing to pay good money for hot machinery that still bore a reasonable resemblance to the production line versions, and the situation became obvious. At the match races, it was a case of 'run what you brung', and if one of the cars was a little lighter than the regulations allowed, or a little more modified in the wheelbase or the engine compartment, it didn't make any difference. All the spectators wanted was a good show. Since a car could run upwards of 100 match races a year, but only compete in a half-dozen major meets, the practical thing to do was to build a 'cheater' for the match races and not worry about the national meets.[40]

In any case, at the big meets the AA Fueler dragsters still got most publicity but even at national meets there were suspicions that teams could run a cheater to dispose of most of the opposition which would then lose to its own team mate thus avoiding the inspection all winners had to undergo.

In short, like many another modern sport, drag racing began to travel a thin line between sport and entertainment, especially from the mid-1960s when factory produced 'Funny Cars', non-stock but loud, odd and eye-catching, began to gain a lot of attention in the drag media and on the strips, as Garlits records:

> An outgrowth of the FX (factory experimental) classes recently instituted by the NHRA and the AHRA, guys were beginning to mount all kinds of engines inside lightweight, fibreglass, stock-appearing bodies and take them on tour like dragsters. At that point there was no recognized class for the 'funny cars' but the fans were going wild for them everywhere and promotors were beginning to pay big money to have them appear at their tracks. We built a 'funny car' or 'exhibition car'.[41]

Prudhomme suggests that one reason for the development of the 'Funny Car' was that the bodies allowed more space for advertisements and sponsors decals than did the low-slung dragsters.[42] Conversely, devices functional in drag racing were used as non functional styling devices on production autos.

By the late 1960s Garlits was making $80,000 a year from drag racing but expenses were high for in the early 1970s Prudhomme put costs as

$25,000 for a 'Funny Car', $25,000 for spares and equipment and a similar sum for travelling and the salaries of helpers. Nancy, at about the same time, stated that costs in the Top Fuel category were immense and prohibited the one man, one bank account operation. There had to be sponsors but the financial assistance brought added pressures for victory:

> Obviously nobody wants to sponsor a losing car. Some sponsors expend quite large sums and they understandably expect results. The racer's problem is that there can only be one winner at a given event and winning in a sport as demanding as drag racing can be extremely difficult. And 'winning' means consistently wiping out the competition, not just now and then, once a year . . . It's not possible for one victory – even a major one – to carry a racer in this sport a year or even two as is the case for Indy 500 winners. In drag racing there are so many national events that even winning the biggest – the Indy Nationals – lasts about a month. And with competing sponsoring organizations – NHRA, AHRA, IHRA, etc. – all staging 'national' events, all putting on 'championship' meets throughout each year, it's not just a joke for drivers to stand in the 'hot car' pit area and ask one another, 'Which national champion are you?' At times they even ask themselves the question! I'd like to see the sport of drag racing organized in such a way that there is truly one National Championship each year.[43]

Up to 1961 the NHRA held just one national event. By 1971 it held seven and was on the way to holding one a month. Nancy points to the confusion this caused but he also records just how valuable a win in one of the big national events could be in gaining publicity for driver and sponsors, when following his win at the big Bakersfield meeting in 1970, his Top Fuel car was featured in *Car Craft* in February, *Hot Rod* and *Hot Rod Industry News* in April, *Car Craft* and *Hot Rod Industry News* in May, *Super Stock & Drag Illustrated, Popular Hot Rodding,* and *Hot Rod* in June; the midsummer *1001 Custom & Rod Ideas* and *Hot Rodding in Color; Car Craft* in July; *Hot Rod* in August; *Rodder and Super Stock* and *Super Stock and Funny Car* in September; *Car Craft* and *Drag Racing USA* in October; *Car Craft* and *Australian Hot Rodding Review* in November; *Popular Hot Roddings Drag Racing Yearbook* in December; *Popular Mechanics, Vogue Magazine, Hot Rod Yearbook 10* in January 1971; *Car Craft* and *Hot Rod* in February; *Argus' Wild World of Drag Racing* in March; *Rodder and Super Stock* in May.[44]

Detroit became deeply involved in the 'sportsman' (amateur) classes too. Sophisticated cheating, e.g. 'stock' cars blueprinted by the factories, and continuous engine development meant a constant re-writing of rules and specifications and negotiation between Detroit and the sanctioning bodies though sometimes a rift did occur between one of the works teams and a sanctioning body. As ever the real point at issue was to find a category in which the true amateur hot rodder could compete with some hope of success. Through the 1960s and after *Hot Rod* would regularly announce that the NHRA had created a category 'to put the little guy' or 'Mr. Joe Average' back in the running but just as frequently letters would soon complain that the category was getting invaded by factory- or otherwise-sponsored cars.

One more major clash was to come in the 1970s between the various forces seeking economic opportunities from the sport and because of the diverse paths they thought appropriate. Saturation coverage was important to pros like Nancy because their main living came from the match racing circuit with the major meets most important for publicity not cash. There were now three sanctioning organisations, the NHRA centred on California: the AHRA based in the Mid-West, and the International Hot Rod Association (IHRA) formed in 1970 to cover the southern USA when NASCAR finally abandoned any attempt to get into drag racing. The three organisations had roughly uniform rules about competition classes and held their major events on separate dates. The prize money they offered for such events was not great. The Top Fuel winner of a national event in the early 1970s got a maximum $6,000 – just enough to cover expenses for the meet. The professionals began to argue that they should be receiving more prize money, especially as basic purses (leaving to one side special 'bonuses' offered by sponsors) was less than the professionals themselves put into events in entry fees. Garlits on a trip to Vietnam in 1971 was disturbed to find both that oval track racers were better known to the troops than drag stars and, that while the best top prize he had ever won was $7,400, the stars of other forms of automobile competition raced regularly for sums of $25,000. He suggested to Parks that the only way drag racing would ever make it 'really big' would be if prize money rose dramatically. The NHRA's position was that the structure the NHRA had built and maintained had been responsible for creating a place for professionals and that the health of the sport depended on a lot more than the money the top professionals made. Parks also argued that the sport simply did not generate the money the professionals wanted. He claimed that a big national event often yielded only around $5,000 in profits but others in the sport found this hard to believe.

In May 1972 the Professional Racers Association was formed with the aim of increasing purses offered at the national meets where one run could cost $250. Its President, Garlits, who held records for all three associations, approached the head of the next biggest organisation in the sport to promote a joint AHRA/PRA race – the National Challenge – to be run in oppositon to the big NHRA event at the Labor Day weekend. The NHRA Nationals were now in their 18 year and were regarded as the fundamental championship of drag racing, an informal attribution the NHRA swiftly got officially underlined by the Automobile Competition Committee for the USA. However, while the prize money for the winner in the Top Fuel category was only $5,000, the PRA/AHRA event offered a basic prize of $25,000. As the President of the AHRA put it: 'The purpose of the event with such large purses is not to start a war with the NHRA, but to upgrade the level of drag racing to get it on a par with many other professional sports where the winners are receiving large purses.' The NHRA quickly announced new deals that raised the top prize money in its professional categories to $7,500 then $10,000 but most of the big names went to the new event and winners in the three professional classes each took a final total of $35,000 greater than the $20,000 on offer by the NHRA, itself a 300% rise from 1971. The end result was a compromise between interests. The professionals had proved a point. They had shown they could 'put on a show' and attract interest. On the other hand as *Hot Rod* put it: 'when it comes to the Big Time, NHRA is it.' They were the association that had the expertise, contacts and con- nections to run really big events and get wide coverage and it was hard to conceive how the sport could be run without them. Still the NHRA had had to acknowledge the power of the professionals in the political balance struck within drag racing and move away slightly from the amateur, civic-minded, non-profit image. In 1973 the total prize money at NHRA's renamed 'US Nationals' was worth over $350,000 and the PRA meet moved to another date.[45]

My aim in this chapter has been to show that there are diverse ways in which a sport or an enthusiasm can be set up to be exploited commercially. There can be struggles between groups in the core who have slightly different interests in the economy of the activity or who believe that a different contextualisation will promote their gain at the expense of others. By the early 1970s a balance had been achieved between various factions within the hot rod apparatus. We shall see, however, that the compromise struck between the forces was an uneasy one, and the battle over just what the drag racing sport's basic nature was to be – 'public service' or 'big business spectacular' – was to be rejoined again in the late 1980s with even greater force.

Notes

1 *Hot Rod* Magazine (*HRM*), 13, December 1960, p. 101.
2 *HRM*, 2, August 1949, p. 11.
3 'More horses thru chemistry', *Hop Up* (*HU*), 1, December 1951, pp. 28–9.
4 *HU*, 1, January 1952, p. 38.
5 E. Jaderquist and G. Borgeson (eds.), *Best Hot Rods* (New York, 1953), p. 13.
6 *HRM*, 6, January 1953, pp. 6–8.
7 'Drag strip competition class rules', *HRM*, 7, August 1954, pp. 34–6.
8 *HRM*, 3, October 1950, p. 5.
9 *HRM*, 7, May 1954, p. 5.
10 *HRM*, 9, August 1956, p. 5.
11 'Will fuel stay legal?', *Rod Builder and Customizer* (*RBC*), 2, September 1957, pp. 18–19, 60–3.
12 'High-powered racing fuels', *HRM*, 14, April 1961, pp. 38–42, 82–4.
13 D. Garlits and B. Yates, *King of the Dragsters* (New York, 1967), p. 47.
14 Garlits, *op. cit.*, pp. 64–6.
15 *Rodding and Restyling*, 5, June 1958, p. 60.
16 *HRM*, 11, May 1958, p. 7.
17 *HRM*, 11, June 1958, p. 5.
18 *Custom Rodder* (*CR*), 2, April 1958, p. 64.
19 *CR*, 1, July 1957, p. 4.
20 *RBC*, 3, August 1958, p. 6.
21 'Hot rodding's big merger', *RBC*, 3, August 1958, pp. 8–9.
22 Garlits *op. cit.*, p. 99.
23 *HRM*, 12, April 1959, p. 5.
24 *HRM*, 12, October 1959, p. 5.
25 *HRM*, 13, July 1960, p. 22.
26 *HRM*, 13, August 1960, p. 9.
27 *HRM*, 13, July 1960, p. 116–17.
28 *HRM*, 13, December 1960, p. 5.
29 *HRM*, 16, December 1963, p. 88.
30 *HRM*, 19, December 1966, p. 8.
31 Gary Cagle, letter, *HRM*, 31, July 1978, p. 12.
32 *Popular Mechanics' Hot Rod Annual 1961* (Chicago), pp. 70–2.
33 Garlits, *op. cit.*, p. 170.
34 Garlits, *op. cit.*, p. 139.
35 Garlits, *op. cit.*, p. 178–81.
36 Garlits, *op. cit.*, p. 149.
37 L. Levine, *Ford: The Dust and the Glory* (London, 1960), p. 407.
38 T. Madigan, *The Loner: The Story of a Drag Racer* (Englewood Cliffs, New Jersey, 1976), p. 23.
39 Madigan, *op. cit.*, pp. 85–6.
40 Levine, *op. cit.*, pp. 414–15.
41 Garlits, *op. cit.*, p. 191.
42 H. Higdon, *Six Seconds to Glory: Don Prudhomme's Greatest Drag Race* (New York, 1975), p. 81.
43 Madigan, *op. cit.*, p. 111.
44 Madigan, *op. cit.*, p. 99.
45 The best account of the 1972 struggle is contained in two articles in *HRM*, 25, November 1972: 'Tulsa vs. Indy', pp. 106–7 and F. Gregory, 'Tulsa vs. Indy:

who really won?' pp. 120–1. See also S. Alexander, 'All over in 6 seconds', *Road and Track*, August 1974, p. 78.

E

Chapter Six
Sporting politics: big business and the state

THE WHITE HOUSE
Washington

October 20 1972

Dear Mr. Edelbrock,

Your kind letter of October 4 has come to my attention. While I was not able to be with you during the World Points Finals in Amarillo, I did want you to know how deeply I appreciated your gracious words of encouragement and support.

Professional organizations such as SEMA are contributing in a significant way to our country's well-being by seeking solutions to the problems of automotive safety, noise control, and emissions. Of particular importance is SEMA's determination that the nation's young motor enthusiasts be a part of this effort, and I welcome this occasion to commend you and the members of SEMA for all you are doing in this work.

With every good wish,

Sincerely,

Richard Nixon[1]

As the sport of drag racing developed so did the hot rod economy, despite internal tensions. However, sports and enthusiasms do not exist in their own enclosed world. Those in the apparatus often need to struggle with institutions quite outside sport so as to maintain their own position and source of livelihood. While the last chapter covered some of the issues that structured the internal politics of rodding this chapter will detail some of the external battles in which the hot rod apparatus had to engage and the threats they had to ward off which might not only have meant the loss or curtailment of particular economic opportunities but, possibly, the disappearance of the whole sport and almost all the points of specific exploitation. All too often in social analysis the 'incorporation' of an activity into 'commodity consumption' or 'monopoly capitalism' is regarded as a straightforward process, simple and friction-free. It is not and this chapter will discuss how the hot rod apparatus struggled, and had to struggle, with truly big business and with the state so as to maintain the specific realm of the hot rod economy.

Detroit

On the face of it the most obvious danger to the integrity of the economy of the enthusiasm appeared to be Detroit. And most of the few academic accounts of rodding that have appeared do represent it as a case of an initial creation 'at the grass roots' 'incorporated' by the mainstream motor industry[2] but, as I tried to suggest in the previous chapter, to adopt this as a 'explanation' of the development of enthusiasms is to coarsen the economic and cultural processes at work and over-refine their outcomes. It is true that aspects of the sales effort of Detroit did present the hot rod apparatus with some problems. The steady move of Detroit into 'hot' advertising, performance and 'muscle' cars caused some friction. For, in trying to counter the argument that it was auto-sports which caused the high level of traffic accidents, the hot rod apparatus was forced, in part, to point the finger at Detroit and the power it built right into the standard American automobile. As early as March 1956 the editor of *Hot Rod* had to ask: 'Is Driving Being Made Too Easy?' for: 'Big trend among automobile manufacturers these days is to see who can pack the most automobile into each new model car. Items that come in for most attention include easyride, effortless steering, racy designs and much, much brute horsepower.' He was doubtful whether they could also supply the average driver with social responsibility. While the hot rod literature generally argued, along with Detroit, that accidents were usually the result of 'the nut behind the wheel' they had to protest from the late 1950s that Detroit was simply providing too much power.

Then, the introduction of limited-run factory hot rods and factory teams in drag racing as part of the increasing use of performance as a sales tool, also caused disquiet in later years about the complexity they were creating in the competition classes and whether there were simply too many categories and 'winners' to make sense[3] and whether rules could be framed so as to still give the ordinary, unsponsored rodder a chance. In 1967, after some years of this, *Hot Rod*'s editor agreed: 'The complexity and variety of the current Detroit car have made establishing drag classifications almost impossible' and noted that some tracks were moving to a new form of bunching cars for competition based on expected elapsed times not 'type' of car, a development I will return to later. Also, on the face of it, if Detroit was selling speed straight to the mass market this was in direct competition to the hot rod economy, a straightforward takeover of the hot rod market.

On the other hand, Detroit was always an important ideological reference point for the hot rod apparatus. From the earliest period of its efforts at ideological persuasion it had argued that what rodders innovated became standard issue on mainline vehicles after the practical experimentation and speed testing of the amateur sport had proved its worth. In the early 1950s the editors of hot rod magazines and office holders in the NHRA were asked to talk at various conferences of the Society of Automotive Engineers.[4] While it seems likely that the Society probably regarded such meetings as providing news of what young people were interested in or as suggesting new lines for stylistic development, they were hailed in *Hot Rod* as evidence that rodders as mechanics were 'getting their ideas across', were making the already remarkable American auto into an even more versatile and tougher piece of transportation and so were fulfilling a useful function in the broader economy and for the broader public. The intellectuals of the hot rod world seized any chance to assert that rodding and the major auto companies were partners in one enterprise. So when the 1960 National Drag Races were held in Detroit the magazine argued:

> The paved quarter-mile of Michigan corn field has at last bridged the gap between hot rodder and American public in general and automotive industry in particular. Motor city men by the hundreds from engineering to presidential status, came to see what all the shouting was about . . . I am sure that the men who masterminded the modern American automobile are realizing that their efforts are best appreciated, most fully utilized and understood almost exclusively by that energetic character called 'Hot Rodder'. We speak the same language, fluently and with respect.[5]

The hot rod apparatus constantly claimed that the 'automotive data' and ideas that drag strip competition produced influenced the regular American automobile: 'It would seem there is hardly a manufacturer in the business that hasn't picked up on the young American influence in automobiling . . . the more we look behind the scenes, the more we realize how tremendously vital is the part the hot rodder and sports car enthusiast plays in the development of next year's product.'[6]

All the 'hot' publicity and production of Detroit did not really disturb the symbosis the apparatus claimed existed nor, in fact, did it upset the hot rod economy. With a twist that was ideologically inconsistent but pragmatically useful the hot rod texts argued that 'track tested' production cars would be better suited for the tough going on the highways and would provide the motorist with 'the reservoir of power' which would enable him to avoid trouble when it threatened in traffic. As the Detroit companies came to make their cars look like race machines and used quarter-mile elapsed times (authenticated by the NHRA) as part of their advertising for regular automobiles, drag racing seemed to gain in social recognition and acceptance. Moreover, Detroit never put *all* the 'hot' in. The, widely defined, hot rodder would always modify or develop whatever Detroit produced, for looks certainly, but for speed too. The package was never completely tied. In effect, the hot rod economy soon found a multi-million-dollar niche within the wide automobile industry, a place that was strengthened, not weakened, by Detroit's emphasis on 'go', not just as a teenage kick, but for all age groups. The magazine had to note that 'the money route' was not really the proper way to be a hot rodder which was through the application of elbow grease.[7] Some readers wrote in to complain about factory cars with a couple of decals added being regarded as 'hot rods' and arguing that competition on the strips was now based on cash spent not the classics of ingenuity married to aching back muscles, but such views were repulsed for the definition of the enthusiast had got much wider now and: 'the hot rodder has been an elusive fella to define. Characteristically he is an individual who soaks up automotive information like a sponge.'[8] The real problem for the hot rod apparatus was not Detroit but how to secure this niche market.

Trade association and trade journal

From the mid-1960s *Hot Rod* began to promote the manufacturers of performance equipment especially after they formed themselves into a trade organisation – The Speed Equipment Manufacturers Association (SEMA) – in 1963. They were presented as being an essential part of the whole 'hot rod project', people who offered a vital service to the rest of the community of rodders and who deserved credit for their enthusiastic dedication:

> I am often prone to wonder where the sporting auto hobbyists that comprise the hot rod world would have been today had it not been for those among them who took it seriously enough to make this fascinating sport their life vocation. Not often looked upon with the high esteem, even reverence, given to some of the loftier 'professions', automotive businessmen do constitute,

however, the biggest, most powerful, single operation in our fair land, and by this fact deserve due recognition. The speed equipment phase of autodom alone is a world within a world, predicting, producing and perfecting thousands of speciality items for increased performance, durability and safety.[9]

Often these men were presented as the heirs of those 'early hot rodders' Henry Ford and the brothers Chevrolet, dedicated to producing the same high quality, durable, safe and affordable items.

In September 1966 the Petersen Company began publishing a monthly trade magazine – Hot Rod Industry News (HRIN) – whose subtitle was: 'Voice of the Automotive and High Performance and Custom Industry'. The first editorial, written by a veteran of the dry lakes, underlined a no-nonsense business line whose tone, at times, was to be at odds with the message for enthusiasts. This editorial also revealed some of the connections perceived to exist between the enthusiasm and a variety of economic interests:

Why are we getting into this trade magazine business? Very simple. As goes the high performance and custom industry, so goes Hot Rod magazine and the other automotive magazines in the Petersen stable. If you think this sounds brutally commercial, then you've got the right idea for that's the whole story. We want manufacturers to make, advertise and sell more products. This they can only do if there is a demand (created by our consumer magazines) and the thousands of retail outlets are moving items rapidly. HRIN is designed to promote action in this latter area.

Two years later HRIN sought to tighten all these bonds in a new feature, an 'editorial preview', which was to inform the speed shop owners in advance of stories that would be carried in the specialist magazines thus providing:

An advanced tip on what several million high performance enthusiasts will be reading about next month in these popular Petersen Magazines . . . which will enable you to anticipate the products that may be in demand by the consumer and to prepare for it with adequate inventory, additional promotions, special sales, etc.[10]

By 1966 SEMA had around 120 members. Many of the founder members were the companies formed by vetrans of the dry lakes and the image the magazine tried to promote of this sector of the hot rod economy *to itself* was of successful business heads who still had rodders' hearts as in the description of a SEMA annual meeting:

The present market is growing. The future looks good, and when we talk to

these men about the past, they're in their element with tales of that first hot
rod, what they did to it, how fast it went and about how the times have
changed over the years . . . You can take the boy out of the hot rod, but you
can't take the hot rod out of the boy.

Or as in:

This high performance and custom industry has come a long, long way. It
used to be run-what-you-brung at the dry lake beds of southern California
and sometimes on the side streets. Now it has come to 220 mph plus quarter-
mile dragsters and factory hot rods that'll turn over 100 mph in the quarter and
run 130 mph without breathing hard, right from the showroom. This industry
didn't just happen – men built it. The men we're talking about started out as
hobbyists, but underneath the dirty T-shirts and grease covered hands they
were sharp businessmen who could look into the future and see a healthy
business outlook.[11]

The retail segment was altogether another matter and presented one
of the two major problems which seemed to threaten the vitality of the
hot rod economy in the late 1960s. The new trade journal posed the
problem directly:

The high performance industry is a $200 million a year business. At the retail
level it is a lumbering slow moving giant that is slowly giving ground to a
thing called a discount house. In two short years the discounters have become
a power in the bolt-on accessory business. Manufacturers are wooing the
mass merchandisers and it appears that it is not just a summer romance. The
traditional speed shop owner has let this happen by not keeping up with the
times.[12]

Hot Rod Industry News's attempts to invigorate the retail element were
to reveal tensions in the hot rod economy, between retailers in competition, of course, but also between manufacturers and certain types of
retailers, and between both and a middle network of wholesalers and
dealers. *HRIN*'s basic aim was to professionalise the retail segment and it
outlined the reason for its mission in subsequent editions. In two years,
all auto departments based in discount stores had taken over 17% of the
market. The discounters had entered the arena because they had perceived the opportunities to sell accessories and components arising from
Detroit's new stress on 'muscle' and 'performance' in 'normal' cars,
because half the American population was under 26, *and* because of
pressures from the supply side of the industry, the manufacturers. The
traditional speed shops, which had grown up around and to service the
hot rod sports from the 1930s, had simply not been doing the volume the
manufacturers wanted and the discounters had been quick to sell

components to new clienteles for hot rod parts: 'the Saturday mechanic and the teenager on a budget', groups, so *HRIN* averred, the speed shop had never really had. A good deal of the trade journal's effort, and it was obviously very closely linked with SEMA, was devoted to revitalising the local speed shop which had always been the final link between production and consumption in the hot rod economy. The magazine promised to help retailers by passing on details about new products, by alerting the whole industry to the opportunities now available to them via the moves of the major automobile companies through a monthly Detroit Report, and by quickly spreading the word on trends that started in one region and which 'often take several months to spread to other areas through normal word-of-mouth channels'.

As well as this information disseminating role, the magazine adopted a missionary zeal aimed at a moral change in the speed shops by constantly hectoring owners to abandon old ways in the face of an increasing challenge from the chain stores and large mail order houses. Thus *HRIN* offered a series of rather elementary advice on good business practice: 'the best way to set up a purchase order file is alphabetically', and a number of educational articles on aspects of retailing such as pricing: 'mark up is the basic tool in the retailer's toolbox', and on such things as basic insurance, legal problems, inventory control, zoning regulations and the like. The aim was to shape up the speed shop owner and get him ready to compete in a brisker world of business: 'Someday soon you may have a desk-sized computer next to your boring bar. When that day comes the racer who built a speed shop on drag strip records, rather than on sound business principles will have to look elsewhere for work. There is no room for this type of shop in a highly competitive field.'[13]

American affluence and Detroit's stress on 'performance' and 'options' in the 1960s were not seen as a threatening takeover but as creating new opportunities for the speed industry which could thrive as the specialists in a sub-market of the general automotive field now given a wider span through Detroit's broad approach. The trade journal got annoyed by bellyaching about Detroit's new interest in power: 'As Detroit has borrowed from our bag of tricks and transformed their ugly ducklings into beautiful swans, we have been carried along by their momentum and have had more products to create and ultimately more items to sell to an ever-increasing clientele.[14] Retailers had to look for the spin-offs, check out what Detroit had left off its factory cars and see what the standard hot engines were likely to require in the way of extra components. The hot rodder vendors could carve out a lucrative place for themselves as the emphasis of Ford and General Motors on 'go' created customers for those who could step forward with convincing expertise and compelling qualifications.

An article by two insurance men, 'Muscle Cars – Newest Threat to Traffic Safety', gives some indications of the close relation between Detroit and hot rods at this time. They point to an expensive sales pamphlet published jointly by Lincoln-Mercury and Coca-Cola to push hot cars and cold drinks which associated drag strips with street racing. They quote a *Wall Street Journal* article of 1968 which avowed that advertisements 'make obvious attempts to depict their cars as racing machines' and note two Dodge commercials where a small town policemen stopped the advertised, production-line, vehicle because he thought it must have strayed off a race track. Cars were called 'Marauder X/100', 'the street sweeper Cyclone C. J.', 'the prowler Cougar' and the like.[15]

Automotive contests were seen as a vital ingredient in the cauldron of opportunities. Drag racing was especially important with, so the magazine declared, 3,729,242 paying spectators; 325,857 contestant entries and 1,629,285 timed runs at NHRA events alone in 1966.[16] To begin with, the sport served to expose greater numbers of the ordinary, spectating population – the interested public or even the 'mass' – to high performance products: 'Whether it goes on on a '66 stocker that is driven only on the street, or an AA/FD, the need has to be stimulated from somewhere, right? Granted all the items on your shelves don't go in racing machines, but the guy that bought them didn't get his ideas from the fancy skin packaging.'[17] In effect, all real hot rod enthusiasts, even amateur ones, came to serve as marketing devices to sell quantities of equipment to a less-involved and less-knowledgeable group who wanted only the style of 'speed' – the 'dress-up market' as it was known – or easily acquired 'bolt-on' performance. The magazine pointed out how the used cars adverts in newspapers now underlined the hot rod components they carried. Contributors to the trade magazine sometimes advised speed shop owners not to bother to display parts required by the 'hard-core racers' for they already knew exactly what they wanted. Shop displays were more profitably aimed at a much less assured market peripheral to, though interested in, the core activities. However, maintaining a distinct enthusiast ambience in shops was still of importance:

the displays serve the function of giving the waiting buyers something to do (hopefully to whet their buying appetites). They can mill about and examine all of the display items. And very possibly they will see items they didn't originally intend to buy, forgot about, or thought they couldn't afford. Meanwhile, the psychological technique of filling the air with relaxing music is applied. A congenial atmosphere is created. Customers can look over new products, read the weekly and monthly racing papers and magazines, ask questions of sales people, and frequently run into friends and get involved in bench racing sessions. All this while waiting to be served. The 'world of wheels' atmosphere in the buying situation resembles that of the local drive-in restaurants. It's friendly and relaxed . . . the 'money guard' stands a better chance of being broken down.[18]

Then involvement in racing clearly stamped individual retailers with an expertise and credibility which was one of their biggest advantages in the struggle for the consumer dollar against the larger, cheaper, yet impersonal organisations of big business. Forms of capitalist retailing which were apparently more developed appeared to threaten the traditional outlet, but, so the magazine argued in stories and interviews, the local specialised speed shop could prosper partly through a clever cultivation of their enthusiast credentials. As one veteran put it: 'Knowledge of the sport pays off in increased sales and return sales. Today's young people are sharp. They want to buy from a specialist who knows the score. They want to 'bench race' and find out what they need to know from an expert, preferably someone who is a leading competitor or involved in racing aspects of the automotive scene.'[19]

However, the trade magazine presented participation in sport as having a double edge for retailers. They were urged to give prizes at the local drags and to sponsor radio shows which broadcast Sunday's drag results. They were told how to incorporate the big races like Indianapolis into their marketing ploys (from decals, through pick the winner contests, to welcome home parties). But while personal involvement in the sport provided the credibility, glamour and personality which could give the edge in the retailing race, it could also be a drain on resources and detract attention from business matters. Owners were enjoined to make a careful appraisal of the real retail value to them of sponsoring cars and to consider all the dangers involved in any help they might give to drivers. Letting them work in the garage after hours, for example, might lead to all manner of problems of theft, lack of insurance cover and so on. Personal or staff involvement in the sport could mean the use of the firm's phones to 'bench race', a tendency to disappear from duty to attend the big national meets and a lowering of the general value of labour power: 'Most serious drag racers dismantle their cars each week to check for parts wear. Doing this midnight oil burning not only cuts down on a man's family life but also . . . cuts down on his production ability, since most of the time he is tired during the day from a night before spent in a cold and draughty garage, working late on his racing machine.'[20]

In the trade journal, which was not for sale to the general public, a much more distanced and colder view of the enthusiasm was adopted; it was discussed in a more evaluative way in contrast, of course, to the tone of the features in the enthusiasts' magazines published by the same company and sometimes written by exactly the same people. In business the danger was that enthusiasm could take over the head as well as the heart and the traditions built round the sport could deflect staff from the truly serious purpose of selling speed parts. So, while *Hot Rod Industry News* sometimes carried scare stories that the mass merchandisers were trying to hire hot rodders as salesmen to increase their own credibility or were entering cars in races to gain publicity, such concern coexisted with much more sceptical comments about immersion in the sport like: 'selling ability and what the men could do when the store was open was far more important than how fast and quick his machine ran at the races last Saturday'[21] and:

> even if a speed shop operator knows who had the quickest time at the local drags, what gear ratio is the best for a certain car or what car has the most lift, all of this knowledge is for nought if he fails to say, 'Good morning, Sir, may I help you?' to a potential customer entering his store. The same is true if he is wearing a dirty T-shirt, continues to race with old cronies while a new customer waits, or stands behind a counter covered with empty coke bottles.[22]

In the retail segment involvement in the hot rod enthusiasm had to be manicured, managed, spruced-up and refined as an oil to smooth the wheels of exchange, so that the speed shop could survive against the truly mass merchandisers: 'I look for the demise of the shops that exist only for the purpose of racing. By that, I mean a shop that was opened by a guy who only wants to support his AA/F rail and doesn't really care about building a business that will stand the test of time and competition.'[23]

In all these ways *HRIN* tried to enthuse, direct and protect the specialist hot rod economy which, among other things, the magazine estimated from its own survey, consisted of over three thousand speed shops around the nation, with total sales in all outlets of half a billion dollars in 1966. Other bodies were involved. I have mentioned some, and a Speed and Custom Equipment Dealers Association was set up in 1967 to represent the independent retailer, there were organisations of strip operators and so on. But, Petersen Publications with its magazines right at the heart of the enthusiasm was well placed to co-ordinate and shape patterns of consumption. In the trade journal, *Hot Rod* and the other magazines for enthusiasts were promoted as 'traffic builders' for the shops. They got people inside the outlets to purchase them and reported on, editorialised about and advertised all the other items the stores sold. Thus, there was a complete commercial circuit through the enthusiasm which Petersen Publications played a large part in keeping 'live'.

Hot rodding and the state

If big business offered one threat to the hot rod economy another came from the state. The 1960s saw a growth in what *Hot Rod Industry News* frequently referred to as 'anti-automobile publicity' in good measure due to the activities of the 'professional automobile fault-finder' Ralph Nader. *Unsafe At Any Speed* was first published in 1965 and argued and documented the case that many auto deaths and accidents were due to the dangers designed into the standard American automobile, including too much power. It warned of the dangers of 'hot' advertising and indicted the automobile as a polluter of the enviroment. Nader was not very complimentary and not very accurate about specialist auto-magazines: 'Most of the auto-buff magazines are run on a shoestring with a small group of car-infatuated, articulate people editing or writing the copy'[24] but it was the political momentum that he represented and stimulated that really bothered the hot rod apparatus. The danger was that legislation to regulate the standard American automobile would curtail the feast of opportunities the relatively unfettered 'hot' car field presented in the mid-1960s.

The hot rod magazines increasingly began to warn not just about the dangers to hot rodding but to the American automobile and, indeed, American liberty if auto-criticism went too far. In July 1963 *Hot Rod*'s editorial warned: 'Red Alert! Auto enthusiasts the country over are under attack and we have got to do something about it. Here's the scoop – and your cue to act. The whole plot was discovered by a Washington rep of one of our companion magazines, Sports Car Graphic, the editors of which have already initiated a campaign to: Support Your Right To Freedom of Purchase. We join them.' Three bills to regulate cars had been introduced to Congress and were being considered. One sought to prevent the sale or transport of any automobile which had parts and equipment which were not the standard ones for that make and model:

> There are too many repulsive ramifications to deal with in this brief space but I'm sure you can grasp the trend of the movement from the few highlights mentioned above. What it amounts to is the fact that your rights to tailor a car to your personal needs or desires are in jeopardy; similarly your rights to purchase and drive; not to mention the rights of auto and speciality manufacturers to build and supply their merchandise as they see fit and proper. And this is not all – more such tripe is in the mill for future assaults on your rights. Its time for action. I strongly urge that you get in touch with your Congressman today.

Nor was this just a problem with the Federal government for local states also started to seek to exercise more control over the car in American life as revealed in this discussion of a Californian initiative:

> But the biggest potential danger to members of the speed and custom equipment industry lies not so much in the anti-smog laws themselves as in the interpretation of them by the various law enforcement bodies, such as the highway patrol and city police departments. It is well within the realm of possibility that such departments, should they be against all 'hot rodders', could interpret these public laws (especially if they contain ambiguous phraseology) to allow for cracking down on all modified automobiles and even the speed shops which offer high performance equipment for sale.[25]

The activities of the state were the other danger the trade journal set itself to deal with. A correspondent (who worked for several other Petersen publications) provided a monthly 'Washington Report' which scanned the business before Congress to inform the industry of the likely effects of proposed and actual legislation. This column regularly commenced with lines fit to make a real hot rodders blood run cold: 'Next Congress, look out for anti-hot rod legislation . . . According to their sponsors, these measures were not intended to work hardship against any particular industry. What they will do, however, is strike at the heart of hot rodding. The industry could conceivably be destroyed – even outlawed – by legislation.[26]

Legislation on emissions, certificates of fitness, to limit the modification of an original car etc. all threatened the speed industry but in the 1960s the main issue was 'so-called automobile safety' as the magazine put it. A large part of the state's concern about automobiles was the human toll on the roads and here the speed industry's link to racing was

133

unpropitious. *HRIN*'s first issue had to admit that there had been a lot of accidents at the strips and a high death to accident ratio. Insurers were becoming reluctant to cover dragsters. SEMA started issuing specifications for various parts – helmets, chassis, etc. – designed to stress safety. Significant too, of course, was, as always, the rippling connotations of the informal sport. In 1969 NBC TV put out one of its 'First Tuesday' documentary programmes which directly linked drag strips to street racing and dwelt on crowd accidents and traffic deaths in ways which a lot of writers to *Hot Rod* found quite inadmissable.[27]

Some believed it had been inspired by followers of Nader but the view was quite widespread. As the Washington correspondent put it in his first column:

> The term, 'hot rod' to Washington, means racing on the streets etc. Too bad hot rods aren't called 'improved performance cars'! This is important. The purpose of the proposed law, as defined in HRI 3228 is 'to reduce traffic accidents and deaths and injuries to persons resulting from traffic accidents.' Because of the stated purpose of the bill, anything associated with 'hot rod' enters the picture with two strikes against it.[28]

The correspondent noted that the Secretary of Commerce had held two meetings of people outside government most interested in automobile safety but no members of hot rod or high performance fields had been consulted.

In the face of this threat of state action the industry lobbied politicians, produced a standard letter to be sent to Senators or Congressmen about controls over automobiles and announced the formation of a National Automobile Enthusiasts Association.[29] Then the magazine reported on and tried to initiate public relations and presentational moves designed to counter the stereotype. *HRIN* heartily approved when SEMA altered its name, changing the first term from 'speed' to 'speciality'. 'The name change came as the result of discussions based on the possibility of misunderstanding of the term "speed" by state and federal legislators currently anxious to propose laws to encourage safer automobiles.'[30] Or as the president of SEMA put it: 'there are still too many influential people in the country for whom the word means only reckless and dare-devil driving. For these reasons the less controversial word 'speciality' was chosen.' In the same vein the journal urged speed shops not to oversell equipment to customers which led to noise and pollution and sought to incorporate street racing into drag strips by arguing for a relaxation of the complex of rules that had grown up around the formal sport.[31]

In all these ways *HRIN* tried to meet and deflect the arm of the state but, just as with the activities of Detroit, not *all* the actions of the state were bad for the industry, the trade journal tried to impress that some offered increased or totally new opportunities. For example, Jackie Kennedy's drive to beautify America might well affect the piles of junk cars – thirty–forty million – lying around the country and: 'Junk parts and hot rod equipment compete in the market place. Many is the potential customer who has modified, changed or altered junk parts instead of buying new equipment. Both new replacement parts and the speed equipment trade stand to prosper should the Federal Government find some practical or useful means of disposing of junk cars.'[32] Or as an editorial on compulsory seat belts argued: 'What we are trying to point out in this editorial, is that there is often a way to make a profit when your state Motor Vehicle Department starts rewriting the rule book. All too often, we have a tendency to gripe rather than look a little deeper to see where a profit can be turned.'[33]

The tone in the magazine for enthusiasts gradually altered. Faced with horrors like: 'a proposed Department of Transportation that could inflict federal control on the basic design of your automobile, including such factors as acceleration!',[34] *Hot Rod* at first relied on a sturdier defence of Detroit: 'let those who know how see to the cars that we drive', while sneering at Nader: 'Maybe we ought to all gather around and remind ourselves what freedom really is instead of what is required to produce a best-selling book on auto safety.'[35] Any difficulties there may have been in the enthusiasm's relations with Detroit got submerged in the growth of a common danger to the whole automotive industry. It was annoyed that governmental agencies did not ask those qualified to give their opinions. It now tried to stress the safety aspect of high performance: 'There is nothing quite so dangerous as a low-horsepower station wagon filled with one complete vacation-bound family plus dog and luggage trying to pass a slow-moving truck on a steep mountain grade on a warm summer day . . . Horsepower limits and speed governors are not going to save lives. We strongly believe that the opposite would take place.'[36]

But it also urged rodders to co-operate with various laws. The fear was that rodders in the course of their modifications or because they resented the 'power robbing' effects of some legislation might well just yank out exhaust control devices and air pumps, presenting the state with an opportunity to legislate the whole aftermarket industry out of existence by insisting that cars only contained standard components or were not modified from their condition when they left the factory. SEMA was pushed to greater prominence in *Hot Rod*: 'SEMA will have to work with the legislative groups to decide what can and cannot be done in the way of automobile modifications and this information will have to be passed along to the hot rodders by means of the various automotive publications, and the hot rodders will have to comply with the requirements'[37] and was eventually allocated its own page in *Hot Rod* to put its views across.

The magazine began to carry a little gentle political philosophy as part of its regular fare. There came to be a musing about how far the state should oversee the individual's right to choose, about state rights *vis-à-vis* the federal government and debate about what the actual intentions of the drafters of the Constitution had been. Along with the reports of national meets and the how-to-do-it articles, worries about what Washington was up to became a standard part of the output of the hot rod literature. When, in 1969, Nader suggested that auto advertisements should be reported to the President's National Commission on the Causes and Prevention of Violence *Hot Rod* burst out: 'And the performance enthusiast thought that air pollution controls were going to offer the most formidable front for the progression of his hobby!' 'Political elements' were suggesting you could clean up the air and juvenile delinquency at one and the same time and were set to invade the hobbyist's space by restricting the right to work on cars and/or having to get all work done certified by a registered commercial mechanic. Hot rodders should take action or: 'by 1970 you could hear someone say, "Yeah, I remember that 12-second supercar I saved for all the time I was in Viet Nam. Too bad it went off production. Don't bump your head on the roof of my rubber car, there!"'[38]

From 1970 the tone got ever more strident. This, though not really explained in the magazine, was because it was at this time that the Clean Air Act was strengthened. California was to be the test bed and was to set standards and plans to achieve these by 1977, which would then apply to the rest of the USA. The Clean Air Act, the Enviromental Protection Agency and state regulation became the open targets of *Hot Rod*'s venom as not only did the automobile come to be seen as the main means through which clean air could be achieved but also as Detroit began to suggest to the state that, if it was to comply with all these new provisions, it should be granted a monopoly over the production of automobile parts. While Detroit could always shift sales pitches the speed equipment manufacturers had, really, only one rationale and they had to fight to defend it. By 1972 the magazine was asserting: 'the whole pollution thing has gotten out of hand', that laws were going to be introduced soon to ban the internal combustion engine and that officials in Washington couldn't care less how legislation affected the auto enthusiast and the industries who supplied him. Plans to prohibit vehicles with modified or altered exhausts were being pressed again which would promote monopoly and stifle free enterprise by outlawing the aftermarket in exhausts. Encouraged by some drag racers being invited to a White House reception SEMA invited President Nixon to a Championship meet and informed him:

> At a time when legitimate performance vehicle enthusiasts and the speciality equipment industry are being scrutinized and often misunderstood by those outside automotive circles, it is reassuring to believe that your administration is cognizant of our industry and the vast number of young adults comprising motorsports activities across the nation.[39]

but still the bad news came and *Hot Rod* was soon insisting that hot rodders had to take action, especially with the voting age at 18: 'It is a matter of survival for the automotive enthusiast.'

In December 1972 another political pulpit was added to *Hot Rod* – the Petersen Publishing Company Editorial – which was carried in all the group's automotive magazines. The editor explained that regulation gone too far and that 'freedoms are becoming affected'. The magazine was worried about: 'impending safety legislation which would require seats the driver couldn't see around and air bags that might render a small child deaf while saving him from minor injury'. Petersen had 'set up a consumer research group under a longtime hot rodder' who would report what was happening in the broad areas around the car and society. 'The way times are going, it isn't inconceivable that you may not be allowed to work on your own car before too long. You may not even have any choice as to what equipment you can run. You may not be able to modify your car, even if it results in a better and safer machine.'[40] The flavour of these Petersen editorials can be grasped from their titles. The first: 'Have We Gone Too Far On Smog Control?' was followed by 'Auto Inspection: Will It Be Another Boondoggle?' then 'Bad Laws May Hobble Auto Enthusiasts', 'Clean Air Act Strikes Again – Now It's Gas Rationing' and so on. From here on in a quite overt political content became a big part of the hot rod journals. Some editions of *Hot Rod* carried a Petersen editorial, a publisher's memo, an editorial, a 'SEMA scene' page and a special feature *all* devoted to repelling the drive of state advance propelled by the 'anti-automobile bureaucracies'. Increasingly, these messages did not just rail but sought to enthuse their readers to take political action. They urged hot rodders to become truly active citizens. They were to write letters, form pressure groups, study local bills, get involved, vote and make their vote count. The May 1973 Petersen editorial: 'Here's How to Make Yourself Heard' was a regular seminar paper on empowerment with advice, addresses and a booklist to enable readers to 'overcome the powerlessness when facing the awesome bureaucracies that confront them'. Rodders were urged to read, for example: 'the Sierra Club's Ecotactics and Handbook to give you some ideas on the means you can use to successfully present your point of view. The environmentalists have developed some successful tactics that may work for you.'

Hot Rod's attack on the various proposals was manifold. It too was for auto safety and for clean air but the supposed cures were going too far and too fast. To begin with these plans were going to be costly for the ordinary motorist. They would put up the cost of fuel, the price of cars and garage bills. Higher taxes would be needed to pay for all the bureacracies and inspections necessary. Then there would be a definite cut in performance which would make starting difficult and there might well be 'hesitations' as cars accelerated onto freeways. This was but one way that state regulation would not achieve what it purported to want. It would produce sluggish cars without the power to deal with sudden hazards on the highway and it would not allow modifications to produce performance. Indeed, it was so ridiculously over-zealous that it would not even allow modifications to promote *safety*. Then all this state regulation was not aimed at the real causes of noise or pollution or traffic deaths. The automobile was being used as a scapegoat when the state would not take on big industry or restrict the sale of alcohol. Moreover, these restrictions were a threat to individual liberty, personal freedom, choice and to rights enthroned in the Constitution of the United States. The Federal government was blackmailing individual states into doing its bidding by threatening to withhold badly needed highway construction funds. In any case, owning a car or cars, and using an automobile as you pleased was an American birthright like 'the right to bear arms' and so a little enviromental cost had to be paid. But then all these laws weren't being enacted by regular guys. They were being brought in, for the most part, not by elected officials but in the self-interest of self-perpetuating bureaucracies. These were the arrogant 'do-gooders' or worse who were quite ignorant of the workings of motor vehicles and so drew up: 'loose laws open to a variety of interpretations', who set up arbitrary codes and standards based on no data (whereas what *Hot Rod* called for was the use of 'statistical and scientific data') and whose desire to have a 'locked-hood' America revealed they had no feel at all for the national pride involved in car maintenance, modification and competition.

From the 1970s it was hot rodding in a hostile environment, and as noise pollution and energy conservation got added to the original charges of road safety and air pollution as ways the automobile compromised the environment, articles with titles like 'Hot Rods May Get the Ax on Wednesday' or 'Motoristic Freedom' became standard fare.

> If you don't believe in government of the people, by the government, for the government; if you don't want to ultimately have to drive the same kind of car as everybody else; and if you don't want to drive your car in a state where there is a police car hiding behind every on-ramp on every highway with radar, VASCAR and a radio, waiting to stop you, see what you're carrying in your trunk and stick a sniffer up your tailpipe, then you had better start working on the problems. *Now*.[41]

The hot rod apparatus argued that it was for reasonable and realistic legislation but what was proposed was often far from that and it railed long and hard against the 'Big Brother' state, the 'federal monster' and the like. Still it was more and more called to negotiate with the state in all its forms to preserve the sport and enthusiasm. So in 1975 all motorsports, and drag racing especially, were threatened by new restrictions aimed at controlling noise. Local ordinances enforcing curfews operated at most strips but with Washington under pressure from enviromentalists and threatening to enact federal regulations on noise levels such 'Motor Racing Facility Noise Regulations' might well threaten strips. The NHRA and SEMA initiated a plan to prepare the sport for this which involved a pilot muffler evaluation programme, opening lines of communication with all the state and government agencies involved in the proposed standards and the creation of a reference data bank on noise levels at tracks around the country and of vehicles competing in the sport with 'sophisticated methods of computerized correlation and analysis . . . being employed to identify the problem areas'.[42]

There was a growing nostalgia for the days when the 'underground hot rodders' in the engineering shops of the big companies of America had sent out real muscle machines on to the open highway. While *Hot Rod* occasionally hailed the top Detroit manager who might not think that 'performance' had become a dirty word and, indeed, was the real quintessence of not only the American auto but of American life, things just got worse and worse and the magazine greeted 1976 in truly rebellious mood. To celebrate the anniversary it announced it was to establish a 'Hot Rodders Bill of Rights'. It wanted:

> Letters about government, its relation to the kinds of car enthusiasts drive. We want you to tell us about problems in your locality, or your own views on what is right and wrong with some of the federal statutes and bureaucracies currently involved with auto design and construction . . . We need letters that will help us frame a model Bill of Rights for the auto enthusiast at some time in the future, a bill that can be presented with the backing of Hot Rod magazine and four million readers to those who make the laws.

Under a logo of the bald eagle grasping the Stars and Stripes the magazine printed a series of letters from straight men with simple views: 'I'm prepared to join any group that wants to fight the seat belt laws and helmet laws and stop this waste of time and money at the federal level. I'm just a good driver who knows what he's doing and wants to be left alone.'[43]

By the late 1970s the whole argument of the hot rod apparatus was directed against an over-regulated America where government action to achieve various goals had lost all semblance of reason, where government controls squeezed out the independent businessman and played right into the hands of the monopolies, where bureaucracies sought to dictate the kind of car you could have, where the most simple modification or DIY could land the average Joe in the middle of a legal situation and where 'consumer groups' kept themselves busy trying to save Americans from 'that dreaded four-wheeled monster – the car'. They wanted to depersonalise the automobile, take the mystery away and get everyone driving 40 mph top speed shoe boxes all painted in an olive drab to cut down eye-pollution. In disgust *Hot Rod* repeatedly claimed that the Red Indians themselves, way before the invention of the automobile, had referred to the Los Angeles Basin as 'the Valley of the Smokes' and that natural emissions from trees were now worse than those from cars. SEMA prepared an 'Industry Position Paper' whose aim was to educate government entities prior to government action, especially about the facts of the auto market, the economic importance of the whole industry and the relation of the new car manufacturers to the aftermarket. It called for socio-economic impact studies to be mandatory for proposed legislation before it was actually implemented. SEMA also argued that in the future there was a distinct possibility of 'police raids' on autosport events to check whether competing vehicles violated the countless laws and unless everyone got involved: 'the machines you're playing with now could wind up under a canvas, never again to have their rubber taste asphalt.'[44]

Hot Rod announced the setting up of a Supporting Member/Enthusiast Division' for SEMA in the late 1970s and then a National Drivers Association. Increasingly there were envious references to the National Rifle Association and the good work it did for its million members in combating 'anti-gun' legislative controls.[45] In June 1979 the editorial began:

> If your doctor told you that you had only ten more years, at the most, to live unless you took certain preventive steps, would you take those steps or would you vow to live those remaining ten years to the fullest come what may? Well I'm giving you a chance to make that choice today, concerning the hobby/ sport we all know and love – hot rodding. That's right; unless you, the automotive enthusiast, take an active role in championing your cause, hot rodding as we know it will be a dead player in 10 years.[46]

and made the now obligatory reference to the National Rifle Association which it hoped rodders would emulate.

One task of the local intellectuals of any enthusiasm is to protect the 'bounds' of the activity from incursions by other social institutions, especially those which threaten to limit or takeover the specific political economy. Most accounts of the development of consumption do not allow for this defence, preferring the broad sweep to the inconvenience and inconsistencies of detailed outcomes. Actually the hot rod apparatus found quite a congenial way to live with Detroit and tried to sustain the speed shops against big mass merchandisers, but it lost a lot of battles against the federal and local state. The increasing pressure on the American automobile, its nature and use via legal regulation, the result of pressure on politicians from consumers and enthusiasts for other things, added to the net of problems already posed for the sport by growing professionalism and the use of fuels. All this ensured that the 1980s were likely to prove troubled terrain for hot rodding. I will consider the events of that decade in Chapter Nine but, before that, I want to pause from the narrative account so as to consider some of the specific ideologies that the hot rod apparatus promoted in the sport and through the enthusiasm.

Notes

1 Reprinted in *Hot Rod* Magazine (*HRM*), 26, March 1973, p. 36.
2 R. Denney, 'The plastic machines', in *The Astonished Muse* (New York, 1957),

pp. 138–56; R. H. Boyle, 'The hot rod cult' in *Sport – Mirror of American Life* (Boston, 1963), pp. 135–77; D. Neuman, 'The quarter mile in 5. 78 seconds: a social perspective of drag racing', *Journal of Popular Culture*, 8, pp. 168–76; S. Conroy, 'Popular technology and youth rebellion in America', *Journal of Popular Culture*, 16, 1983, pp. 123–33.

3 *HRM*, 21, November 1969, p. 10.
4 For two accounts of one of these see *HRM*, 4, January 1951, p. 12 and *Society of Automotive Engineers Journal*, 58, December 1950, pp. 66–8.
5 *HRM*, 13, November 1960, p. 5.
6 *HRM*, 15, November 1962, p. 5.
7 *HRM*, 20, January 1967, p. 10.
8 *HRM*, 19, October 1966, p. 8.
9 *HRM*, 18, June 1965, p. 5.
10 *Hot Rod Industry News (HRIN)*, 3, April 1968, p. 46.
11 B. McVay, 'High performance & custom industry, past present and future', *HRIN*, 1, September 1966, p. 22.
12 D. Pierce, 'Speed merchants', *HRIN*, 1, September 1966, p. 31.
13 *Ibid.*, p. 40.
14 *HRIN*, 2, April 1967, p. 6.
15 W. Haddon and A. Kelley, 'Muscle cars – newest threat to traffic safety?', *Journal of Traffic Safety Education*, October 1970, pp. 7–8, 29.
16 *HRIN*, 2, June 1967, p. 21.
17 B. Leif, 'Drag racing's growth', *HRIN*, 3, December 1968, p. 20.
18 J. Gross, 'Fill 'er up', *HRIN*, 1, October 1966, p. 31.
19 *HRIN*, 1, September 1966, p. 38.
20 B. Leif, 'Race car sponsorship', *HRIN*, 1, October 1966, p. 23.
21 *HRIN*, 3, June 1968, p. 30.
22 *HRIN*, 3, July 1968, p. 6.
23 D. Pierce, 'Information file', *HRIN*, 2, May 1967, p. 50.
24 R. Nader, *Unsafe at Any Speed* (New York, 1965), p. 15.
25 *HRM*, 20, March 1967 and see *HRIN*, 2, February 1967, p. 6.
26 *HRIN*, 1, October 1966, p. 10.
27 *HRM*, 22, October 1969, pp. 12–18.
28 *HRIN*, 1, September 1966, p. 18.
29 E.g. *HRIN*, 2, August 1967, p. 6; 3, May 1968, p. 6.
30 *HRIN*, 2, June 1967, p. 48.
31 *HRIN*, 2, March 1967, p. 6; October 1967, p. 49; November 1967, p. 6.
32 *HRIN*, 1, October 1966, pp. 10–11.
33 *HRIN*, 2, December 1967, p. 6.
34 *HRM*, 19, May 1966, p. 5.
35 *HRM*, 20, December 1967, p. 14.
36 *HRM*, 20, December 1967, p. 6.
37 *HRM*, 20, December 1967, p. 121.
38 *HRM*, 22, January 1969, p. 6.
39 *HRM*, 26, March 1973, p. 36.
40 *HRM*, 25, December 1972, p. 7.
41 *HRM*, 28, September 1975, p. 7.
42 *HRM*, 28, November 1975, p. 13.
43 *HRM*, 29, January 1976, pp. 7–8.
44 'Sema scene', *HRM*, 31, January 1978, p. 24.

45 E.g. *HRM*, 31, July 1978, p. 4.
46 *HRM*, 32, June 1979, pp. 4, 116.

Chapter Seven
Ideologies in the enthusiasm:
the work ethic

How much, in spite of all the canned entertainment and packeted provision, the urge to express oneself personally and freely by mending and making persists. How strongly 'odd-jobbery', 'doing things about the house', survives, even when the husband is not particularly a 'good un' in his other habits . . . From there it is an easy step to real 'handymanship', and to hobbies proper. The counters of working class papershops, towards the weekend, are crowded with a great variety of what the trade calls the 'hobbies Press' . . . In these activities, as is sometimes pointed out, working class men still exercise personal choice, act freely and voluntarily. Their regular jobs are often undemanding and undiscriminating, but here, by their integrity and devotion to a craft, however curious some of the crafts may seem, they can be specialists.[1]

Sports and enthusiasms are one social site in which meanings are promulgated and made manifest through activities and by results. In this chapter I want to critcise certain prevalent assumptions in social analysis by considering what the hot rod apparatus had to say about 'work' and how rodders seemed to react to it. However, I must stress that I do not think rodding is particularly unusual here. For me, hot rodding is only an example of a host of other enthusiasms which could be scrutinised, all of which have their own institutions, literature, heroes, calendars and their own ideologies, which often seem to draw on what is glibly referred to as the 'work ethic' but which, in hobbies, enthusiasms, interests and passions, are not related to paid labour. So hot rodding is far from unique or odd.

'Work' and the 'work ethic'

In social analysis few concepts are more used and less thought about than 'the work ethic'. Indeed, acknowledged or not, a good deal of the central areas of social analysis *have* to rest on a notion that the dominant values of capitalist society do, or at least once did, promote work as the arena for male life for only through such an assumption can issues of

144

subjective perception as opposed to objective reality be simplified so as to permit a host of other concepts, theories and moral positions to be maintained. In my first chapter I argued that this belief in the power and moral import of some 'work ethic' is a major force which not only shapes the theoretical contours of much social analysis but has also structured the supposed importance of various topics and sub-disciplines. In the trains of thought which dominate social analysis where 'leisure' is thought to be determined, derivative and secondary, not much attention has been paid to claims made by those who have studied sport that it often is a mechanism for promoting or perepetuating some 'work ethic' and, in any case, there has been little attention paid to the specific ideologies which the intellectuals of enthusiasms or sports promulgate. In this chapter I want to consider what the hot rod apparatus said about 'work' and how this relates to widespread, though little investigated, assertion of the significance of some 'work ethic' in capitalist society.

In post-war America full employment and the changes associated with a general rise in real incomes caused a number of analysts to ponder the changing nature of work, its meanings, and its effects on the individual. Quite often the targets of this attention were workers in the automobile industry, and it was in this period that labour in automobile factories (this labour very narrowly conceived) was elevated to an iconic status, such that labour on the track or line became, somehow, the explicit or implicit model of what most modern work is like, or would soon be like, and in which major guidelines for investigation were provided such as repetition, boredom, degradation, de-skilling, and so on, all spun round the central thread of alienation. Such studies helped establish an orthodox tradition in the social analysis of work which is still dominant today, given added weight, but little more depth, by a renewed Marxist interest in the labour process from the mid-1970s.

One of the largest of these post-war studies was by Kornhauser. His book, pregnantly titled *The Mental Health of the Industrial Worker*, emerged out of interviews with over four hundred male Detroit workers and their spouses carried out in 1953–4. Kornhauser, like so many other students, had no doubts that 'work' was synonymous with paid labour, or of its significance for individuals:

> . . . clearly work not only serves to produce goods and services, it also performs essential psychologistical functions. It operates as a great stabilising, integrating, ego satisfying, central influence in the pattern of each person's life. If the job fails to fulfil these needs of the personality, it is problematic whether men can find adequate substitutes to provide a sense of

145

significance and achievement, purpose and justification for their lives.[2]

Such confident proclamations underpin many other, much more recent, studies of work, its meanings and effects, but Kornhauser departed somewhat from the orthodox tradition in that he at least tried to establish whether his workers found 'compensations' in other aspects of their lives for what he believed to be their routinised work. However, his search led him to conclude that only 10–15 per cent of his sample were engaged in hobbies or pastimes which: '. . . are of genuine current significance in their lives as sources of pride and enjoyment'.[3] The destructive effects of modern work were not, it seemed, checked by engagement in any other activity.

Kornhauser, despite this excursion, was able to swing back into the path of orthodox analysis by deploying a few more assumptions. He exemplifies an approach to the study of work which is both quick to assume the crucial existential significance of some conceptually muddy 'work' and which also demands that, if *other* activities are to enter into consideration as possible sources of pride, fulfilment, identity formation and affirmation, they must pass the most stringent scrutiny as to their *moral* worth. The dismissive use of terms like 'hobbies', 'pastimes', 'entertainment', 'amusements' is indicative here and Kornhauser's analysis abounds with phrases like *'serious* reading', *'shallow* routine pastimes', *'genuine* self-expression', *'challenging* quests for knowledge' and the like, where some undisclosed and undiscussed moral evaluation merges with what purports to be detached scientific appraisal, and operates so as to exclude various categories of action as being impossible and unworthy sources of meaning, purpose and self-definition. So Kornhauser excluded that considerable percentage of his auto-workers who insisted that all their spare time was devoted to house, car or garden. He excluded those who referred to gambling or drinking and the 20 per cent who alluded to sports (including hunting). All these were joined by those who said visiting or TV watching was their main leisure activity. Kornhauser's residue was composed only of the boat builders, violin makers and short story writers. Such value judgements, concealed in commonsense concepts and taken for granted connections, reek of the power of the 'work ethic' which may, or may not, have penetrated the minds of most workers but is certainly lodged as a moral ideal in much of what purports to be the sober scientific analysis of work and of its meanings.

I have made rather similar criticisms of another of these post-war studies, a true unthought-about classic, Chinoy's *Automobile Workers and the American Dream*, and will not repeat them here[4] but, actually, some indication of the crux of the matter is contained in the introduction to Chinoy's study written by David Reisman. This is highly complimentary in tone but raises the issues in ways which actually jar with the main text's orthodox approach. Reisman is much more insistent than Chinoy that workers are more or less forced to find self-expression and a meaning for their life outside the factory. Reisman is troubled by Chinoy's gratuitous rejection of the satisfactions of non-employment and his unease crystalises around one of Chinoy's respondents who insisted that his chief interests in life were 'baseball, girls and his car' and whose immediate concern was to be able to purchase the latest model of the automobile company he was employed by. Chinoy, like Kornhauser, simply could not accept this as a valid statement of life interests but Reisman did and mildly suggested that cars certainly could be a way of life for some people.[5]

Now these criticisms of two post-war studies are not designed to pick off some easy targets, for their assumptions still underpin *most* orthodox study in this field and still serve to simplify the real puzzle of issues which lie around 'work', its meanings and effects. As I suggested in Chapter One by far the most important of these assumptions is that 'work' is equated with employment. Recently, a critique of such lazy scholarship has been developing within, as it were, the sociology of work itself. In their books Rose and Pahl both point to the fallacy of treating 'work' as equivalent to the regular paid labour of, usually, men and both point out that what are all too often claimed to be 'new attitudes' or 'departures' from 'old' values invariably rest on comparisons with an implied or idealised past based on no or inadequate evidence as to exactly what such attitudes or values were in earlier periods.

Rose concentrates on the issue of whether some 'work ethic' has *ever* affected the behaviour of most workers. His scepticism about this is refreshing, but his analysis tends to dwindle in force because his attention is directed at paid labour and so other activites, other labours, do not attract the careful scrutiny he applies to the meanings of 'work' as conventionally understood. Indeed, he is led to argue that a 'work ethic' cannot now represent truly bourgeois values since modern economic performance depends on avid consumption. The activities of the modern sales effort '. . . reinforce a broader hedonistic frame of mind which is directly at odds with the bourgeois doctrine of deferred gratification.'[6] He refers to: '. . . an immensely competent advertising and promotion industry whose creative elite possess every skill needed to reassure people of their personal right to self-indulgence, to frequent escape from social obligation, and work commitments, to an undue concern with time, or from worries over budgeting.'[7] In such quotes Rose reveals that he has not entirely escaped the frameworks imposed by the assumptions of the dominant tradition. He certainly simplifies the accomplishements of the groups in modern capitalism who work with and on culture and symbols, and assumes they produce an undifferentiated, one-dimensional, ideology of 'easy indulgence' in 'leisure' time.

Pahl's text concentrates on discussing the various types of work that were and are done in society and insists on the important distinction between employment (paid labour) and work, which is conceived of as a very broad category encompassing all productive activities (paid and unpaid), reproductive activity and some consumption. Within a broad duality of production and reproduction Pahl provides a typology of ten types of work with eleven qualifications or subdivisions. The reproduction aspect itself, a category covering a lot of what most analysts would label 'leisure', contains four kinds of work with six subdivisions. Such a broadening of the key term should have great implications for orthodox study (though up to date it really has not), for *if* 'work' is where 'man makes himself' and *if* 'work' is an unclear concept, with many dimensions, then it is by no means clear which of these *works* is to be afforded centrality in identity creation, or perhaps all are, or perhaps relative weights change through history or through a life. Each work may have its own ideologies and preferred meanings which can vary through time and space. Pahl catches part of what is at issue here in his concluding remark that: '. . . the work ethic is alive and well: people enjoy working and there is plenty to do. Often they may not particularly enjoy their employment.'[8]

Pahl's intervention has been damned with much praise. It has quickly gained the label of a 'classic' but has provoked very little change in the direction of research or extra thought by those content to plough along in the orthodox furrows. It has not received the criticism that such an important text deserves. For it does contain faults some of which turn on deep problems about 'meaning' and exactly what the term 'work' is supposed to cover. Although Pahl begins his study by saying that one of its starting points is people's changing *experience* of 'work' his study is curiously silent about meanings and their sources. The main text provides a rather formal account of 'work' of which the typology just referred to is a good example, while a couple of case studies here and there hardly deal with the issue of what messages people are receiving about 'work' and how they interpret them. Pahl concentrates on examining the work done and tends to neglect questions of meanings and associated ideologies and occasionally lapses into the normal and quite unwarranted suggestion that the existential significance of various works can be illuminated by quantitative measure: 'The assumption must be that, if more time is spent on one activity than another, then that activity ranks as more important or essential',[9] whereas what is really of the essence here is the varying *quality* of labour times. Moreover, Pahl's stress that work (in all its forms) is a strategy of households directed to a project of 'getting by' and 'cosiness' means that he both neglects independent, individual work strategies, as he recognises, and tends to adopt far too instrumental a view of what work is done for. So he has little to say about work in relation to expressive needs, self-presentation and status display. He does appreciate that such labour is done and is promoted in society: '. . . this development of consumption as a form of work is, perhaps, the dominant new element that capitalism has imposed on household work strategies'.[10] but he does not investigate the qualitative significance of such work and relegates mention of it to footnotes or throwaway lines. As with Rose, Pahl tends to assume that modern advertising and marketing always link to 'new' needs and 'new' commodities.

My point is that even these important new critiques of the orthodox tradition do not really touch on all of the vital issues involved in recasting the study of work. In particular, if there are many *works* and the meanings of each can vary, then there is a great need to focus on the way people learn about work and are socialised to various meanings. For there is no intrinsic meaning to any piece of labour. Meanings have to be attached, sustained, promulgated and learned. As I have said, most analysis rather vaguely assumes that the dominant values of capitalist society do present some 'work ethic' which is both smooth and unequivocal in tone and paramount in the messages emanating from the major institutions of society. Neither of these assumptions is obviously correct and, at a bare minimum, students of the meanings of work need to be alive to a diversity of dominant sources presenting rather different messages about work, and also to the fact that while dominant values will provide a good deal of input, albeit in a more complex and contradictory fashion than is often suggested, other sources exist with their own institutional supports which will mediate and mix with dominant views. Specifically, class, gender and ethnic cultures will make complex inputs, as will quite precise occupational ideologies formed in varying workplaces which will have both formal and informal expressions: from union rule books to workgroup norms. Acceptance of even this point makes it clear that the meanings of work are not likely to be neat and simple or form some uncomplicated 'ethic' but are rather likely to be jumbled and variegated, so that any individual has a whole range of types and levels of meanings on which to draw and with which to understand or appreciate the labour they are doing at any particular moment. Any appeal to a 'work ethic' as central to the experience of work – even when that term is only understood as paid labour – totally simplifies this issue since it picks out only a few of the extremely heterogenous meanings which circle around labour and *asserts* these to be 'the most important'.

One of the fullest descriptions of the work ethic is provided by Rodgers when considering nineteenth-century America: 'The central premise of the work ethic was that work was the core of moral life. Work made men useful in a world of economic scarcity. It staved off the doubts and temptations that preyed on idleness, it opened the way to deserved wealth and status, it allowed one to put the impress of mind and skill on the material world.'[11] This formulation is preferable to most, if only because Rodgers understands that worry about the dangers of sheer idleness form part of dominant ideologies about work. In all too many analyses the 'work ethic' has been slimmed down to equate to a craft ethic or professional ethic – work as a vocation – in which it is argued, or rather asserted, that the job *should* yield a sense of mastery, control over materials and techniques, command of technology, an engagement of hand and brain in solving problems and so on. This then becomes linked to another aspect, as alluded to by Rodgers, that the job should allow the opportunity for development in personality, and, though the rather imprecise connections are usually quickly skated over here, an opportunity for advance and mobility in material terms.

One problem with this kind of formulation of the 'work ethic' is that is posits far too simple a relation between objective task and subjective perception. The most routinised and paced paid labour requires some workers' knowledge to be applied if the task is to be done in the optimum way and thus virtually *all* jobs provide the raw material for workers to regard themselves as 'skilled' even if this is not institutionalised in the labour market. Then pride can be obtained from doing any job, even the most menial, well in the eyes of bosses or other workers. The respect of significant others in the workplace can be what is sought and valued, and this does not depend on the abstract quality of the task to be done. Or work can gain meaning by being defined as a sacrifice, through which the individual yields him or herself to unpleasant tasks or routine in order to meet obligations to others – usually wife, husband or children – and so gain respect. However, and crucially, the tendency to align 'a work ethic' with a craft job ethic has meant that there are numerous meanings around work which have received – from history, sociology or Marxism – little attention. Even Rodger's formulation misses a lot of these. The meanings of work which circulate around its role in marking passages in the life-cycle – adulthood, retirement – is a good example. Meanings can arise out of the job's location in a quite particular context. Thus purpose and identity can be summoned out of working for a well-known firm or in a glamorous location or from being linked with broad ideological notions of 'scientific progress' or from being associated with a desirable product. Car workers call on all of these to locate their work and infuse it with meaning. Nor has work as an area for the experience and display of sheer strength, endurance and courage been much discussed, yet, for males at least, such values are of some importance and by no means nestle easily with the craft ideal. Much hard, routine, labour is infused with meaning because it allows a physical confrontation. Life in any industrial concern is fraught with danger. Many labour processes routinely produce potentially dangerous incidents. The radical response to this has been to detail why such processes have come to be in the service of profit maximisation, but much less analysed is the response of workers to such recurrent situations and the way danger and bravery, drawing on notions of masculinity, become important in the meanings surrounding work. Men can gain pride, respect, assert and confirm identity, by pitting themselves against fear or furnace.

So, and while the ones I have mentioned certainly do not exhaust the stock, there are many ideologies which lurk around work and which provide meanings and only some of these are caught in the routine appeals of orthodox sociology and Marxism to the power of some 'work ethic'. What I am arguing is that the intellectual problem confronting the student of work is extremely complex, for there are *many works* in a capitalist society and *many ethics* or ideologies about work. The task has to be to trace what ethics apply to what kinds of work, for only if some activities can be shown to be intrinsically trivial and devoid of any ideological underpinnings, should they be written-off by social analysis as irrelevant sources of pride, identity and the understanding of social relations.

The presentation of labour in hot rodding

The ethos of hot rodding, expressed through the specialist magazines and books of post-war America, was not one redolent of passivity or indulgence but rather contained urgent prescriptions to labour, to strive, to plan, to exercise skill, to compete, to succeed, to risk; themes like those supposedly typical of some traditional 'work ethic' but directed at unpaid time. In the early days the main myth of the culture was of buying a junked Ford for a few dollars, of reclaiming various parts from it and reassembling from these and some other standard and custom accessories, via a great deal of hard and skilled labour, a high performance vehicle. Jaderquist's manual *New How To Build Hot Rods*, first published in 1957 and through to its sixth printing by 1977, is, like other books, full of pictures revealing how to do it yourself. The emphasis is on study, problem solving, initiative, making do and saving money by 'knuckle scraping' and 'back breaking' in an overall tone that would have heartened Benjamin Franklin: '. . . Tools, remember, are only extensions of your hands, arms and fingers. Unless the original will and muscle is there, the finest tools in the world are useless.'[12]

In Horsley's *Hot Rod It: And Run For Fun* of 1957 the bias of the text and photography is on the never-ending business of understanding the machine, especially the engine, in theory and practice. This kind of theme coexists with messages which stress not occupational success but, say, that working on your hot rod after paid labour is a source of satisfaction whatever your occupation or that all rodders form a special community of interest or that there is a relation between your rod and personal style and identity. Mass produced automobiles, it is held, are standardised as the result of an inevitable compromise: they are, therefore, nobody's 'dream machine', whereas 'Your rod expresses you in more than just looks. Its quality of workmanship and roadability, as well as its power advertise your status and power as a rodder. You want to be able to point to your car with pride and say, "want to take a ride?".'[13]

Hot Rod presented a variety of themes, values and ideas but a large part of its message was taken up with the ideologies of activity, involvement, enthusiasm, craftsmanship, learning by doing, experimental development, display and creativity, all circulating around the motor car as an object in use. In this chapter I trace some of the themes of this message as it related to mechanical labour, but it could as easily be illustrated in other aspects of hot rod activity, about fuel for example: '. . . on page sixteen is the first of twelve enlightening articles on fuel and carburation', or about driving. Many articles urged that, whether on the strips or streets, a true hot rodder should be a top class driver: skilled, knowledgeable, cool, able to marry mental awareness to manual dexterity to foresee and forestall danger. So what follows is but an aspect of an ideology which covered many other rod-related activities.

Hot Rod's conception of its younger readers was that they were a group of normal males who, being American, were attracted to mechanics, tinkering, competition and the search for success. Because these combined speed and the automobile, readers were always on the brink of lawlessness. They could succumb to temptation. They must not be allowed to be idle. They must have the right path constantly set before them. They required leadership, organisation and a sympathetic control. The magazine tried to accomplish this in part via the individuals and cars it featured as the measures of success in this pursuit and in part by its overall ideological tone. The magazine never presented hot rodding as an activity for the idle or for the spectator, it is not about triviality or passiveness or easy hedonism. The bottom line is that nothing good comes easy:

> Stuart has been developing the same engine, a 1934 Ford for the last eight years. He has constantly improved it and hopes to improve it even more in the future. At one lakes meet a rod went through the block, shattering a four by eight inch hole in the side of the engine. He salvaged the pieces, welded them together and welded that piece into the hole. Performance was not altered.[14]

In its early years more or less each month the magazine carried a story about someone who worked several hours a day, three hundred days a year, on their rod. Nor could or should success be a matter of money. In 1949 when the editor asked for snapshots of readers' cars to be sent to the journal for publication he remarked: 'By the term "good car" we do not necessarily mean one that has thousands of dollars sunk into it. Most of us cannot afford that. We do mean a car that reflects good workmanship and ingenuity.'[15]

The hot rod project was presented as a serious one. Indeed the magazine argued it was just this that distinguished the true hot rodder ('the million of us') from the 'shot-rodder'. These kind of messages spilled out of the numerous technical articles about engines, components, fuel, etc.; through DIY pictorial strips, in the assessments

153

F

of featured cars, in stories of individual achievement, in the technical question and answer section, on the readers' letters pages and in the editorials. So in January 1951 when the magazine tried to get a hot rod (with a truck engine) into the Indianapolis 500 track race, it mused: 'Whether it qualifies or not, the car will still long be remembered as a tribute to American inegenuity and the average man's desire to build something of his own design, with his own hands.'[16] The emphasis was not simply on working with metal but on theoretical understanding, scientific knowledge and designing skill: 'In many cases you can improvise, but when you can't take it easy. Save your muscles for the gym and use your head in the garage.'[17]

An outline of some typical articles may indicate what I mean. In November 1948 the magazine printed the first part in a series of 'Building a Hot Rod'. The titles of the successive monthly articles were: (i) Glossary of Terms; (ii) Classification and Selection; (iii) Running Gear Part I; (iv) Running Gear Part II; (v) Power Plant Part I; (vi) Power Plant Part II; (vii) Power Plant Part III; (viii) Power Plant Part IV; (ix) Roadster Completion. If this does not give the flavour, then consider the subheadings of the Power Plant I article: (i) Dissassembly of Engine; (ii) Inspecting and Reboring Block; (iii) Increase in Power Output; (iv) Reasons for Porting and Relieving; (v) Methods of Porting; (vi) Methods of Relieving. And so it went on through the years with articles on: 'Crankshaft Stroking: More Engine Torque And How to Get It' one month, 'Do A Better Valve Job' another or 'Formulas and Math Every Hot Rodder Should Know' which began:

> Scientists say that the world and everything in it are based on mathematics. Without math the men who are continually seeking the cause of and the reasons for the many things that make the world go round would not have any means of analysing, standardizing and communicating the things they discover and learn. Math and the formulas that allow it to be applied to different problems are therefore, essential to any scientific endeavour. Hot rodding is a science. It's not as involved as determining what makes the earth rotate on its axis or building a rocket or putting a satellite into orbit but it is, nevertheless, a science.[18]

Long debates often broke out in the letter columns about, for example, what the 'coeffecient of friction' *was* precisely. Theoretical knowledge was not, however, regarded as important in its own right; what mattered was its application or, put another way: 'Never mind all the fancy words, what it all boils down to is how effeciently air and fuel are converted into usable power.'[19]

The magazine had a particular philosophy both on the reasons for 'American economic success' and on the importance of applying and testing knowledge in a practical, down to earth way. This was a theme constantly stressed in the Korean War period. In 1951 an editorial reflected that hot rodders were doing the job in the motor pools at the war front and in the training camps. The mass media was proud of this but was quick to condemn 'the schools of experience' in which this pre-eminence had its birth. It was not a natural trait nor could it be learned from text-books, rather: '. . . young Americans must learn to do by *doing*, there is no substitute or shortcut for actual experience.'[20] This stress on learning by practice, and not via books, was a repeated theme in the magazine and was underlined as a characteristic, indeed crucial, American trait. In general, 'experience is the best teacher'. The magazine was always sceptical about all the 'experts with slide-rules' who could impose restraints on invention and imagination. In 1952 it reported how two rodders were trying to create a car capable of 300 miles an hour. Many said this was impossible: 'But it is an accepted fact that hot rodders don't always *know* what can't be done, so they go ahead and *do* the impossible anyway.'[21] The hot rodder was the practically oriented underdog who could exasperate theorists and match Detroit's best. The Motorama car show of 1954 provided an opportunity to show that: '. . . backyard built cars and the people who build them are capable of matching or surpassing the world's finest.'[22]

When individuals were featured it was as enthusiasts or mechanics, their paid occupations were either not mentioned or mentioned in passing – they were not significant. What mattered was their absorption in the activity, the technical details of their car, their sweat and dedication to their task. The theme of this kind of article was on the unity of mental and manual labour. So when the magazine featured Fred Iges's roadster in February 1950, after plenty of technical data, the article ran:

> Using a 1925 Model T body, Fred filled and smoothed all the contours and added many original ideas to the lines of the car. The turtle back was welded to the back of the body and leaded in smooth. The deck lid is made of sheet aluminium to save weight, and the joined edges have been filled with a special cold solder. A metal worker by profession, Fred has done all of the body in his backyard garage. Faced with the problem of getting short louvres punched in the curved edges of the hood and side panels, Fred manufactured his own jig and dies and stamped the louvres himself. Power behind the dies was provided by use of a heavy hammer.[23]

This is a fair example of featured individuals. A craft-like approach to the task, attention to the smallest, apparently insignificant detail, was usually held up as the route to success in building or racing and was sometimes contrasted with attitudes to be found in paid labour. In 1948 an industrial designer praised hot rodding as: '. . . it encourages the development in our youngsters of the art of mechanical artisanship. This artisanship is seldom found in the auto-brotherhood. There is so much sloppy work performed in the great majority of garages that it becomes a rarity to see a mechanic who is proud of his work.'[24] While in 1959: 'Incompetency among mechanics in garages and new car agencies has become a major problem for today's motorists.'[25]

Akton Millar, dry-lakes veteran and elected official in hot rodders' associations, presented a concentrated statement of the magazine's ethos in his article: 'Hot Rods, I Love 'Em' of 1951. He never mentioned his paid occupation, except to joke about being an infantry private in the war, but talked about his first hot rod: 'Working nights and Sundays, I spent approximately four months building my car and enjoying every minute of it while I learned many new angles to car construction which cannot be found in a book.' And went on:

> I have always felt that successful participation in hot rod activities, as in any other form of activity is based on the age-old law of compensation in that the amount of effort one puts forward on a project determines the degree of education, fellowship and satisfaction which he may expect to enjoy in return. I have seen boys come into the organisation, compete in one or two meets and drop out because they found the competition too tough or the financial demands too great. Others work hard, sacrifice time and money, and remain in year after year eagerly awaiting the next event and the challenge it has to offer. One can compare the sport to a ladder; some take one step, others ten or more. But one thing is certain in all cases: the boys learn that there is a relationship between man and machine which cannot be found in any other sport. Words cannot describe the rewarding satisfaction of doing things with one's own hands, then seeing, hearing and feeling the gratifying results of hard labour and sacrifice. Nor can mere words ever convey the sensation that the hot rodder experiences when he gets behind the wheel of 200 plus horsepower and begins a run against the clock with the knowledge that he is about to demonstrate the union of speed and acceleration as personified in a hot rod of his own making.

Moreover: 'Progress within the Association makes it necessary for one to change ideas, methods and styles constantly if he wishes to keep pace with the top men.'[26]

As I have indicated here and there through this text, *Hot Rod* was not adverse to printing intellectual reflections or musings about what the activity 'signified' or 'meant', and such analyses often suggested to rodders that what they were involved in was a re-working of old values in new contexts. In 1951 it reprinted an article about the enthusiasm from an academic journal[27] and a year later it published a long article by Dr P. E. Siegle, once on the staff at the University of Illinois but then consultant psychologist to the Maremont Automotive Products Corporation, which, remember, was the major sponsor of ATAA. His article: 'Psychological Components of the Hot Rodder' related the sub-culture to a wider American culture which stressed initiative, competition and free enterprise. It was about the '. . . opportunity to make more and better things. The ideal dream is that of a man alone with his raw materials, using his ingenuity and know-how along with his industriousness to produce a better *thing*', and Siegle went on: 'There is an almost mystic quality to the picture of the young American boy working from scratch in the shop hoping to build a better hot rod. It fits with the American shibboleth of recognition for the ability to pull oneself up by the bootstraps. Hard work and luck are key ideas in the American success story.' Hot-rodding allowed this. Indeed, it was perhaps *more* in tune with the older virtues than was the modern 'conspicuous consumption' society where status came from the acquisition of goods and which was, anyway, frustrating and anxiety-provoking since the result of competition was not clear cut, a point that many modern analysts of consumption might ponder. Siegle also explained to his readers that rodding allowed an outlet for aggression and the achievement of mastery over machines, in a society where the relevance of older standards of personal success were by no means unchallenged. In Siegle's portrayal the hot rod movement involved a more vital working out of basic cultural values than the rather flabby and cluttered life of advanced capitalism now allowed.[28]

I could give many other examples of the inspirational message of this magazine, only one of a number centring around car knowledge, modification and maintenance. As readership increased, those in control obviously realised that it was being purchased by large numbers of people who were not hot rodders in any pure sense and, as I indicated in Chapter Four, the magazine began to broaden the definition of what could be considered a 'hot rodder' so as to cover all 'the mechanically minded' or 'motor minded Joes' as the publication put it. These were people, so it said, who wanted to know more about the automobile than was available in other publications and who wanted to get a better performance out of their stock models. The magazine was often scathing about the so-called technical details printed in the truly mass media or in the advertisements of the Detroit companies. It sneered at the ordinary motorist who believed that because his speedometer registered 120 miles per hour he was actually *doing* 120 miles an hour. While Detroit's advertisments might claim their engines could develop 300 horsepower those who read the magazine knew that 'horsepower' lost much of it's meaning once a salesman took the reins and that the automobile industry knew fine well that there wasn't one production car that could pull an honest 300 hp. over any length of time in an 'as installed condition'. The magazine proclaimed itself as for the insider, the knowledgeable, and so while the technical articles and question and answer pages changed somewhat from the mid-1950s, so that a lot more attention was given to mechanical details of new cars and new engines, still, the DIY ethos, urgings to learn and to strive, to improve, to work on your car and make it better – better looking and better performing – remained central in this magazine, were paramount in this magazine as it spoke to its million and more readers each month.

Alterations in presentation

Now, since I am arguing in this book for the importance of tracing the *specificities* of enthusiasms and the cultures of consumption it is important for me to admit that through the years *Hot Rod*'s editorial focus did alter as the overall policies of the Petersen Group dictated that it pursue and emphasise new facets of the general enthusiasm for motorized vehicles that could be labelled 'hot rodding'. This meant that sometimes *Hot Rod* encompassed the drag racing sport but at other times it covered drag racing partially, sometimes very partially, while concentrating on a lot of other automobile-related activities. At times the magazine focused on street rods and customising, on 'show' rather than 'go'. Vans, go-carts, motorcycles, dune-buggies, and other mani-festations of 'the' automobile also took up a lot of space for a while. This also meant that at periods *Hot Rod* moved away from a detailed concern with the theory and practice of backyard modification and towards an alignment with a simple buying of performance and/or looks, particu-larly so in the era of the 'muscle car'. So through the 1964–70 period *Hot Rod* broadly catered for those who were concerned with performance but who didn't have the time, talent or inclination to build or modify much their own car and wanted to purchase power in the showroom or as a simple 'bolt-on', in a decade where it was Detroit who 'put the hot in'. My admission might appear clinching evidence for those who adhere to a simplistic 'incorporation' notion of 'free-time' activity or who think the complexity of issues surrounding modern consumpton, including the promotion of the values that surround unpaid labour, can be dismissed by uttering magic phrases like 'market provision' or 'commodification'.

The 'radical' response to Hoggart's perception at the head of this chapter is to refer to 'capital' shaping 'leisure' and to dwell on 'commodity provison'. *Hot Rod*'s deviations from the early spirit of make-your-own from the mid-1960s seem a classic case of the desire for craft pride and pursuit of the work ethic snuffed out in an avalanche of mass produced commodities. However, the real questions are whether and how far the search for skill and information Hoggart referred to gets altered or 'deformed' because it is organised through what are conventionally called 'hobbies', and because the commodities which are specialist magazines try to promote the sale of other commodities? In fact, the slightest investigation of the invocations often uttered here reveals them to be cheap sleights of hand. It is hard to see quite what the causal connections are supposed to be especially because, as always, the 'radical' critique of 'commodity provision' rarely if ever discloses the *other* method by which needs could be met. The argument has to be that packaged provision takes over *all* the possible activities and that, somehow, this is subjectively experienced as such by participants. Otherwise, throwaway references to 'capital' or 'commodities' merely become the mystical incantations of a certain philosophy of man not the empirical science of social structures.

The movements of *Hot Rod* throw some light here. To begin with, its various deviations did not pass without protest. Complaints abounded at all the shifts of emphasis along the lines that 'Hot Rod has become a snob book for the high-roller' and the like. More significantly *Hot Rod* was bounded by its own ideology. The magazine was a commodity and helped to sell commodities but its pitch was that it was for the backyard, shade tree, mechanic who was the heart and soul of rodding. Part of what Petersen Publications came to sell were detailed manuals on all aspects of car maintenance and modification.[29] I won't delve into these here but I trust the point I am making is an obvious one – but perhaps it isn't, for the hot rod apparatus was intent on appealing to the grease-under-the-fingernail crowd not the musers of post-modernism. The lower classes of capitalist society use their unpaid time to develop expression, drama and personality through projects which may well be judged as mundane when viewed from the heights but may be of great moment to them.

In addition every so often, shadowing its various shifts, *Hot Rod* would announce that it had drifted too far from the basics of hot rodding and that it was going to get back to the little guy and DIY and carry plenty of articles about affordable projects that the average man could carry through with a few tools. A new editor in April 1972, making one of these promises of new but old good intentions put it:

> If you want it all in one sentence, HRM's primary editorial direction is showing you, with clearly illustrated, authoritative, understandable articles, how to perform easily accomplished modifications which will improve your car's performance (acceleration, braking, cornering, gas mileage etc) or appearance while staying within your financial reach.

Or as with another a decade later in May 1981 announcing a new 'how-to-do-it' series:

> Until the advent of the aftermarket, hot rodders did it all themselves. Now, many rodders have come to rely upon store-bought parts and assemblies rather than take the time to hone their own tool twisting talents. This is not to imply that every hot rodder has to master the intricacies of butt-welding aluminium, porting heads, beatin' on rusty bodies or owning your own spray booth or trim shop. That's dreamland. But that doesn't mean you shouldn't be made aware of some of the basic approaches to hot rodding, such as the techniques behind fabrication, hammer welding, parts making, tin-bending or metal working while using nothing more than simple hand tools.

Hot rodders were still asked to test their knowledge in quizzes as well as in their projects:

DO YOU KNOW?
Answer True or False

1. Slider clutches and automatic transmission converters have little if anything in common . . .
4. Static holding force (spring pressure) increases in direct proportion to engine rpm. since high engine speed is associated with strong spring forces . . .
5. In terms of centrifugal pressure plate loading, release lever position in the pressure plate has little bearing on the amount of total loading once the clutch reaches high rpm. . . .
10. The thicker the clutch/disc (within reasonable limits) the more holding pressure will be accomplished when using a diaphragm clutch pressure plate . . .[30]

The first sentence from the first-ever editorial – 'Hot Rod is published to inform and entertain those interested in automobiles whose bodies and engines have been rebuilt in the quest for better performance and appearance' – became almost a sacred incantation and was repeated over and over again in the magazine across the years to declare what *Hot Rod* and hot rodding were truly about. In November 1985, for example, the editor argued that less is more: 'Replace cubic money with hard work, talent and ingenuity. Be an individual, build the car you want to build – not what the standard is. If you do a good job by stressing craftmanship you'll be accepted.' In recent years on-board electronics and electro-mechanical devices could be viewed 'objectively' as commodities stripping away skill and, indeed, dealing the death blow to the mechanical basis of rodding. But this is not how they are presented to those who read the magazine. They simply represent new challenges. They lead the way to fascinating problems such as whether rodders are about to witness the end of the carburettor and: 'all of us are going to be faced with the requirements of becoming electronic hot rodders as well as wrench wizards. Either way tomorrow is becoming increasingly exciting.'[31] State action to regulate automobiles, new technologies, even gizmos, were presented as just laying new matters on the bench to think about and to work with because, as in the words of an early article: 'Squeezing more power out of an internal combustion engine will always be a fascinating business to me because it will never be a cut-and-dried deal. There's always some weird new angle that comes up; some difference of opinion to hash-out.'[32] Of course, some people know more than others but, in hot rodding, now as ever: 'nobody has all the answers'.

Rodding and employment

The hot rod sub-culture of post-war America can be dismissed as a trivial topic, one to be shunned by the serious minded, of little moment to the analysis of work and its meanings. However, if it is granted that 'work' is a multi-faceted activity and that the meanings of work are not to be encompassed by invoking the power of some immutable 'work ethic', then there is a real necessity to consider exactly what social sources are promulgating what ideas about what work at any particular period and here I am arguing that the specialist literature that hangs around popular pursuits is of some significance. The more or less unexamined activities and ideological material of gardening, angling, cooking, do-it-yourself, boating, motoring, home-computing, knitting, sport and so on, all have plenty to say about labour and identity, skill and self, craft and commitment, the necessity of combining the mental and the manual. Of course, there are powerful arguments which suggest that in the post-war period a basic cultural shift occurred with a devaluation of paid labour as a significant area of life, with people's prized images becoming focused on the weekend-self or holiday-self, but regardless of such hypotheses about the varying importance of sectors of life, true students of work do need to consider the social organisation of a lot of enthusiasms and interests, and the kinds of ideologies which surround them for, so far, the organisation and re-organisation of 'free time' has not received the examination it deserves.

My review of the themes contained in the specialist literature of one particular enthusiasm indicates that the weight of a lot of its messages stood very close to that melange known as 'the work ethic'. The desire of the lakes enthusiasts to safeguard their sport or at least a sport, and the mutation of some of them into a creative elite who also sought to protect a bundle of economic opportunities which grew up around the sport, meant that hot rod literature rang out with a serious tone. Its fire was trained on idleness, time was to be filled with skilled activity and success seeking. The journal addressed its readers through an idiom stressing excelling through effort, progress by trial and error, advance via defeat and learning from mistakes. Benjamin Franklin's nostrums that: 'There are no gains without pains' or that 'God helps those who help them-selves' echo again and again in an enthusiast's argot and were pursued in action by the magazine through its influence over the local and national organisations.

Hot Rod did not seek to challenge commonsense categories of 'work' or 'leisure'. Its language was, in the main, quite conventional. It spoke of hot rodding as 'a hobby', as 'tinkering', as an 'avocation'. However, as the quote by Akton Millar detailed earlier indicates, *Hot Rod* often tripped over the definitional problems more sophisticated analysis has now come to. In August 1950 the magazine featured the 'Recuperated Coupe': 'The entire process consumed many hours in time and consider-able expense in parts, but like many other car builders he took great pride in his work and enjoyed the work he was doing' while another featured car is: '. . . a real tribute to the craftsmanship that makes car building a great hobby'.[33] Such, unrecognised, conceptual confusion (mirroring, of course, most orthodox social analysis) rippled out into mass media surveys of the subculture. *Hot Rod* was instrumental in presenting its version of the activity in a well-selling novel, a number of low-budget films and in popular radio and TV shows of the 1950s and

1960s. A *Life* cover story in 1957 (heralded with some suspicion by *Hot Rod*) did speak of illegal street races but also told its readers: 'These cars are usually hand built with much ingenuity and affectionate care by avid teenagers.' *Life* featured the 'Dream Boat' of 24-year-old Norman Grabowski, much admired in the Los Angeles drive-ins: 'By working for five years on a poultry farm and as an extra for the movies Grabowski has earned the money it cost to hand make his machine – $8,000.'[34] So a wider audience was made aware of craftsmanship and expertise ethos of the hot rod world as they were in later movies like *Hot Rod* (1979) and *Heart Like a Wheel* (1985).

Of course, the levels of achievement reported and honoured in the magazine were symbolic, not representative of the average level of effort or achievement in the enthusiasm as the apologetic tone of most readers' letters about *their* cars indicates.[35] The specialist literature and its echoes in the mass media presented a mythological version of the hot rod endeavour: stating what should be done if you wanted to reach the pinnacle. It was an optimistic version too. Nothing is said about botched jobs or cars that look aesthetically awful or perform badly as a result of home tinkering. There is little about racing accidents (when that racing is legal) while disasters – engines blowing, cars turning over – are presented as challenges, as opportunities for progress, not as being physically or financially crippling. The ethos is positive and exuberant, with little time to dwell on failure except as a stepping stone to success. The route to honour, status and self-satisfaction is still labour, and practical manual labour at that, but the appeal here is to something much higher than working for wages. Often the magazine suggested that the purpose of employment is merely to provide the wherewithal for this finer pursuit. In general though the magazine and most other hot rod literature, had very little to say about paid labour. Sometimes, but by no means always, the employment of featured rodders is mentioned but such references carry about the same significance as their home town. Of the jobs that are mentioned in this random and peripheral fashion, a high proportion (though not *that* high given the place of automobile work of *all* kinds in the American economy) are in automobile-related employment and the vast majority are in skilled manual or petit-bourgeois occupations but there is not nearly enough evidence here from which to draw any firm conclusions about the precise social background of participants in rodding.[36]

Hot Rod's constant search for respectability for the enthusiasm did lead it to suggest sometimes that 'know-how' could lead on to employment.

In 1952 it reprinted a NHRA pamphlet – 'The Hot Rod Story' – whose author argued: 'That hot rodding provides an incomparable proving ground for amateur experimentation and research is not open to question. That out of such activity – be it classified as a sport, hobby, or avocation – may arise some of our foremost engineers or designers of tomorrow is a reasonable speculation.'[37] Or in 1953, in reply to the decision by the National Automobile Dealers Association not to sell to hot rodders, the editor proclaimed: 'The thinking men of Detroit's industry are increasingly aware that from such enthusiasm and enterprise can come the skilled manpower pool necessary to keep American wheels rolling.'[38] This theme was reinforced, as the magazine's circulation expanded, by regular full page advertisements which also suggested that hobby could be turned into employment. From the mid-1950s the Army and the Air Force regularly sought 'men with mechanical skill' while correspondence courses counselled:[39]

> If you eat, sleep and live cars
> TURN YOUR HOBBY INTO A CAREER
> Get America's big-time, big-future
> AUTO MECHANICS, DIESEL COURSES
> at home, in your spare time.

Then too the development of a paid elite of racers, greeted none too enthusiastically by *Hot Rod*, suggested another way that personal interest and paid employment could be combined, in advance to professional ranks. The hot rod literature does sometimes suggest that any rodder's ideal would be to marry hobby and payment. Bill Kenz, a racer and speed shop owner, remarked in 1951: 'When cars are a man's hobby as well as a livelihood, there is always something new and interesting coming up . . . there's *never* a dull day.'[40] Don Garlits, who metamorphised from Florida street racer to world champion, recalls that when he left school in 1950 he took up a book-keeping job: '. . . it was just taken for granted – including by myself – that I'd get a job of that kind. It was awful. Working conditions were all right. It simply boiled down to my dislike of the day-in, day-out drudgery of working with invoices and receipts, bills of lading. It was an utter drag.'[41] Hot rod expertise gave the chance of a career to: '. . . the kid who wasn't very good at schoolwork, especially all that English, but who could speak to engines. He could rest his fingertips on the hood of any car and detect its illness.'[42]

However, being a professional is not painted as an easy, simple, or always desireable option, as I will sketch in Chapter Eight. It requires total dedication, single-mindedness, perseverance and luck. There is a stress on the costs of success – injury, lack of friends, broken marriages, loss of family life. Moreover, it is not presented as necessarily that enjoyable, as in Prudhomme's weary description of drag racing:

> Six seconds sometimes feels like a lifetime – especially when you look out the side and there's a car right next to you. There are so many things that can happen. Tyre vibrations. The car gets out of shape. While the car is out of shape and while the tyres are shaking, not only are you concerned about beating the guy next to you, especially in a big race like Indy. , but you're thinking "I've got to fix that before the next round". There must be a million thoughts that go through your mind driving the six second run. Then people look at me at the end of the day and say, 'Boy you sure look tired'. Doggone right. I have thought about every thought in the world.[43]

The stars of any enthusiasm are important in the production of meanings as they serve both as the embodiment of ideological principles and allow lower-level practitioners to relate their immediate experience to mediated experience through similarities of circumstance and event. Stars exist at a higher but essentially parallel plane. However, heroes are not necessarily portrayed as entirely successful. In the hot-rod literature there is more than a hint that the drive required to reach professional status could involve failure as a human being. *Hot Rod*'s stress was on an *amateur* ethos. It was quick to point out that professionalism could bring a displacement of goals so that running for fun could easily shift down into earning a living. The professional elite were regarded both as craftsmen with mysterious secrets and also as having sacrificed some spontaneity and enjoyment. Prudhomme speaks those words that echo oddly to the amateur enthusiast of most sports: 'Racing isn't fun it's a business. Of course, it isn't fun. This is serious. We like to win. We race to win. But we don't enjoy ourselves at the track. It's not fun. It's a serious business.'[44] Moreover the degree and kind of sponsorship they received from parts companies meant that they began to transgress the basic code of rodding. As Garlits put it around the same time about his fellow professionals: 'The bulk of the guys out there know how to change pistons, but they don't know how to tune a motor. They're parts changers. The guys have been programmed to this type of procedure.'[45] Amateur endeavour was not only seen as a more authentic experience, untainted by an instrumentalism which could lead to scandals and cheating, but could be combined with calls to high standards of morality, close attention to unwritten rules, and, indeed, financial *sacrifice*, in short, much more than could be expected from any mere job.

In all, the hot rod literature tends to be silent about any paid labour which is not connected to automobiles and while reference to the possibility of moves into rod-related jobs can be found, they are by no means a major element in the specialist literature. In this, and in its incorrigible stress on importance of manual labour (albeit founded on contemplation and study), *Hot Rod* presented a highly romantic vision of work and what it was for. The rodder was enjoined to see himself and, as I will discuss in the next chapter, *herself*, in the roles of craftsman, inventor, the independent artisan and as practical dreamer, whose garage improvements and drag-strip experiments were, the magazine constantly asserted, monitored by Detroit and paid off in the form of better cars for everyone. As well, the literature stressed the nature of the experience to be gained through racing. This gave existence a rare quality of excitement, found when you are out there, at the edge, wheel to wheel, in competition, waiting for the light to turn green and you have to get out of the hole. The magazine enjoined that fine workmanship and controlled aggression could be fused in a way which allowed identity to be tested, celebrated and displayed. Unlike the confusion of much of the rest of life, racing on the lakes or strips offered plain measure of success and failure. There were clear victories, intelligible defeats, comprehensive standards of personal achievement and progress, laid down by the exact second hand of a timing device or the line across the track at the finish. So complex cultural imperatives of all kinds surrounding 'work' could be easily understood, obeyed and applied in the drag race.

My example of the hot rod literature is designed to show that injunctions to strive, to create, to study and achieve are around in plenty in 'leisure' activities. Most people are touched by them in some part of their life. What is revealed when we look at the specialist media of the hot rod world of the 1940s and 1950s and right on into the 1980s are directives in its pages, and the carrying out in practice, of personally chosen projects unconnected to paid labour: 'work' as hobby, as relaxation, as fascination, as something *you really want to do* rather than being constrained to do. About feeling *good* by working hard. This I am sure is true of the literature of many other activities, but, I would argue, is especially significant in automobile pursuits. The automobile is a machine, it is technology and people confront it, handle, know, master and enjoy it in ways which may be routine for some but for others is often very satisfying: as it was for the hot rodders. The automobile also has important connotations as a product. Words which are 'naturally' associated with it – mobility, freedom, pace, progress, competition – have parallels in other, apparently more 'important', areas of culture and metaphors, allusions, if not direct substitutions from one cultural sphere to the other, are plentiful.

The assumptions which underlie a lot of social analysis define many areas of life as unimportant. The orthodox tradition of the study of 'work' and its meanings has largely ignored 'leisure' and when it has noticed it there has been a depiction in broad brush strokes like 'trivialisation', 'passive response', 'incorporation by the mass media', 'hedonism' and so on. Such categorisations flatten out the varied configurations of non-paid activities, avoid issues of the relative quality of time and ignore ambiguities inherent in the way life has developed in capitalist society. Special interests and specialist literature with their 'insiders' dope, 'expert' opinion, assurance of 'community' and assertions of the importance of the search for authenticity, abound in modern capitalism but have been neglected by social analysis. In *Hot Rod*, as in much other literature, social identities were offered, arcane language was explained, mysteries of craft were laid bare, tasks were invested with purpose, each reader was addressed as part of a wide movement and everyone was held to be implicated in 'scientific progress' and 'technological advance'. Those who operate as the cultural entrepreneurs of unpaid time, working through an unexamined literature and disregarded organisations, do draw on grander and long established (though not necessarily socially effective) cultural themes in order to defend, explain and promote their activities and make them respectable, but, in so doing, they alter the accents, replace essences and shuffle significances so that older messages ring out in new areas of life. Part of what they do is to *really* re-work the 'work ethic', locate it to unpaid labour and so, quite possibly, make it *more* psychologically meaningful for the bulk of the population than it was in earlier periods of capitalist society. Until sociology and Marxism give such moral entrepreneurs and the transformations they attempt a lot more attention, then, I suggest, we will not know too much about the various meanings of a variety of works and their differing significance for the individual. It might be as well if analysts now laid aside the texts of Franklin, Alger, Marx and Weber and picked up instead some other examples of this type of the popular literature of contemporary capitalism. Then we might be able to judge how far the argument presented here for hot rodding holds true for other sports and for other enthusiasms.

Driving ambitions

Notes

1 R. Hoggart, *The Uses of Literacy* (London, 1957), p. 326. I am grateful to Cambridge University Press for allowing me to use some material first published in my chapter in P. Joyce, *The Historical Meanings of Work* (Cambridge, 1987) in this section.
2 A. Kornhauser, *The Mental Health of the American Worker* (London, 1965), p. 7.
3 *Ibid.*, p. 199.
4 H. F. Moorhouse, 'American automobiles and workers' dreams', reprinted in K. Thompson (ed.), *Work Employment and Unemployment* (Milton Keynes, 1984).
5 E. Chinoy, *Automobile Workers and the American Dream* (Boston, 1955), pp. xix–xx. The only contemporary academic piece on early rodding was G. Balsley, 'The hot rod culture', *American Quarterly*, 2, 1950, pp. 353–8, subsequently used by R. Denny in another early analysis of rodding in the *The Astonished Muse* (Chicago, 1957), pp. 138–56. Balsley was a student of Reisman's.
6 M. Rose, *Reworking the Work Ethic* (London, 1985), p. 19.
7 *Ibid.*, p. 105.
8 R. E. Pahl, *Divisions of Labour* (Oxford, 1984), p. 336.
9 *Ibid.*, p. 106.
10 *Ibid.*, p. 106 fn.
11 D. Rodgers, *The Work Ethic in Industrial America 1850–1920* (London, 1978), p. 14.
12 E. Jaderquist, *The New How to Build Hot Rods* (6th printing, New York, 1977), p. 33.
13 F. Horsley, *Hot Rod It and Run for Fun* (Englewood Cliffs, 1957), p. 151.
14 *Hot Rod* Magazine (*HRM*), 1, April 1948, p. 5.
15 *HRM*, 2, March 1949, p. 4.
16 *HRM*, 2, December, 1949, p. 4.
17 *HRM*, 4, June 1951, p. 6.
18 *HRM*, 14, January 1961, p. 94.
19 'Shop series', *HRM*, 32, February 1979, pp. 42–5.
20 *HRM*, 4, September 1951, p. 5. V. Papanek, *Design for the Real World* (London, 1971), p. 34 remarks on the oddity of design schools in the USA still following basic courses developed by the Bauhaus which seek to allow students to get a sense of the 'interaction between tool and material' when most male teenagers have already spent a lot of hours under automobiles souping them up.
21 *HRM*, 6, May 1953, p. 6.
22 *HRM*, 7, January 1954, p. 51.
23 *HRM*, 3, February 1950, p. 19.
24 *HRM*, 1, November 1948, p. 11.
25 *HRM*, 11, February 1959, p. 5.
26 A. Millar, 'Hot rods I love em', *HRM*, 4, March 1951, pp. 10–11, 24–5.
27 Balsley, *op. cit.*, reprinted in *HRM*, 4, July 1951, pp. 8–10.
28 P. Siegle, 'Psychological components of the hot rodder', *HRM*, 5, August 1952, pp. 24–5, 48–9.
29 For early examples of this kind of literature see: F. W. Fisher, *California Bill's Hot Rod Manual* (Los Angeles, 1949); Editors of Hot Rod, *Hot Rod Your Car* (Los Angeles, 1952); G. Hill, *Popular Mechanics' Hot Rod Handbook* (Chicago, 1953); L. Hochman, *Hot Rod Handbook* (New York, 1958); R. E. Petersen and the

168

Editors of Hot Rod, *The Complete Book of Hot Rodding* (Englewood Cliffs, New Jersey, 1959); J. Christy, *Hot Rods: How to Build and Race Them* (New York, 1960), etc. etc.

30 'Shop series' *HRM*, 34, November 1981, p. 86 (answers at end of article).

31 *HRM*, 41, May 1988, p. 7.

32 'The almighty inch', *HRM*, 7, December 1954, p. 22–3, 69.

33 *HRM*, 4, May 1951, p. 13.

34 'The drag racing rage', *Life*, 29 April 1957, p. 78.

35 Of course, one of the ways in which social analysis has presented an idealised view of 'work' in the past has been the pervasive assumption that every skilled worker was actually a good or even competent craftsman.

36 Surveys of the readers of *Hot Rod* suggested that they tended to be slightly younger and have less college education than the readers of most other auto magazines. *Advertising Age*, 55, 26 July 1984 reported that the 85 per cent of the 800, 000 buyers of the magazine were male and 65 per cent were between the ages of 18 and 34.

37 *HRM*, 5, March 1952, pp. 30–3.

38 *HRM*, 6, May 1953, p. 5.

39 *HRM*, 8, January 1955, p. 4

40 *HRM*, 4, September 1951, p. 26.

41 D. Garlits and B. Yates, *King of the Dragsters* (London, 1967), pp. 18–19.

42 B. Ottum, 'Is there life after hot rodding?', *Sports Illustrated*, March 1981, pp. 40–1.

43 H. Higdon, *Six Seconds to Glory: Don Prudhomme's Greatest Drag Race* (New York, 1975), p. 95.

44 'Musings from the old man', *HRM*, 31, June 1978, pp. 23–5.

45 'A day in the life of a working class champion', *HRM*, 30, July 1977 pp. 30–2, 118.

Chapter Eight
Ideologies in the enthusiasm: an all-American way

I want to make one point very emphatically: I believe very firmly that a love for the automobile is a wonderful thing. Hot rodding as a sport has been tremendous therapy for literally millions of young men all over the country. In fact if the automobile still had the interest of the young people today that it did when I was young – and boys devoted themselves to it and to other hot rodders as we did – I wouldn't have been called upon just recently to make a film exposing the dangers of marijuana. Gangs of guys engrossed in learning about and tinkering with cars were – and are, when you can find them – good for this country.[1]

Which American dream?

It is often claimed that certain activities represent, perpetuate and promote particular ideologies or social institutions. Often, however, such claims are so all-embracing in scope as to be tautological and also tend to avoid the troubling consequences of comparative reference. As far as automobiles are concerned this is a major problem with Blaisdell's search for the values in magazines of the car culture which is not only coloured by the author's concentration on sports cars, which he admits are a European import to the USA, but also, following Dettelbach, traces 'values' around some grandly amorphous themes: 'youth', 'freedom', 'success' and 'possession'.[2] Certainly, sports and enthusiasms do carry certain general ideologies but via the specific forms of their basic activity, purpose, history etc. It is vital to consider these in particular detail and not deal with them just in grand sweeps of 'victory', 'freedom' and the like. For sports are not all of a piece nor are ideologies about, for example, what it is to be an 'American'. That such matters are all too often simplified, as in references to an 'American Dream' which can, conveniently, be just about what any author wants it to be,[3] is all part of the simplification of the issue of 'cultural domination' in a lot of social analysis. All too often concepts like ruling ideas, dominant values or hegemony are used as if they *provided* an analysis rather than being just the starting point for analysis. The other side of this coin is that 'the consensus', 'consumer society', 'commodity provision' and the like are usually viewed as being straightfoward, simple matters when they are, as I have already tried to argue, usually complex and multi-faceted phenomena.

I indicated in the previous chapter that drag racing was a mechanism for passing on certain ideologies or, to be precise, the local culture industry that worked around hot rodding used it as a vehicle for giving life and specific point to general ideologies and values thought to be important in America. Such cultural work, the repositioning and re-livening of general propositions (often themselves contradictory) is no simple matter. So while *Hot Rod* and the other material of the enthusiasm spoke about what it meant to be an 'American', this was a specific track of the all-American way and for a particular audience – publishing industry data for the late 1960s shows the median age of readers of *Hot Rod* as 21.6 years with 43 per cent having attended college.[4]

To begin with, the ideal hot rodder was addressed as a blue-collar man or, at least, readers were told they belonged to the no-nonsense, practical, grease-under-the-fingernails brigade. As I have argued, this did not exclude the exposition of theory or even philosophy, the hot rod media certainly did not speak down to their audience, but all abstraction had to connect, fairly directly, to the related realities of working on cars and dealing with life:

> all that Madison Avenue stuff is more plastic than a McDonald's '6 Trillion Burgers Sold' sign. There's nothing phony about lying in your driveway at night and trying to put the LaSalle trans back in your Caddy V8 '51 Ford and the splines won't line up with the clutch disc (even though you know they fit 'cause you took it apart the night before last) and there's nobody to help you and that sideshift box is lying there on your chest and the junk keeps falling in your eye and it's dark and you've got to go to work at 7. 30. in the a. m. I mean *that* is reality, and the Hot Rod staffers know it because they've all *been there* at one time or another. All this business of skiing in St. Moritz is only true in the toothpaste and cigarette commercials on TV.[5]

Hot rodding was for those with the 'right stuff' and it was quite appropriate that Chuck Yeager started appearing in a series of advertisements in *Hot Rod* in the 1980s. The hot rodder was a man, and later a woman, whose motto was, oddly enough, 'don't go where there's a trail' and whose feet itched to move to that different drum.

I will come back to this 'class' location of rodding again but in this chapter I want to try to begin to explore the exact kind of Americanism involved in the hot rod sports by considering what connection it had or was presented as having to four broad cultural themes: (i) the precise nature of the American genius; (ii) patriotism and involvement in foreign wars; (iii) masculinity and feminity; (iv) the outlaw image and Western man.

A home-spun sport

Part of the distinct 'Americanism' on offer was the way the hot rod apparatus conceived of the relation between technology and the American 'genius'. Much of the structure and language of automobile sports is of European derivation. 'Roadster', 'speedster', 'hot rod' and 'drag racing' are some of the few phrases connoting cars and car contests which were born in the USA. I have already decribed how the hot rod sports were looked down on and ignored for quite a while by the main automobile sports organisations in the USA because they did not accord with the *pur sang* of European-created and sanctioned auto competition. Given this it is not surprising that one aspect of the ideologies which the hot rod apparatus spread, especially to legitimate the activity, was to explain rodding as a typically American activity, natural and untainted by foreign notions. As *Hot Rod* put it in July 1952 when it was urging rodders to spread the word to papers and police about all the good things they were doing: 'Hot rodding is part of the American scene. We have no secret police here ferreting us out and therefore no reason to be obscure and furtive about activities. From a technical viewpoint, we are more likely to make contributions to American technology than any other sport. If for no other reason than this we should be openly proud of our interest in hot rods.' Hot rodding was seen as representing the spirit that had made America: ' "All-American" can be applied to the sport of drag racing and its participants as appropriately as to other organized athletic activities, for drag racing was truly born and raised in America and its early fledglings showed the same rebellious, adventurous traits as the pioneers who conquered the wilderness and turned it into a nation.'[6] Hot rodding certainly pulled on some Protestant work ethic associated with the founding fathers, as I tried to suggest in the last chapter, but it also married this to an indigenous, earthy, non-conformity.

One point this turned on was what made a 'hot rod' different from other cars and what exactly it looked like. In the early years this centred on the distinction between 'hot rods' and 'sports cars'. Several articles and letters were devoted to trying to establish what the difference was. In post-war America there was an estrangement and, indeed, antagonism between the two groups of aficionados, for the sports car was a European creation and was argued to be a 'European solution' to the task of making cars go faster, handle better and improve, while the 'hot rod' supplied the home-spun answer to similar problems. But another element forging links between rods and the American way was introduced here, for sports cars were also expensive items. The edginess between devotees of the two types of car did not simply reflect the distance between two continents but two 'classes' too. The ideology of hot rodding always involved a definite strain of poor kids versus rich kids and, as part of this, the humbling of many a 'millionaire sportsman' driving the best European machinery money could buy by a 'backyard-built special' was lovingly chronicled. At first *Hot Rod* upheld this distinction but later the tone changed. In 1954 the reply to the repeated question 'was a sports car a hot rod?' was now in the affirmative: '. . . a sports car being merely an older and international term for a "hot rod" '[7] and features on sports cars could then be labelled 'International Hot Rod' or refer to a 'hot rod in disguise' which led to readers' complaints.

This outcrop of a deeper definitional conundrum: 'what is a hot rod?', reached its peak in 1955 when the magazine promoted the concept of a 'Hot Rod Road Race Team' to participate in a Mexican road race. Individual rodders (sponsored by the magazine) had entered 'the Caballo' in previous years but now the journal suggested a full team should enter paid for by reader subscriptions. It noted that, to be successful, the two cars would need to be sleeker and more streamlined than before. This proposal provoked a good many letters enquiring, in the main, why hot rodders should contribute for cars that looked suspiciously like sports cars. In May the vice-president of a New York State hot rod club wrote:

> If you wish to get the hot rodders of the entire nation behind your effort, body and soul, why try to get them to build two sports cars? Now don't go off half-cocked; I'm not one of these guys who tries to perpetuate the hot-rod – sports-car feud. But I still think they're two basically different vehicles, even if you do call them two different approaches to the same subject. There's a hot rod look and a sports car look . . . when you build the car from the ground up and encase it with a body that looks for all the world like a Ferrari, where do you have the grounds to call it a hot rod? The romance is gone!

In the June 1955 issue a long letter (interspersed by defensive editorial comments) was printed: 'selected as representative of many asking that the old Caballo be kept rugged and square'. The letter ruminated on earlier efforts:

> What you had was a meat ball hot rod of fantastic design, slapped together like Saturday's soup gleaned from decades of forgotten chowders. Olds here, Model T there. Anyone among your worshipping legions had seen better hot rods . . . better looking. The appeal of Caballo was bound inseparable with your Quixotic charge at Ferrari's windmill . . . and how all of us wanted a rebuilt 'T' beating Ferrari!

A car in this hot rod tradition: 'would be an achievement for the common man'. The debate rolled on and a correspondent from Purdue University posed the issue and gave the maximal answer the journal now approved: 'What is a hot rod? Is the term limited only to Ford roadsters? Or are we broad minded enough to admit that all competition cars are forms of hot rods?'[8] Still as drag racing and drag machines developed this distinct American input into the European-dominated world of autosport was celebrated as when the NHRA joined various international racing regulatory bodies.

Then *Hot Rod*'s conception of its younger readers was that they were a group of normal American males who were, therefore, attracted to mechanics, tinkering, competition and the search for success. It saw them as in a great American tradition of, for example, Henry Ford and Thomas Edison, practical tinkerers whose backyard experimentation led on to great discovery and, often, personal wealth. As I have mentioned the hot rod apparatus enjoined a suspicion of the science certified in books and of what experts with slide rules said was the limits of the possible. It argued that the true 'American genius' was to translate and improve on a basic invention and: 'American youth is the most advanced among the nations of the world in mechanical know-how, the attribute which has kept this country foremost in progress. Building cars, studying engines and learning basic mechanics, the essence of hot rod activity, is one of the greatest contributing factors to such progress.'[9]

Wars

Not surprisingly perhaps this theme intersected with American military might. For the history of hot rodding spanned three major wars. One way in which the hot rod apparatus could show the sport as respectable, useful and downright American was to link the innate mechanical aptitude it expressed and increased to patriotic duty and military service. The *Colliers* article of 1941 reflecting the ways, it believed, the 1930s street racers had been incorporated argued: 'In sharp contrast to three years ago, the jalopy driver has come into his own. Today you will find him, and an endless stream from the same mould, pouring into sprawling aircraft factories, well equipped for his task in the defense industries. At aviation schools he is being turned out as the master mechanic, the designer, creator of horse power.'[10] As I have already noted, many 1930s hot rodders were drafted and some of the stars and office holders of the pre-war associations died in action. Many in the hot rod apparatus could recall the period when they carried a carbine on foreign soil and yearned to return to the normality of the dry lakes sport. By the time of the Korean War *Hot Rod* was in command and the drive to save the sport was at its height. Part of *Hot Rod*'s pitch was to launch a National Hot Rod Blood Donor's Week: 'Remember Joe? . . . the guy with the full race cam who always seemed to nose you out in the drags? He's in Korea now . . .'[11]

Forging a link between the special skills of a sport and the pressing needs of the nation at war was one way of illustrating not only the basic respectability of rodders but their usefulness to an imperial power. In 1950 *Hot Rod* argued that rodders maligned as 'delinquents' would be better prepared for the improvisations and emergencies which were a necessary part of war than the ordinary person. In 1951 an editorial reflected that hot rodders were doing the job in the motor pools at the war front and in the training camps: 'We take pride in the fact that we possess great mechanical know-how. In a measure, the very essence of American armed might rests in our ability to maintain technological superiority over the rest of the world.'[12] While an article: 'Hot Rodders and the Defense Program' asked what rodders could do for their country. A lot had been called up but it called for the others to organise locally into 'flying squads of trouble shooters'. They should take an inventory of the capabilities they could offer but: 'The sheer mobility of an organization of hot rodders, the capacity to meet quickly at a given point and to move to a critical area without a loss of time, in themselves constitute an inviting prospect to civil defense directors and planners.'[13] And besides, it would be 'a solid PR job'. *Hot Rod* began carrying a special letters section for men serving in the armed forces from 1951 and printed many a wistful letter from men whose rodding had been halted by Uncle Sam. It carried their pictures of jeeps, tanks even large warships recording their top speeds and elapsed times, and their stories of hot rod clubs formed on military bases in far away Europe or Asia.

Some of the men who became top professionals believed their war experiences contained lessons about participation in the sport:

> The ultimate price extracted from a few drag racers is permenant injury or even life itself. I don't enjoy talking about this aspect of a drag racer's life, but it is part of the story and, unfortunately, a lot of psychologists and others say it is one of the reasons fans attend drag races . . . When I was sixteen years old the Korean War was in full swing. Like vast numbers of other kids I ran away and joined the Marines. In a fox hole just south of the 38th. parallel I ate, slept and lived among dying or even dead man for days on end. Somehow all my fears of meeting my Maker were buried in that small hole.[14]

All the danger wasn't in the trenches, however, as deaths on American roads numbered around 38,000 a year and in 1954 President Eisenhower held a road safety conference in the White House which pointed out that traffic deaths for 1952 exceeded American fatalities in the Korean War.

The Pentagon too perceived some correlation between military service and the sport for they became big advertisers in the hot rod literature in the late 1950s and 1960s as in:

In Today's World
What Does It Take To Feel Like A Man?

> It takes *action* to feel like a man. Takes *pride* too and good skillful *Training*. Join the modern Army's Combat Arms program and you'll have all three . . . The whole Army is like a huge well-oiled engine – with men and machines closely interlocked. It takes *men* to fit into this kind of picture. And the Army *makes* men like this - technically skilled, competent, confident.[15]

The forces produced films which inter-related recruitment and hot rod themes for distribution to high schools, e.g. *The Hurrying Kind* (1960), and they helped sponsor the campaigns of some professionals. So Prudhomme's car or Garlit's would carry 'Army' or 'Navy' as one of the logos. In fact, the services ran their own drag racing teams that appeared in certain of the Stock classes.

More wistful letters from servicemen started to appear from another battlefront in the mid-1960s: 'I am presently serving in Viet Nam and, needless to say, your magazine is hard to come by . . . Since receiving the issue it has been in more hands than a pic of a pretty girl. One of my buddies even offered me two (2) *Playboy* magazines for it. Naturally I turned the offer down . . .'[16] A number of other servicemen wrote in about the difficulties of getting *Hot Rod* in south east Asia and to affirm that it was almost as popular as *Playboy* but this time, unlike the other conflicts, they did not get a special section to themselves, nor, apart from rare references to the effects of the draft, was there any editorialising about the war until 1972. Vietnam was not an easy war for *Hot Rod* to fight. In that year the editor introduced a special piece somewhat nervously and quite untruthfully as follows:

> While normally it is the policy of Hot Rod Magazine to abstain from covering matters of a political nature, we felt that since the situation in Vietnam has had such an overwhelming effect upon the country's young male population Garlits' story should be told. This is the first and last story of this type in Hot Rod Magazine. It should be understood that Don Garlit's sentiments do not necessarily reflect those of the staff or Petersen Publications Group.[17]

Garlits, who had just visited Vietnam with the stars of other motorsports, was allowed space to present his view that, basically, this was not a conflict America should be in:

> I am happy to report that the morale of our troops is good. They are doing their job well and they are obeying their orders. But the guys are deeply concerned about the feelings of the people at home. They want to know if the people in the United States are blaming the troops personally for this war and all the destruction and death it has wrought. I think a lot of guys who come back don't want to talk about Vietnam, don't want to admit their involvement.[18]

Garlits' view was that the soldiers were doing their best, the public's beef should be with the Pentagon and the successive governments who had put the troops in an untenable position and unthinkingly exposed them to the additional dangers of drug addiction. In response to what was said to be an evenly balanced flow of letters *Hot Rod* promised again that this would be the last time a political article would appear in its pages.

Men without women?

If *Hot Rod*'s uneasy stance to Vietnam relative to other wars reveals that there are limits to the kinds of patriotism that can be promoted through the specialist media, everything in this chapter so far indicates that one aspect of the American way which the hot rod press espoused and reflected was that tinkering and racing automobiles was a *masculine* preoccupation. The first editorial in *Hot Rod* began:

> Hot rod is published to inform and entertain those interested in automobiles whose bodies and engines have been rebuilt in the quest for better performance and appearance. In this publication readers will find a chance to air their

views, ask questions (and get the answers) read about racing and timing meets and automobile shows, see the latest in engine and body design, enjoy entertaining fiction and see engine parts displayed with what we call 'the feminine touch'.[19]

The semiology here was pretty overt. In the first issue the 'pin up' section was of great-looking cars but their names – 'Sweet Little Sixteen' and 'Little Beauty' – allow for quite fetishistic analyses of the enthusiasms of the rodders. Often real women and family life were presented as 'getting in the way' of the true passion. If hot rodding was like an idealised version of 'work' then emotional obligations were either seen as interfering with total concentration on the central focus of a man's world or women had to fit in around it. 'We had to squeeze the marriage in between a couple of Regg's races' claimed Mrs. Schlemner in the first issue of *Hot Rod*. The car was often presented as one of the family or a rival: 'After 3 years of sharing his affections, Jack still has a crush on both his wife and his roadster'[20] or even, possibly, something rather darker:

> After building a few street roadsters I found myself at a drag strip and the fire inside me began to burn a lot hotter. Here was the chance to test your ability, knowledge, frustrations, desire for recognition within the confines of 1320 feet of asphalt. I was instantly fascinated. On Saturday or Sunday I could drive fifteen minutes from home, release my pent-up emotions and return home. Being raised by women – my mother and grandmother – somehow made the release I got at the drag strip make me feel more masculine. It satisfied a need.[21]

Other magazines, especially *Hop Up*, did run pin-ups of the 'sweater girl' variety as in: 'A beautiful car and a beautiful woman. Curvaceous Lynn Roebuck accentuates the positive by posing with the sectioned Cadillac Coupe de Ville. The Cadillac is fully explained on the next pages. Miss Roebuck needs no explaining',[22] and such pictures provoked some appreciative letters; but others were not amused:

> This is going to meet with a lot of disapproval and comment from your readers but I will come out with it just the same: please don't spoil those beautiful customs and rods with some model. It's ok. to have the girls but not on the fenders please. It is distracting for the enthusiasts and the wolves. Both the girl and the car are nice but not together.
> John Larsen, Dayton Iowa

To which the reply ran: '. . . we like cars and women. However we felt there should be some reason for putting pin-up pictures in an automotive magazine, hence the cars in the same photo with the girl. OK?'[23]

Even here the lounging blondes had to share the pages with the occasional: 'Mom Beats Son In Drag Race', usually about Peggy (clutch-it-again) Hart[24], and other auto magazines, like *Car Craft*, were made of sterner stuff and the fear that girls might destroy the enthusiasm was plain:

> Look fellows, I'm an ordinary car fan and I don't understand all this show-how stuff. When I look at a magazine I want to see lots of pictures of cars and I don't care how they are built. How about cutting out all this technical stuff and tossing in a few pictures of pretty girls. Lots and lots of girls. And preferably lots of pictures of cars, any kind of cars.
> Yours for more girls,
> Francis X. Riordan,
> New York

The editor advised the writer to look at the masthead which declared it to be 'The show-how magazine', while an editorial two issues later responded to the correspondence that had come in: 'Car Craft will never go pin-up. We just thought the lad that liked girls had a right to get up and speak his piece. If he likes girls he likes girls; as for us we like em too but not to the exclusion of automobiles. So peace fellows.'[25]

In the early *Hot Rod* 'parts with appeal' was the section where rather decorous cheesecake was supplied to increase the magazine's pulling power. The attitude to the engaging properties of 'a pretty face' was, I suppose, the flip side of the sterner messages the magazine promoted of hard work, study, effort, patriotism and so on. If hot rodding was to be a 'healthy avocation' then 'the boys' surely needed to relax sometimes. Seigle's analysis of the 'psychological components of the hot rodder' in 1952 set the activity in Adleresque waves of 'power drives', 'the will to power', 'floating agressions' and the like and while he perceived hot rodding as having taken boys away from delinquent or destructive behavior such as sex clubs or teenage scandals, it was not surprising, in this perspective, that one element the boys required in 'letting off steam' was girls. For him hot rodding was: 'CREATIVE, EDUCATIVE, COMPETITIVE, CONSTRUCTIVE, and MASCULINE all of which are desirable elements in furthering the best in the American way of life'.[26]

So the early specialist literature certainly did address the 'hot rodder' as a male being. When *Hot Rod* spoke, as it frequently did, of 'fellowship', 'fraternity' and 'motor-minded Joes' it meant just that. Rodders had experiences: hanging out in restaurants drinking coffee and bench racing, and rodding offered possibilities: army service or transition to an airline pilot, couched in male terms. The whole idea of rodding as some 'outlet' for deep-seated aggressions engendered from the competitive problems of everyday life and as allowing 'mastery' were right in the American vernacular, of course, but served to exclude females from front seat participation. It seems that some of the early drivers at lake events were female but by the mid-1940s, at least, the timing associations had banned females from competition on the grounds that it was far too dangerous an activity for them.

Thus, for most women who had anything to do with the enthusiasm, the early hot rod sports seem to have been an extension of the 'normal' adolescent dating rituals among which, and much intermixed with the street rods, was 'cruising' or 'cruising the strip' in which teenagers developed a solution for finding places to mix with other young people in the evening using the car as a medium of movement and meeting.[27] The slow paseo along main street and in and out the drive-ins and parking lots was a way of seeking sexual contacts and, as already suggested, street racing certainly could be an aspect of the night's adventures. Goldberg, considering some cruising areas in California in the late 1960s, argues that prowess at drag racing or, at least, the appearance of having a 'hot' car, was an important aspect of the flirting, teasing and excitement going on.

> Whereas the high school dance is the resulting social spinoff following a football or basketball game, so may cruising be considered a social gathering complementary to drag racing. The most striking feature of the strip is the massive predominance of cars altered from their original appearance to the image of the drags: the competition aesthetic, the hot car look. Wide racing tyres, magnesium hubs, radically lifted suspensions, and air scoops are some of the more obviously visible signs of a hot car. For those who really know, these are only the prerequisites to a fully-competitive car. Subtleties of engine sounds, brand name racing parts, and types of suspension sort out the higher status cars. The car which capsules the driver is as much his success story as the letterman's sweater is the athlete's. Each alteration has a meaning translatable into terms of power and speed on the drag strip, into status on the cruising strip.[28]

This was for males. Females, who drove the strip mainly in pairs or trios, were not expected to drive image cars, they were spectators, those for whom the display was put on.

Nor was this anything new. The lexicographers of the slang used on the drag strips in the early 1950s note the use of the term 'drive-in cam' to denote: 'An attempt to stimulate a full-race cam. This term refers sarcastically to the practice of pulling out the hand choke on a 'stock' engine to make it idle as if it had a ground cam in it, said to be indulged in by some would-be hot rodders who frequent the drive-in restaurants late at night.' While 'sex wagon' meant: 'a car which appeals to the female sex: the type of car sometimes derisively referred to as a "hot chrome" '. Such terms were, of course, as much a condemnation of women's lack of knowledge about technology and love of fashion and frippery as they were of the 'shot rodders' who ran these things, a judgement made harsher by the fact that the Pasadena rodders used the term 'virgin' to connote 'A "clean", "sharp looking" stock car with the original equipment'.[29] Nor was the function of the car as a sexual arena forgotten in the hot rod press as in the advocation for 'a padded headrest, handy for mild traffic tiffs . . . and drive-in movies!'[30] Of course, the ideologies involved here were underpinned by a differential access to cars. In the *Life* pictures of the games teenagers played on wheels referred to in Chapter Two and in the novels, plays and films about hot rodding girls were always the passengers, never drivers.

The early trips to the dry lakes were, probably, an extension of the dating rituals of Saturday night, a weekend away from under the eyes of parents. Certainly there were girls at the lakes. Photographs and reports detail them as spectators, crew members and as minor officials. The role of women in the early sports then mirrored the parts on offer in the wider society. They appear as the touring-professional's spouse keeping him in clean T-shirts under difficult conditions, as understanding parent or loyal wife, in the background, cooking and caring for the husband or sons as they obsessively build a hot rod out of the family coupe in the family garage:

> Although I tackled the job alone-my buddies seemed to have been swallowed up by the earth when help was needed – I was joined in the project by the most loyal of assistants, my wife Vivian. She devoted countless hours to the job when four hands were needed; cutting strips of metal, helping me set the top and body in place, and even aiding in overhauling the engine. By proffering gallons of coffee, bandages for my flattened or burnt fingers and occasional pats on the back in times of stress she kept my morale from sagging too low.[31]

Hot Rod's and the NHRA's attempts to persuade the early car clubs to try other activities than racing and their emphasis on scenic tours and reliability runs, with picnics, almost ensured that women had to be taken on board as necessary ingredients in these more sedate pursuits. When *Hot Rod* indicated 'How To Stage Your Own High School Hot Rod Show' part of the advice was to get pretty girls to doll-up prizes and cars to ensure that the local papers carried pictures. Often marriage was seen as the big divide in the enthusiasm, for the everyday responsibilities and costs often took the boys out of hot rodding. As professional Tony Nancy put it: 'marriage does have a way of slowing a guy down'. However, some male car clubs spawned parallel female clubs as with the Smokers of Bakersfield: 'The meets are very well run, speaking well for the cooperative spirit of the club. Even the "Smokerettes", which is the ladies' auxillary, turn out to help at the gate and refreshment stand'[32] or the Torques of Blue Lake: 'The wives and girl friends of club members have formed a club called the Torquettes. Recently they had a pillow raffle and contributed $92 toward the future dragster.'[33]

Given these patterns in the sport and their presentation, it would be easy to understand hot rodding as just another patriarchal sport or, even more, a quite archetypal patriarchal sport in which some of the major elements of a rather crude form of masculinity were passed on in unadulterated fashion. The whole emphasis on speed, competition, aggression, carelessly collected oil stains and dirty clothes reinforces this assessment. There is a lot to it, and as the big meets and car shows developed, each with their own beauty contest at which 'Miss Top Eliminator', 'Miss Torque Wrench' and 'Miss Winternationals' would win her crown and a photographed cuddle from the male champion, this was a dominant theme. The advertisements for Army and Air Force mechanics which became quite prominent in *Hot Rod* were not aimed at women. So American values about 'normal' masculinity and feminity did permeate the sport, in its language and its presentation, but there were diverse nuances and facets and these are just the salients along which ideologies and identities can alter and change. For, oddly, drag racing not only became one of the few sports in which women compete directly against men and in which a woman became a world champion, but is also the source of one of the few major mainstream films to seek to portray the tribulations and successes of a top-class *female* sportsperson.

In fact, the exclusion of women from racing on the lakes was never that well-founded. It was based not on presumed physical differences in ability but on saving women from danger. Since the sales pitch of the emerging drag racing sport was that it was safe it would have been difficult to exclude women on the grounds that it was dangerous. Even the post-war lakes organisations had allowed one female to run in trials. Veda Orr, wife of a top competitor and speed shop owner, was allowed to compete on the basis that she had been driving since 1937 and had edited the mimeographed monthly programme notes of the SCTA. She had clocked 115 mph. Professional drivers too often acknowledged the driving capabilities of their spouses. Thompson met his wife through an impromptu street race and would sometimes tell the disgruntled loser of an illegal drag:

> Aw, forget it. Not only can I beat you. I can put my girl in the car and she can beat you too!' And that's just what used to happen. I loved it because it really sank the needle into my competition; really was humiliating. And it proved that it was more than my driving that made me a consistent winner. It proved that my workmanship was all right. And it proved that I had a very, very special girl.[34]

This nod to the mechanical and driving abilities of women was patronising, of course, and even Thompson's girl poses the question: 'either racing goes or I go' before accepting that his greatest infatuation is with the car. Still, such exceptions did allow that some women did know about automobiles and might want to race them. When *Hop Up* conducted one of its 'What d'You Think?' features among girl spectators at the Saugus Drag Strip, asking them: 'how would you hop up an engine?', four of them replied on the lines of:

> How would I hop up an engine? Let me see. First, I'd . . . let's see . . . I don't know what I'd do. I guess I'd get a book and find out. Oh, I don't know. I'd learn what I'm doing first. I don't like Edelbrock heads but I do like Evans heads. Why? Well, because it sounds better. Oh . . . I don't know!

reinforcing the male readers sense of superiority about the correct approach to technology and, indeed, what 'technology' actually is. But Jann Parry responded:

> First, I'd get a '49 block, have it ported and relieved, bore it out an eighth over Merc. Then I'd stroke the crank an eighth . . . that makes it ⅛ x ⅛. Well . . . I'd get a set of Evans heads an Evans three jug manifold, Harmon & Collins cam and mag and a set of headers. If it were just for me, I want a street and drag car because girls are not allowed to drive at the lakes, I would then drop it in a '40 Merc with a Carson top.[35]

Just as the story 'The Lady of the Lakes' about a woman at Bonneville – 'although she prefers to do most of the work on her car Doris is not opposed to the idea of her husband helping out'[36] – contained some 'normal' overtones (especially as the husband did the actual driving) but did reveal that some women might want to take part and even compete in this 'man's world'.

As early as 1949 a letter to *Hot Rod* asked whether there could be a girls' club in the SCTA to which the answer was sure, why not, why don't you call yourselves the Racing Darlings? While by 1951 the magazine noted that there were two female hot rod clubs in California. The parallel clubs to male ones which I have already mentioned also had a role here. Often these were involved in the charitable, 'good works' aspects of the car clubs which *Hot Rod* tried to foster as part of its theme of respectability, still some women certainly got involved out on the strips. When the magazine featured a club from Ohio it had to remark: 'No doubt a certain share of the success is due to the fact that there are no 'hot rod widows' as a result of the Pipers club. Their wives have effectively solved this problem with the formation of another group, the Piper Puffs, condescending graciously to see things hubby's way . . . until that starter drops the flag!' The 'twelve active girls, all married and most with children' were very active in community work, organising the donation of 300 pints of blood to a hospital, donating $350 raised through the sale of Christmas cards to local charities and:

> Between drags – and occasional class wins – at the strip, the attractive wrench wielders blend their domestic talents for lucrative fund drives with bake sales. Their big heart for charity appeals is attested by needy females in town, and the Mid-Ohio timing association can best vouch for the girls 'spare' time. So the next time someone raises an eyebrow at the mention of an all-girl hot rod organization, challenge them to match the Piper Puffs of Columbus, Ohio – tough competition in any man's language.[37]

Of course, these women were constituted reactively and were addressed in a patronising way: 'how strong the feminine touch can be' etc. None the less, these women were shown as working on cars, driving in events and even, occasionally, beating their husbands. The hot rod apparatus had to allow that *in principle* women could drive cars as well and as fast as a man. Indeed, as I mentioned earlier, one female competitor was featured quite regularly in the early hot rod press as in: 'Proof that drag racing is not an all male world is pretty Peggy Hart, mother of two teenagers, wife of a drag strip operator and one of the gamest throttle trompers.'[38]

I am, of course, not arguing that women had equal opportunities in drag racing and women were often confined to a special 'powder puff' section at the strips in the 1950s, nor am I arguing that drag racing was not in its form riddled right through by male preconceptions, most things were in post-war America. What I am saying, and a reason why Mandell quoted in Chapter One, for example, might need to reconsider his view of what constitutes a 'proper' sport, is that the nature of drag racing allowed women to compete on grounds of formal equality with men, they could not be kept out nor could they be forever ghettoised in their own section. Moreover, the ideology of the NHRA made it difficult to exclude women. The whole hot rod apparatus's representation of rodders was as a bunch of misunderstood people regarded as 'deviant' who were discriminated against by ignorant people. Since they sought to counter discrimination and prejudice they had to be open to *all* those who heard the call of the enthusiasm. A NHRA bulletin board of early 1952 was at pains to point out that there was no racial, colour or creed barriers to joining the organisation. Hot rodders had been persecuted as 'a kind of minority group' so they could not now discriminate against sections of the population. An NHRA advertisements in the first issue of *Hop Up* was quick to point out: 'Remember – Membership is Restricted Neither to Age Limit Nor To Sex'.[39] If the bug bit and the technology was grasped then women could compete.

Even the trivilisation of women through pin ups was somewhat at odds with the seriousness of the presentation of rodding in the magazines of the enthusiasm. In *Hot Rod* the 'parts with appeal' pictures were dropped in 1950, came back in 1951, were dropped again to return in 1953[40] and then virtually disappeared for over twenty years as a part of the editorial content though many of the ever increasing advertisements combined sex and sales appeal in quite overt forms as in the mid-1970s regular: 'Stacked and Quietly Waiting For You' which was supposed to apply, presumably, both to the boxes of mufflers and the bikini-clad girl or in the famous sales pitch for vans: 'Adult Toys From Dodge' carried by models across the front of their wet T-shirts. So the magazine continued to project a stereotyped version of 'femininity' but increasingly this had to contend with the rise of just a few women to important positions in the sport in direct competition against men.

In March 1967 *Hot Rod* carried an article 'The Female and the Fueler'. It featured five women who were doing well in the sport, including Shirley Shahan, who had been chosen as one of *Hot Rod*'s top drivers of the year for 1965 and who in 1966 had become first woman to win a major NHRA title. Basically, all these women ran in the Stock classes of competition where speeds were lower and vehicles ran on gas. The article was about the concern in the sport as to whether women, 'the rolling pin set' or 'kitchen brigade' as the writer archly referred to them, should be allowed to compete in the quickest classes of drag racing which used fuel. Professional drivers had to be licensed, after a physical examination and study of techniques in observed runs, by one of the sanctioning bodies

185

G

and: 'To-date, there do not appear to be any women who are holders of the so-called "unlimited" licences. Of course, any woman can compete in stock-type cars but as soon as they begin the transition from these to gas, sports or modified production machinery the licencing aspect comes directly into the picture.' The views of the sanctioning bodies questioned were cautious but relatively open 'to the proper type' as with Jim Tice of the AHRA:

> I doubt many people will deny that the American woman has emancipated herself to the point of doing almost everything anyway. But I question that there will be more than a few who will brave the possible consequences of the really fast cars. We're not trying to licence 9 million housewives to drive AA fuel cars. But just because I don't think we can legally stop them from participating if they can pass the proper tests, doesn't mean this many will take a crack at it. Drag racing is very big now and we feel a woman who has sufficient driver experience and can pass our licencing requirements should be able to run.[41]

This article provoked a letter in July 1967:

> Although I was pleased to finally read that something good is being said for the female competitor, I was disappointed to discover that no mention was made of me or any of the other drivers back in the East. I hope the Female and the Fueler story will maybe make it a little easier for the girls who are just starting a career in drag racing. This can mean a lot of heartaches because I had a steady diet of being pushed around for a good many years at drag strips opposed to female drivers. I don't have much to worry about now, but thinking back over nearly ten years of drag racing cars . . . I can remember a lot of tears that came in trying to get through the tech. lines at strips . . .
>
> Mrs. Shirley Muldowney
New York

It was Muldowney who became the first woman to gain a NHRA Top Fuel licence in 1974 and who became the first female Top Fuel World Champion in 1977. She became the subject of many articles: 'The Quarter-Mile Queen' and the like and was the subject of a major film *Heart Like a Wheel*, released in 1983 loosely based on her life.[42] In this film, drag racing, as ever, especially for pros, is not pictured as an easy life but success in the sport, albeit at the cost of the emotional life, is revealed as possible for women as well as men. Her career begins in classic fashion in mid-1950s street racing in New York State. Her boyfriend chokes in one illegal race and later she takes on the opposition. They settle down to a marriage where he works in a garage and is the mechanic for a car which she races. At an NHRA meet she meets Garlits, sits in his dragster and dreams of turning pro. Her husband scoffs but after she drives to Detroit to get sponsorship he relents and builds a dragster. He handles the entry procedures, adherence to regulations etc. she is to 'take care of the kid and drive'. In 1966 at a drag strip she meets Kalitta, the Bounty Hunter, and, when the officials don't want her to enter and she requires three signatures from NHRA accredited drivers to race, the husband cautions: 'look at it from the NHRA's point of view . . . if a woman had an accident it could set the sport back ten years', but Kalitta and Garlits help her get in and she takes the track record. Later she beats off Kalitta's advances: 'the only thing I do fast is drive', but the husband yearns for: 'a regular wife' and is disenchanted by the dragster: 'we built it for fun, a hobby, now it's our life.' She leaves him, goes to California, becomes 'Cha Cha Muldowney' combining sex appeal with drag racing as the 'Bounty Huntress', gets emotionally involved with Kalitta and becomes world champion in the Top Fuel class in 1977 and in 1980 and again in 1982.

So drag racing was not stuck in some simple red-neck masculinity.

Women In Rodding

For well over 50 years – infact from the automobile's inception – not only the world of motorsports but all aspects of automobile operation, maintenance and construction were strictly a male domain. Thankfully, that is changing in the 1980s. And in all facets of hot rodding, though we may not be fully aware of it yet, we are seeing rapidly increasing female participation. We're not talking about fender or front seat decorations here – we mean builders, drivers, tuners and owners of hot rods of all types . . . If you thought hot rods were boys' toys think again. Welcome women,[43]

'Women's liberation' was accepted in hot rodding as part of the modern American way but was grasped in a quite limited way.

To begin with, the rather few women drivers who did make it to the top had, in effect, to become 'one of the boys'. As Muldowney put it to *Hot Rod* in April 1972 when asked 'What is your position on Women's Lib.?':

I like being the weaker sex. But I do think it's about time that women were treated equal. When I started racing people discriminated against me because I was a woman. I like having doors opened for me. I also feel that some of the Lib. people go to extremes. I want to be able to go to the track and look like a lady but still be able to do a job like a man when I'm racing and get paid the same amount of money.

And the male drivers often suggested they had a particularly driven attachment to the sport. They often explained the impact of hot rodding in terms akin to a love affair, terms like 'fever' or 'fascination' were often used:

> I maintained the car myself, although we normally had plenty of volunteer assistance. In fact, literally hundreds of eager helpers could be found at almost any strip, most of them young men who would have gone with me on a full-time basis at the drop of a wrench. Many of these boys were so involved with racing that nothing else mattered, including their schooling, and they looked toward me and the other touring professionals as a means of escaping their day-to-day responsibilities . . . Without exception, I tell young men with racing fever to complete their education before even considering the sport of drag racing. The more formal technical training, the better, so I tell them to stay in school at all costs if they want to become top-notch racers – or top-notch anything for that matter.[44]

However the wise words of the professionals scarcely disguise their own obsession. This is no 9 to 5 affair, there is no weekly paycheck, no quiet nights in front of the TV with the family. This is addiction. You become 'hooked'. You're preoccupied, involved, you lose friends and maybe more:

> It takes a certain kind of woman to to understand a man's feelings about any activity that consumes most of his time. As my career began to grow so did the problems at home. When my marriage failed I was pushed deeper into a world of isolationism. I'm not shirking the blame for the marriage break-up; it becomes a matter of circumstances in my case and in lots of similar ones. Too many days away from home, what appears to be neglect of everything except one's own interests, hundreds of hours around, under and inside a race vehicle, money seeming to pour out like water for parts – a very steep price tag almost every professional racer's family is faced with . . . if he has a family.[45]

Fans, recognition, self-satisfaction, and the camaraderie and sexual opportunities of a gypsy life of motels and pits, fill the emotional gaps. Part of this is to learn the omnipresence of competition and the fluidity inherent in a mechanical sport where there are always problems, uncertainties, mishaps to handle and modifications to be made:

> One of the things that keeps drag racing so interesting is that just when you feel you have a car that is the perfect combination of body and powerplant, and nothing can stop you now – your 'world' seems to fall to pieces: you start getting beat. You are forced to realize that even though you have applied a lot of time, money and good ideas to come up with *your* 'unbeatable' race car, a lot of other guys have been doing the same thing![46]

Part of the ethos of war, drag racing and certain masculinities too, is to learn that involvement requires detachment. Enthusiasm has to be spliced with coldness if you are to be a perfectionist or a professional, especially as regards accidents and the ever present possibility that fear will eat the soul:

> I fought a mental battle that afternoon and finally arrived at an attitude I could live with, an attitude every mature individual must maintain: whenever an unfortunate incident happened I would do what I could for the person in trouble; then I had to put the incident in mental storage and return to the job at hand. If a person – any person – can't learn to do this he is defeated at the starting line of life's race.[47]

Or put more laconically by another male pro: 'Garlits had got burned but we didn't bother too much about that.'[48] This is not to say that one should be foolhardy, all precautions should be taken and there should be the insider's assessment of the risks being taken, but that said a real hot rodder had to do what a man's got to do even if she was a woman. Muldowney's career took a particularly classic turn after her World Championships. In 1984 she had a near fatal crash in which she suffered major injuries. She required five operations but returned to racing again in 1986 in a car specially built to allow for the fact that she had, amongst other things, lost part of her foot. She received *Hot Rod's* ultimate accolade: 'Shirley was – and still remains – the master of her craft.'[49]

In addition women who suceeded in drag racing were frequently sexualised in the sense that their looks, way of dressing and appearance became part of what they were 'offering' the sport as a sales proposition. Muldowney ran in countless lucrative 'Battle of the Sexes' match races against Garlits and other male professionals in the early 1970s for example. Letters to the magazines from girls who wanted to break into drag racing or get into the professional ranks tended to receive supportive but sexist replies, the respondents probably realising that their car had more chance of being shown in the magazine if they, or a friend, posed on top of it in a bikini. The clearest indication of this form of incorporation came in the late 1980s as *Hot Rod* switched back to providing some pin-ups on its editorial pages. In April 1987 the magazine introduced its 'first annual swimsuit edition'. It explained this by saying it was following an example set by *Sports Illustrated* and harked back to the 1950s and the 'parts with appeal' tradition. 'So, we rounded up some typical, healthy, beach-type girls; dressed them in real swimsuits like you'd see at the beach; and then had two of our best free-lance photographers pose them and our hand-picked hot rods in striking settings anywhere except at the beach.'

In 1988 the editor tried to explain the clean nature of the second swimsuit issue through 'a letter to his Mom' plus a picture of him cuddling his daughter. The bulk of letters about the first issue had been negative but it was just some 'editorial fun'. However, the occasional letter that had come in suggesting the magazine run male pin-ups: 'make me sick'. Some of the girls who posed in this edition were those actually involved in drag racing as crew or as with one pictured in a red bikini and half in or half out of a red racing suit:

> Women drivers have been an important part of drag racing since the days when Peggy Hart, the wife of famed dragstrip operator C. J. Hart, strapped on her helmet then strapped it on the competition at Santa Ana during the early 1950s with her Cad. "powered, '27 T highboy roadster. And the Shirleys, Shahan and Muldowney, come quickly to mind too. But few, if any, of the current crop of female drag racers have had the distracting influence of 'leaver' Lisa Moscker and her class-kicking, Lambeck and Gottlieb Pro Stock '87 Chevvy Camaro. All Lisa has to do is slowly pull her fire suit over her Hawaiin Tropic underpinnings and it's an instant red light for the guys she's racing.[50]

Which about revealed as far as *Hot Rod* and hot rodding had got with treating women as people: but then, any deeper thinking about 'liberation' might have required a much greater degree of questioning of the tight masculinity which was the ideology of the top stars of the sport and about the role of automobile sport and the uses of automobiles in America.

The outlaw breed

I have indicated here and there that one part of hot rodding always involved the common but illegal sport of street racing. This was an activity whose meanings were to alter across the years as it steadily became rather less reprehensible and more of an icon of a vanishing America.

Racing in the streets would never go away despite the growth of organised drag racing, and its association with death on the highways, traffic accidents and the like was felt likely to bring the growing formal sport into a head-on collision with the state. Young drivers were still regarded as a real social problem in the 1960s as the writer of the manual *Teenagers and Safe Driving* suggested. In 1966 drivers under 25 made up less than 20 per cent of licenced drivers but accounted for over 33 per cent of drivers killed in accidents. Or, to make another deadly contrast: 'Between 1961 and 1966, motor vehicles killed nearly four times as many *servicemen* – most of them on our own roads – as the Viet Cong killed in Vietnam.'[51]

Often, but wrongly, Los Angeles is held to be the unique site of this sport, but right across the country in 1961 Boyle interviewed half a dozen of the Glen Cove Road Panthers of Long Island, New York who had now 'reformed' into a model hot rod club, but who all admitted to illegal racing in the past and asserted that they still got four or five invitations a day to race either from 'squirrels' or, a favourite line of hot rodders, from 'little old men and women' at stoplights. Leon Schorsch, 'a hot rodder of the old school', was a vetran of two thousand street races and had run for say $10 a gear or 'gears for beers' and all the variants of combining illegal auto racing and gambling. 'Guys still come up to my house and say, "Hey man, you got a bad El Camino?" And I say, "Yeah". I've gone out and raced them. Bad means it goes.'[52]

So the illegal sport is truly a national one but, still, the Los Angeles scene certainly is its most documented arena especially for the more organised and unspontaneous manifestations of street racing. I have already alluded to various 'outbreaks' in the 1940s, while in 1957 *Life* pictured illegal racing there both in the streets and on the concrete bed of the Los Angeles river. A *Los Angeles Times* photo of police in 1962 has a caption which reads: 'Drag racing check up – automobile drivers are questioned by police in a suprise raid. Tuesday night drag races being staged by youths on Vista Del Mar in Playa Del Ray. More than 200 hundred youths were watching the 100 mph. drag races before police cordoned off the street. Thirty eight were taken to Venice Division station for booking.'[53]

The scene in the city in 1966 was documented in another *Los Angeles Times* article though, to repeat, the claim for uniqueness is quite inaccurate:

> In other major cities, drag racing on the streets and parkways is an occasional phenomenon, a freak thundershower. In LA. there is a squall every night. Last year, for example, the LAPD issued 2, 120 citations for 'speed contests', an astonishing figure considering that it represents only a small fraction – certainly no more than a tenth – of the actual number of races. Moreover, street racing is not confined to a section or two of the city, like smog, it is ubiquitous. Even the otherwise sacrosanct streets of Beverly Hills have a piece of the action.[54]

A youth from Houston stated that 'the average guy' either raced himself or knew someone who did and that if you went to practically any drive-in, but especially to Bobs in Van Nuys, you would find guys ready to race:

> There's lots of action around here and lots of bread to be made. You can run on the boulevard, or there's Riverside Drive at Griffith Park, or Forest Lawn Drive off the freeway. A friend of mine made a hundred bucks at Forest Lawn a few weeks ago. There are regular run-offs there, sometimes 200 cars. Well, there were until last week. Some guy totalled his car, so now the heats on.

The writer argued that, in fact, there was not too much the police could do about it and then made another point of some significance in understanding this sport – it was by no means the preserve of teenagers, middle class or otherwise, but plenty of adults were involved too: 'They come, usually, from among the city's poor, and to them, street racing isn't a game, it's a living.'

The underground sport had developed its own organisations and the writer interviewed 'Stretch', a 32-year-old negro, President of the Western Avenue Street Racing Association: 'one of a dozen or so such groups in southern LA. On Friday and Saturday nights, the 50-odd Association members gather in a parking lot at the corner of 78th and Western. Here the real business, arranging street-races, is transacted.' A hundred people gathered and over thirty cars. There was beer, noise, dancing and challenges were struck for bets of up to $300.

This report contained a mention of Big Willie a 'promotor of street races in the area of 43rd and Vermont' and Big Willie Robinson was to gain a long-lasting prominence in the LA. street racing sport as *Newsweek* began to detail three years later: 'the sport has changed from a casual duel at a lonely traffic light into a highly organized, if illegal, urban phenomenon . . . thousands of supercharged dragsters are challenging the police themselves for after-dark control of the streets. Moreover, they seem to be prevailing.'[55] Willie, a 26-year-old gymnasium manager, had established the National and International Brotherhood of Street Racers in 1966 which now claimed to have ten thousand members and had nowhere legal to run. The simple answer to this lack of facilities was that every Saturday at midnight: '1,500 to 3,000 speedsters wheel their souped up chariots into a huge parking lot at the foot of the Baldwin Hills section of the city. While the drivers and their motor molls talk of heads and cams, scouts hunt for likely courses.' The scouts checked the road and the lighting to see if the spot was good for competition and spectators, counted the intersections to be crossed in runs and whether the police were patrolling the area. When their report was positive the crowd sped to the appointed place, race officials blocked off the public traffic from the course, the match race was run and then the move was back to the parking lot to plan another race. As a race controller put it: 'We know it's dangerous and illegal but we try to make it as safe as possible. And if the man's not around, that's about as legal as we can get.' In fact this article suggested, as did several others, that the police had a laissez-faire attitude to these activities, which was probably just as well, the author thought, because 'in Fort Lauderdale, the arrests last week of several drag racers triggered a riot that injured 41 persons.'

The Brotherhood had strict rules against drinking and fighting while engaged in the street racing and violators had to surrender their colours and have their tyres deflated. Through a megaphone Willie issued threats of busts to the police so as to maintain order in the parking lot. Under his direction, in what was an old hot rod style, the Brotherhood had a policy of assisting motorists in trouble. They were handed a card: 'You have been helped by a member in good standing of the Street Racers of Los Angeles County – a new breed of brotherhood.' Willie was trying to establish a 200-acre racing park in the Sepulveda basin and was lobbying local businessmen and public officials to support the venture. When the Recreation and Parks department voted not to approve such a project he had organised an 11,000 vehicle park-in on Van Nuys Boulevard during the Christmas shopping period.

The Brotherhood attracted quite a bit of media attention at this time. They can be seen in action, for example, staging an unofficial meet, at the start of the film *Two Lane Blacktop* of 1971, a mainstream 'alternative' movie, which is a hymn to street racing and its associated gambling.[56] At the same time the Street Racers of Los Angeles County were featured in *Car Life* which asserted: 'Anywhere else street racing is a furtive, back alley business, with one wail of a police siren all that is needed to bust things up. Yet in Los Angeles street racing is completely in the open and is so highly organized and structured that it goes on like clockwork every Saturday night in various sections of the city.'[57] There was the same story of the organisation of races, though now the street racers had adopted radio-equipped cars to monitor police calls, but infact events still had the tacit approval of the police, who seemed to prefer to have the sport overt rather than covert, and the racers openly proclaimed their allegiance with jackets and cars adorned with 'Street Racers of Los Angeles' logos. The article dwelt on Willie's expertise in PR and promotion which was now such that he carried an attaché case full of information about the street racers with him at all times. The group was fully integrated racially and males and females were accepted into membership which was claimed to be almost ten thousand. Big Willie had become such a celebrity that he had made appearances on behalf of a candidate to be Mayor of the city. Gambling was still an important associated activity but the organisation frowned on drugs and drink. The racers claimed to have a technical commitee which examined cars before they ran, to have doctors always on hand in case of accidents though they tried to avoid these by blocking off the streets before they ran and never raced in residential areas. All in all Willie appeared to be a rather conformist deviant and: 'is stressing brotherhood and patriotism (he has a replica of the flag stitched on the arm of his jacket).'

He had tried to explain to the NHRA how the way the official sport had come to be organised did not match the requirements of his members:

> In reality the dragstrips located in Southern California, although the finest, do not in most cases adequately handle the racers' needs. To the best of my knowledge the race tracks are only available Wednesdays and Saturdays and sometimes Sundays. An additional problem results from the fact that most strips have some form of noise curfew that makes it necessary to stop racing somewhere around 11 pm. This makes it difficult for the heads-up grudge races to do their thing in the few short hours of availability. Some may say – well, so what? Street racing, that's what.

His argument was that the brotherhood didn't really want to street race but did want all-night drag strips which the curfew laws prohibited. This was why he had tried to get a 'motor sport park' built in the area. The Director of the NHRA told the writer: 'I know the guys that race on the streets. They complain about there not being enough drag strips, or that it costs too much, or that there are too many cars and too many delays. Some of these things may be partially valid, but it doesn't matter. These guys wouldn't come out even if they did exist. They are only psuedo racers.'

At about the same period, and at odds with the claims of the 'uniqueness' of the situation in Los Angeles, the sway of the unofficial sport was detailed for Detroit. *Car and Driver* magazine claimed:

> By day Woodward Avenue is a wide street that all the fat daddies from Royal Oak, Birmingham and Bloomfield Hills use to drive into stolid old downtown Detroit . . . But come sunset, Woodward Avenue becomes the street racing capital of the world. Oh yes, there's some action around LA – out in the valley and in Dawney and along the beach, and a lot of guys talk about Palm Beach

and Miami, and theres even a little street racing going on up in the Bronx and on the South shore of Long Island. But they don't cut it with the scene on Woodward, where maybe two thousand – really – cars are milling up and down the five mile long strip on any given night. Woodward is the Indianapolis of the street racers.[58]

Here, at Ted's drive, 'Like every night it looks like the garage area at a big race. Lined up in the stalls are rows and rows of Super Cars with giant tyres and hunched up suspensions and hood scoops and fuel injection and blowers and mag wheels and smooth, cool-looking paint jobs.' Matches would be struck and then it was out to Interstate 75 to race. There were amateurs who raced for fun and professionals who participated in the illegal sport to make money. There was a pervasive cynicism about organised drag racing:

> Sanctioned drag racing meets are supposed to have stopped all the illegal action on the streets and turned hot rodding into something apple-pie sweet and legal as little-league baseball, but nobody really believes that. The drag strips have become so crowded that a guy is lucky if he can make three runs during an entire afternoon or evening, but on Woodward you might get fifty shots in a few hours. And they're all free. Of course, pros like Cheater can make a lot more coins on the street than on the track, where you get those 19 cent trophies with a phony gold car stuck on top of a cheap wood pedestal.

Again, local police were not really concerned to stop or even harass the unofficial sport. The author even hinted that unofficial factory-based teams operated in this illegal milieu for the purposes of market research, a suggestion which formed the crux of another survey of the Detroit street racing scene in *Esquire* magazine in 1969. This piece argued that the large auto companies believed in the existence of a set of connections between the 'youth market' (defined by attitudes not years), hot cars, word of mouth, drag racing *and* the illegal sport. It was an article of faith that 'if a car can't cut it on the street or drag strip today, young buyers are looking elsewhere.'[59] Both General Motors and Ford were said to have 'undergrounders' (some of whom had been NHRA champions) who kept the companies in touch with what youth thought and some of whom raced on the streets – using factory-prepared cars. This reveals some of the complexities in the relations between Detroit and auto enthusiasms. Winning on Woodward Avenue (and, say, featuring the street sign in mainstream auto advertisements) was an important marketing ploy because: 'If a car is respected on Woodward, it will be a best seller in the youth market anywhere. The automakers know this. If you're looking you'll find some high ranking company boys out there driving casually, taking it all in – and racing. Auto makers know that if they can produce a hot street racer, they're *in*, from New York to California.'

Street racing, that other great hot rod sport, may appear to be at odds with some of the other themes I have picked out in this chapter as illegal, 'deviant' and so un-American in some broadly conceived, quickly sketched 'consensus' but, actually, I think that is quite incorrect. What I have tried to suggest in this chapter is that hot rodding picked up on certain heroic and romantic themes in American culture. Apparently oddly for what seems to be such a modern sport ('dominated by technology' etc.) it revolved around what Rotundo has called a 'Masculine Primitive' ideal of manhood and a vision of America and of being an American which harked back to the frontier, backwoodsmen and cowboys. It related to Roosevelt's 'Western Man' whose whipcord and iron qualities defined the characteristics of a special individual and a special nation, and whose existence was an essential but vanishing strand in the American way.[60] Suprisingly, the sport hot rodding seems to have most in common with is that other home-spun activity, Rodeo. This is true organisationally and ideologically. Rodeo too had close ties between a complex of organising associations and the specialist literature, had problems with professionalism, had a proliferation of 'world champions' and faced an emerging political challenge from animal rights campaigners. Ideologically Rodeo is presented and grasped as an evocation of a 'real life of action' regarded as much more meaningful than everyday existence in contemporary society and one thought to be disappearing fast.[61]

For me hot rodding racing, both its street variant and the official sport, related very neatly to one American archetype in this cultural set, the outlaw. The professionals of the sport were presented as quintessential nomads who dwelt in a lonely place and lived only to confront others and themselves. The ritual of two men 'duelling' from stop light to stop light resonates with the Western myth. This was why, though street racing posed a continual threat to the well-being of the official sport, the hot rod apparatus actually had a difficult line to hold. Many more people bought the literature of the enthusiasm, the speed equipment and accessories than ever raced on the strips for any length of time. It was partly this fluidity in the interested public which, to *Hot Rod*'s chagrin, made hot rodders hard to organise into as potent a political force as the National Rifle Association. Still it seems likely that the outlaw image was and is an essential part of the term's selling power and one that has its own pathways into American popular ideologies and legitimations of identity and behaviour.[62] 'Being' a rodder – even amongst the interested public rather than the core participants – allowed the reaffirmation of the truly important, plain, simple, traditional values against all the mush of modernity and the disorientating tangle of red tape that could trip you up in a bureaucratised world. Hot rodding was a way of engaging in a simple 'natural' activity within, even against, the rigidities of advanced capitalist America all, of course, in combination with the skill and pride taken in mastering a craft for 'A young fellow who knows his way around the guts of an automobile will never have to go on relief.'[63] Despite reaching a situation where certain women could take on the pre-existing form of the sport and reach the very top spots, hot rodding stood for old American virtues. For times when boys just wanted to work on automobiles and when a pretty car and a pretty girl went together and no one thought to question the fact.

Through the decades *Hot Rod* began to speak more and more about the over-regulation and regimentation in American life *including* a scepticism about its own early efforts to dragoon everyone into clubs. It began to scoff about the times when 'we all planted trees', 'adopted Korean orphans' and spat: 'it is not essential to the health of hot rodding that all of us band together into a bunch of brown shirt commando units to change flats on the freeways for little old ladies.'[64] Something seemed to have gone wrong in the heart of the country. Too many restrictions, too much legislation about too many things was seen as about to extinguish the old glories of American individualism and as likely to block American advance. The hot rod apparatus began to preach rebellion against such encroachment on *their* brand of America way. In this new world even the clash by night of the street racers began to receive a rather more sympathetic treatment. From the 1970s, as my sketch of the muted reaction to Vietnam might indicate, hot rodding had to exist in a more troubled and troubling America where the automobile was under increasing scrutiny, kids were more interested in smoking marijuana than tyres, women were said to want something more and the whole cultural location of sports in American life seemed to be changing. In the 1980s hot rodding was set to run on dangerous ground.

Notes

1 T. Madigan, *The Loner: the Story of a Drag Racer* (Englewood Cliffs, New Jersey, 1974), p. 108.
2 K. Blaisdell, *Keepers of the Flame: A Search for Values in the Magazines of the Car*

Culture, Ph. D. thesis (Rensselaer Polytechnic Institute, 1984).
3 H. F. Moorhouse, 'American automobiles and workers' dreams', *Sociological Review*, 31, 1983, pp. 403–26.
4 B. Yates, 'Road testing the road testers', *Car and Driver*, June 1969, p. 39.
5 *Hot Rod* Magazine (*HRM*), 26, January 1973, p. 7.
6 Madigan, *The Loner*, p. 45.
7 *HRM*, 7, August 1954, pp. 50–1.
8 *HRM*, 8, August 1955, pp. 8–10.
9 *HRM*, 4, July 1951, pp. 5.
10 E. Lawrence, 'Gow jobs', *Colliers*, 26 July 1941, p. 14.
11 *HRM*, 5, May 1952, p. 23.
12 *HRM*, 4, September 1951, p. 5.
13 *HRM*, 4, April 1951, p. 34.
14 Madigan, *The Loner*, p. 112.
15 *HRM*, 16, March 1963, p. 12.
16 *HRM*, 18, October 1965, p. 10.
17 *HRM*, 25, April 1972, p. 29.
18 'Don Garlits speaks on Vietnam', *HRM*, 25, April 1972, pp. 28–30.
19 *HRM*, 1, January 1948, p. 3.
20 *HRM*, 6, December 1953, p. 39.
21 Madigan, *The Loner*, p. 108.
22 *Hop Up* (*HU*), 2, May 1953, p. 8.
23 *HU*, 2, January 1953, p. 6.
24 *HU*, 2, July 1953, p 12.
25 *Car Craft*, 2, February 1954.
26 *HRM*, 5, August 1952, p. 25.
27 F. Setterberg, 'Cruising with Donny on the San Leandro strip', *Michigan Quarterly Review*, 19–20, 1981, pp. 692–700.
28 T. Golberg, 'The automobile: a social institution for adolescents', *Enviroment and Behaviour*, 1, 1969, p. 165.
29 D. Mansell and J. S. Hall, 'Hot rod terms in the Pasadena area', *American Speech*, 29, 1954, pp. 89–104.
30 *HRM*, 9, February 1956, p. 57. It should be remembered that 41 per cent of Kinsey's respondents noted the automobile as a common place for pre-marital sexual relations, see E. A. Smith, *American Youth Culture* (London, 1962), pp. 170–1.
31 'We channeled and chopped our car at home', *HRM*, 5, April 1952, pp. 20–3, 56–9.
32 *HU*, 2, August 1952, p. 32.
33 *Custom Rodder*, 2, May 1958, p. 63.
34 M. Thompson and G. Borgeson, *Challenger* (Englewood Cliffs, New Jersey, 1964), p. 26.
35 *HU*, 1, May 1952, p. 40.
36 *HRM*, 4, December 1951, p. 60.
37 *HRM*, 12, March 1959, pp. 70–1.
38 *HRM*, 6, October 1953, p. 59.
39 *HU*, 1, July 1951, p. 40.
40 See editorial, *HRM*, 4, March 1951, p. 5 for an example of this equivocation.
41 'The female and the fueler', *HRM*, 20, March 1967, pp. 30–1.
42 *Heart Like a Wheel*, Mainline Pictures, 1983. The NHRA and *Hot Rod* are

prominently displayed in this film and the NHRA and Petersen Publications are thanked for their assistance in making it.
43 'Who'll stop the reign?', *HRM*, 36, 1983, p. 58.
44 D. Garlits and B. Yates, *King of the Dragsters* (London, 1967), pp. 164–5.
45 Madigan, *The Loner*, p. 109.
46 Madigan, *The Loner*, p. 22.
47 Madigan, *The Loner*, p. 76.
48 H. Higdon, *Six Seconds to Glory: Don Prudhomme's Greatest Drag Race* (New York, 1975), p. 27.
49 'It's what I do', *HRM*, 39, May 1986, pp. 60–4.
50 *HRM*, 41, April 1988, p. 111.
51 G. Griffin, *The Teenager and Safe Driving* (New York, 1968), p. 23.
52 R. H. Boyle, *Sport – Mirror of American Life* (Boston, 1963), p. 169.
53 F. Basham *et al.*, *Car Culture* (London, 1984), pp. 4–5.
54 R. Ross, 'A squall every night', *Los Angeles Times*, West magazine section, 20 November 1966, pp. 12–18.
55 'The brotherhood', *Newsweek*, 15 September 1969, p. 51.
56 *Two Lane Blacktop* (Universal Picture, 1971).
57 J. Scalzo, 'Street racing-that's what', *Car Life*, April 1970, pp. 63–6.
58 B. Yates, 'Street racing', *Car and Driver*, September 1967, pp. 62–5, 92–3.
59 D. Jedlicka, 'Gaining respect on Woodward Avenue', *Esquire*, September 1969, pp. 44–58, 112–17.
60 R. Parks, 'Biological thought, athletics and the formation of a "man of character" ' and E. A Rotundo, 'Learning about manhood: gender ideals and the middle class family in nineteenth-century America', both in J. A. Mangan and J. Walvin (eds.), *Manliness and Morality: Middle Class Masculinity in Britain and America 1800 – 1940* (Manchester, 1987).
61 K. Fredriksson, *American Rodeo: from Buffalo Bill to Big Business* (College Station, Texas, 1985)
62 S. Tatum, *Inventing Billy the Kid* (Albuquerque, New Mexico, 1982).
63 *HRM*, 19, September 1966, p. 6.
64 *HRM*, 25, November 1972, p. 6.

Chapter Nine
Drag racing in the 1980s: running into troubles

I think the sport has the ability to grow right now. It won't always. But you can't grow with cash flow. You need financial resources and/or a cash infusion. That's why so many companies in the world go public. I suggested this . . . for NHRA. First, you'd be able to use the cash to upgrade existing facilities; second, you'd be able to borrow money – because a non-profit corporation can't borrow money. They talked about it, but they couldn't figure it out. So I got my attorneys together to see if it would be legal to do. Not only is it legal, but it wouldn't be that difficult. So we did the IHRA program first – it's a kind of backward situation – and then I came to them with this proposal. As a matter of fact I wouldn't be surprised to someday see them attempt it on their own. It was a four-program proposal. 'A' would be the existing corporation, NHRA. 'B' was the corporation we would sell all the assets to. 'C' was my corporation, IHRA. And 'D' would be the final corporation, when you combine 'B' and 'C'. 'A', being NHRA, would stay in existence, but it would sell all its assets, making it very 'cash rich'. It would go back to its original purpose: conduct sportsmanship programs, make speeches at high schools, raise the level of consciousness of drag racing, promote the sport, safety and so on . . . It would not conduct events. Corporation 'B' is really just a holding company while you do this thing, to make it legal. When you come up with corporation 'D', I would put in my corporation IHRA, and I'd get back X amount of stock, say 30 percent if we figure NHRA is worth twice as much. However, you still have to buy the assets out of 'B' and put them into 'D'. My written proposal stated that anyone would have the same opportunity as Meyer to invest in corporation 'D'. If they are unable to participate financially, Meyer would be willing to come up with the extra cash to provide the total amounts to corporation 'D'. Or corporation 'D' could elect to borrow the needed funds to buy 'B's' assets. But part of my pitch to them was that obviously corporation 'D' is no stronger than 'A' and 'C' put together. Is that strong enough to do what we want? If we want the sport to grow we need more. They said, 'Are you willing to sign for that kind of commitment?' I said, 'I'm not going to sign for anything I'm not in control of.' Why would I do that?[1]

In the early 1970s drag racing consolidated as a major American sport.

The NHRA sanctioned around 150 strips and dominated the structure of events with the AHRA and the IHRA (which developed out of a break-away from the AHRA in 1970) as smaller, rival, basically regional, organising bodies. All three had relatively standardised rules. The sport had a professional circus of top stars and there was an increasing coverage by television. There was a base of amateur participation at local strips.[2] The hot rod publications continued to thrive. Detroit and the speed industry, or 'aftermarket' as it came to be known, worked closely together, and the publications of the sport supported both the well-being of the regular American automobile and the the aftermarket industries now being promoted as crucial to the good health of the hot rod enthusiasm which was part of the whole American tradition. Next to a picture of a billowing stars and stripes, roadside posters proclaimed: 'Support Motherhood, Apple Pie and Hot Rod Magazine.'

Four major problems began to emerge in the 1970s which upset this cosy outcome to twenty-five years of strenuous attempts to re-organize and control the nature of hot rodding and continued on worrying those in charge of the sport through the 1980s. These were:

(i) a fall in amateur participation in the form of the sport developed by the sanctioning associations;
(ii) continuing state action on environmental protection which again, through restrictions on noise, among other things, threatened the root of the sport: participation at the local strips;
(iii) a sharp rise in the costs of drag racing, especially professional racing, which, combined with a rapid rise in land values in some areas, threatened the existence of many strips;
(iv) increasing doubts as to whether the public service ideology within which the NHRA had cloaked drag racing was appropriate to cope with these problems and further promote the sport.

Underlying these issues, as always through the whole history of hot rodding, was the fear of an assault on the core of economic opportunities that the enthusiasm offered and which the hot rod apparatus had striven so long and so hard to create and promote. I will now detail the contours of these problems and indicate the ways they intersected.

Bracket racing

The way that competition in drag racing had come to be arranged was, as in most sports, 'artificial' and by no means the only way that racing could

H

be organised. As I have noted throughout this book the delineation of competition classes had been a constant preoccupation of those who controlled the hot rod sports. Classes were constantly amended and revised to encompass all manner of engines, body styles, degrees of modification, types of fuel and, most importantly, to create a basic space where the 'little guy' could run. By the 1970s the competition classes had become very numerous and most complex. Here is how the NHRA tried to explain just *one* of its amateur classes in the mid-1970s:

> Youngest of the NHRA eliminators, Pro Comp, despite the designation, is a sportsman bracket. It is similar to the professional eliminators in that it features heads-up racing involving cars which bear a marked resemblance to some of the pro machines. However, unlike the three professional eliminators, Pro Comp racing involves several different classes of cars which are equalised through fuel and weight restrictions and allowable modification. The classes comprising Pro Comp are double-B funny car (BB/FC), double-A gas dragster (AA/D), double-A alcohol dragster (AA/DA), double-A altered (AA/A), A/funny car (A/FC), A/fuel dragster (A/FD) and B/fuel dragster (B/FD) plus a couple of experimental classes for turbocharged cars. Cars in the BB/FC class are almost identical to their AA/FC brothers except with regard to fuel – alcohol instead of nitro-methane. AA/D and AA/DA cars, by the same token, are very similar to the AA/FD's except that they substitute either pump gasoline or alcohol for nitro-methane. The A/FC, A/FD and B/FD cars are powered by unsupercharged engines which burn nitro-methane and the AA/A uses alcohol in supercharged engines. Throughout Pro Comp – and the professional brackets – a double-A or double-B designation means the car involved uses a supercharged engine. The presence of the letter F indicates that the class burns nitromethane fuel rather than pump gasoline or alcohol.[3]

In fact, as always, each class tended to get invaded by runners sponsored by some commercial interest so that the driver who just wanted to drive in off the street and race – 'the backbone of the sport' – found it harder and harder to compete and could not get many runs down the strip when he and, increasingly, she did. The three major associations administered up to five hundred different classes for sportsmen to race in but in March 1981 *Hot Rod* described these as:

> Although by definition a sporting endeavour – and despite the fact that material returns are notoriously poor – this 'sportsman' competition has evolved, if you want to call it that, into a confusing, expensive, highly technical game of weight breaks, index factors, sponsors, elapsed time breakouts, politics, extremely sophisticated cheating and locked-up front brakes at the finish line.

The true amateur had to find his way through a huge rule book detailing carb. limitations, wheel base dimensions and all the other complexities of making a car go alluded to above. Another writer to *Hot Rod* in 1983 asking about the basis of classes received a very complicated reply which ended with: 'That's it in a nutshell, Steve. So simple any average dentist or brain surgeon could understand it.'[4]

Relatedly, dragging had become an expensive activity. The boy who wrote into *Hot Rod* in 1975 saying he wanted to get involved in the 'Econorail' category of the NHRA classes and how could he build his own machine was told, among other things, to go to a professional SEMA builder or buy a second-hand race car and to save up $10,000 towards his racing effort. Even members of the hot rod apparatus had the feeling that drag racing had got far away from its 'original purpose' and that it had 'lost something'. Drag racing as it had been set up by the NHRA had become too costly, too complicated and over-organised for the weekend racer. Every additional change in the rules to try to make competition fairer annoyed some group and pushed up costs.

A much simpler and cheaper way to organise competition was to concentrate not on what a car 'was' precisely but what it could do. In other words racing could be organised not around degrees of technical modification etc. but around performance – likely elapsed times. This allowed handicaps to be allocated to slower cars so that everyone who came to the track could compete against everyone else with some hope of success or at least could compete in very broad categories based on expected outcomes known as 'brackets'. Such competitions, harking back to the early days at the lakes and to some of the informal rules of street racing, had been tried at some Californian strips in the 1960s, but spread rapidly in the 1970s and came to be known by the term bracket racing.

From the mid-1970s *Hot Rod* started to pay a good deal of attention to this new form: 'Bracket racing is here to stay. It may well be the future of organized drag racing, since for many drag strips, bracket racing provides the economic foundation on which they survive.'[5] It went on to outline the main features of this grass roots sport, though there were all manner of local rules and variations. Racing usually took place within three brackets of elapsed times. Competitors 'dialled-in' their own expected elapsed time and wrote this on the window of the car. As they moved towards the start the strip officials gave a handicap to the faster car so that, in theory, on their chosen times, both cars would arrive at the finishing line together. The handicap was effected through the starting lights which allowed the slower car a electronically controlled start. If a car ran quicker than its 'dial-in' time, an error known as 'breaking-out', it was disqualified. If both did, the one nearest to its 'dial-in' time won the race and progressed into the next round of the elimination contest. So, in bracket racing the aim was not to go as *fast* as possible but to be as *consistent* as possible and hit the time you had posted. The other advantage was that the strict inspections operated by the the NHRA strips partly for safety reasons and partly to prevent cheating within its complex class structure were relaxed in non-sanctioned bracket racing.

Hot Rod hailed its spread as a sign that 'the fun is coming back to drag racing' and as providing the best value per dollar spent for the amateur racer. The magazine noted its devestating effect on the 'class legal' form of racing preferred by the associations:

> Class racing is dying in organized drag racing, since years of development have lowered national records and indexes to the point where only meticulously prepared and very expensive machines have a chance at being competitive. Class and eliminator purses simply haven't kept pace with the expense. As class racing involvement continues to diminish, aftermarket equipment manufacturers will naturally shift their contingency money to bracket competition, which offers a far larger market for their products.[6]

Some already had, and from these and the fees paid by those who wanted to race, some strips were able to offer bracket racers a weekly first prize of $1,000 in the fastest bracket and prize money stretching back to sixteenth place. One of the operators responsible for the spread of bracket racing had established the The United Bracket Racers Association in 1974 with its own championship: the US Bracket Nationals with prizes of some thousands of dollars. By 1978 the total purse for 'the little guys' race of the year' was $45,000. These finals came to be held over the Labor Day weekend too, mirroring the NHRA's US Nationals for the professional racers and class legal amateurs. Bracket racing had its own newspaper from 1977, *Bracket Times,* national events and supporting sponsors, but the emphasis was firmly on fun, the family and the family car.

In short, many of hot rodding's amateur enthusiasts – the 'low-bucks weekend warriors' – found a simpler, affordable, more competitive and congenial form of competition than class-legal drag racing and one which seemed to put more emphasis on the skills of the driver than on how much could be spent in 'cubic dollars' to improve engine performance. The associations acknowledged the popularity of this form by changing some of their rules to incorporate bracket-type competitions and run them side by side with class legal racing. The form went into the

NHRA rulebook – the self-proclaimed 'bible of drag racing' – in 1976 and was supported because it kept individuals in the sport. The NHRA set up regional contests with regional finals and *Hot Rod* studiously boosted this form of drag racing through the late 1970s and into the 1980s with many articles of the 'How to Win at Bracket Racing' or 'How to Build an $1100 Bracket Racer' variety.[7] Such promotion puzzled some readers for it seemed to herald a basic change in goals of the sport. To repeat, bracketeers did not seek to go as fast as they could nor to achieve the lowest possible elapsed time they could but to hit an elapsed time *consistent* with that designated. Some writers objected that, in the brackets, competition was about who was slyest not who was quickest or had the guts to go all out, but *Hot Rod* and the sanctioning bodies accepted bracket racing as a place where resourcefulness could be substituted for the big bucks approach that threatened to drive the amateur away from the sport, and as a form of competition in which the guys who paid the freight at the local strips could escape from the suffocating layering of rules and regulations that had got in the way of simple fun and straightfoward enjoyment.

So, there came to be more of a clear seperation of big-time and little-guy drag racing. Most local tracks operated handicaps as a staple with some professional match races and special events. The associations each arranged a 'season' of top events with the NHRA having fourteen or fifteen national and thirty-five regional by the mid-1980s, (out of around 125 sanctioned strips) attended by professional dragsters and the sponsored amateurs. By the 1980s bracket racing had become drag racing's major amateur form and had developed other organisations. The Championship Bracket Racing Association (CBRA) ran a sixteen-race series, through ten states, with a guaranteed purse of $10,000 in the top elapsed time bracket at each event. Its pitch stressed it was a participant sport for all: 'the most equal opportunity sport in the world' and that it was simple: 'You don't need tons of money and you don't have to be an expert mechanic – all you have to do is drive consistently.'[8] Its guide for beginners, written by a grandmother, announced bracket racing as 'the motorsport for everyone'. It was fun, fair and could be quite profitable. The CBRA was dedicated to providing high-paying bracket racing at already sanctioned first-class strips and promoted numbers of local meets with prizes up to thousands of dollars via sponsorship from camshaft and tyre manufacturers etc. with payouts starting from second round contests onwards. The CBRA had its own newspaper, *United Racer*, and a monthly newsletter, *Bracket Flyer* subtitled 'news for the little guy').

However, this new form of drag racing did not prove immune from the kind of developments that had troubled hot rodding throughout its history. Bracket racing too soon developed professional classes with sponsored cars and the like, though a street class did remain for the sportsman. Then, in the last years of the 1980s, manufacturers began to develop delay boxes and stutter or sputter boxes which were, basically, small electronic devices that aided either reaction time at the start or allowed the car to run a pre-set elapsed time. They were expensive and hit at the 'good-time' nature of this form of drag racing: 'Up until now there wasn't any way to cheat Bracket Racing.'[9] Discussion about these developments took two forms. One was whether they did really constitute 'cheating' or were just another technological development for rodders to conquer and use. The other was whether it was possible to ban them. They were small and very easily hidden anywhere in a car.

Despite this both the NHRA and the IHRA had come to operate their own well sponsored bracket championships, with sixty thousand participants in the NHRA series in 1987. It was promoted as bargain basement fun for the blue-collars, who had always been thought to be the largest element in rodding, and for the burgeoning white collar classes who felt the need to get back to the real world. It was the area of the sport which went right back to an old NHRA slogan 'ingenuity in action' and where 'resourcefulness substituted for cubic $s'. So while these new organisations and the separation of forms of drag racing meant that the associations, especially the NHRA, suffered some loss of control over grass roots racing and some dents in their 'little guy' ideology, from the 1970s and through the 1980s bracket racing was what the hot rod magazines boosted as they continued to urge 'amateur involvement' in what was becoming much more difficult terrain for all automobile sport.

New times old problems

Part of this concerned a continuation of state action on pollution that I discussed in Chapter Six. In 1979 the magazine ran a series with a title that was to be repeated many times in the next decade: 'Hot Rodders – an Endangered Species?' The issue here was 'anti-vehicle discrimination'. There were over a one hundred regulatory agencies operating at the federal level alone, more than half of whose funding was directed at 'cleaning up' the automobile. The future was bleak. In July 1979 *Hot Rod* quoted a Congressman: 'You may soon find yourself with a sticker on your car that tells you what days of the week you can use it.' Some of these agencies had top administrators who had been aides of the hated Ralph Nader. They were pushing 'anti-tampering laws' for the 1980s that could make modifying an automobile an offence. *Hot Rod* rumbled on about the busybody state, bureaucracies, the Sierra Club: 'There are a lot more car owners than hikers' and so on. Much of the October 1984 issue was devoted to the question 'Can They Outlaw Hot Rodding?' which was analysis of the California Inspection and Maintenance Program designed to check air pollution. In California a lot of the modifications rodders had routinely carried out had been technically illegal but the 'smog law' of 1969 had not been enforced. Now, under Federal pressure, officialdom would be 'coming down on individual automobile owners like the Spanish Inquisition'. However, while apparently as combative as ever, this article did suggest the enthusiasm now had to bend with the wind and urged rodders to learn to live with the new rules and so extend the mission of 'hot rodding':

> Hot rodding has been operating on 1950s mentality and technology for far too long. We at Hot Rod Magazine have been just as guilty as the rest . . . We seriously hope that our aftermarket industry will also be awakened by this challenge and will respond with our own brands of high-performance, high-tech smog-control systems . . . this article merely breaks the ice on many topics we have ignored for too long. We will follow up with numerous articles and projects showing how to build 'clean' performance engines, exploring possibilities for more effective and effecient smog control equipment, and beginning what we are sure will be a lengthy educational process for hot rodders into the field of electronics. [10]

Another emerging problem was more difficult to resolve. For the financial viability of many local strips was becoming precarious, especially in areas where expanding populations and rocketing land values ripped at the very surfaces of the sport as surely as high speeds and over-use had wrecked the dry lakes. Nowhere was this more serious than in the birthplace of hot rodding, Southern California. When in December 1977 a letter asked *Hot Rod* what was being done to protect the race tracks in that State the editor replied:

> Unfortunately, not a whole lot. Noise and cars are both under attack, so when the two are found together you can bet 'Uncle Sammy' and 'Sally Sierra' will be out in force. This is not to mention the rising land prices which are making all sorts of low-density land use – farms as well as race tracks – uncommercial.

The answer was to support SEMA, to write to representatives and senators and to push for a reform of the tax structure on property which now made assessments on the 'best use' of land not the worth of what it was actually being used for.

In 1981 another article warned that 'Hot Rodders are an Endangered Species'. California's active strips were now outnumbered by the ones that had closed including some legendary tracks on which much of the early history of the sport had been made – Lions Drag Strip, San Fernando Raceway, Fontana Drag City and a dozen others. Land value was one problem, another was that housing development and retirement villages had spread out and engulfed drag strips which led to increasing complaints about noise and pollution. Many strips that remained had legal restrictions as to the hours they could be used, what kind of cars could run on them, bans, curfews and so on making their economic future much less certain. This was not just a problem for California, though by 1982 Orange County International Freeway could be advertised as 'The Last Drag Strip In Southern California' and it soon closed, for right across the Continent exactly the same issues arose. The operator of the Racing Park of Englishtown, New Jersey was having legal action taken against him by residents of the housing that had come to surround his track, but he was fighting back:

> The judge has to try to make decisions right down the middle . . . The tracks have a right to do business, the blue-collar workers who use the tracks have a right to their recreation, and other people, people around the tracks are entitled to use their backyards. Everbody's entitled to their recreation. But these people should understand that not everybody wants to hit a ball, or throw a ball, or catch a ball for recreation. If you tried to shut down every tennis court because you thought the game was stupid or something, you know some hell would be raised.[11]

Hot Rod ran a series of 'Drag Strip Survival' articles. Basically it was the local strip that was under threat. Professional drag racing had begun to concentrate on new 'super-tracks', stadia purpose-built for automobile competition with all the facilities associated with a modern, sponsored, spectacular sport – TV towers, executive boxes, lounges for the stars and comfortable seating for forty thousand-plus crowds. However and as ever, the danger was that as local strips closed racing on the streets might gain in popularity as a sport. Through the mid-1980s *Hot Rod* began to advocate volunteer efforts to improvise some form of simple, basic competition on any strip of asphalt that might become temporarily available and urged: 'If you drag racers sit and wait for someone else to provide you with a new drag strip, or if you simply park your cars and complain when your local track closes, you're gona be out of luck. To put it another way, dragstrips of the '80s may be where *you* find them.'[12] The tone was uneerily like that of the early 1950s but in a much less favourable atmosphere.

Other echoes sounded across nearly forty years in notes and articles warning of the likelihood of, and dangers attendant upon, a resurgence of the illegal sport if drag strips kept closing. The state was still concerned about the rate of car accidents among young drivers, and street racing had never gone away. It figured in many movies and TV movies e.g.: *American Graffiti* (1973), *The California Kid* (1975), *Hot Rod* (1979) and *King of the Mountain* (1981) as an American institution. But it was not just a figment of the imagination of the entertainment industries. The *New York Times* in 1980 reported on various races with fatalities on Flatlands Avenue in Brooklyn with the police response being: 'as soon as one drag strip is shut down another one opens elsewhere', while a participant argued: 'It's a brotherhood. We could be a bowling league somewhere.'[13]

A *Hot Rod* article in February 1982 told how, with the closure of Brotherhood Raceway Park, the strip the LA Brotherhood of Street Racers had struggled to obtain, three million people in Los Angeles now had no local drag strip. Some of the 'weekend warriors' were moving out to compete on the avenues of the San Fernando Valley. The LA police department said that the street racing problem was bigger than ever and that over an eighteen month period at least twenty traffic deaths had resulted from the illegal speed contests. A 'drag race task force' had been set up by a local politician and the first 'community meeting' attracted a crowd of over a one thousand people and great media interest. Big Willie Robinson spoke from the floor and the LA police representatives were asked to investigate the possibilities of blocking off city streets to serve as temporary race tracks. In short, the situation was something like the late 1940s except that in the 1980s there were no abundant abandoned airstrips to help take the heat off the streets.

In August 1985 *Hot Rod* carried an editorial and an article on the new old menace. The editor admitted that in his youth:

> I did my share of street racing . . . Now the handful of the old gang still involved with cars (like me) doesn't street race anymore. I guess it's all part of growing up and realizing the potential of things that can go wrong – and knowing they most likely will. But everyone doesn't grow up as evidenced by the current crop of street racers who race real race cars on the streets.

The author of the article insisted he was not writing about the 'road racers' of the famous Mulholland Drive in the Hollywood Hills, or the Banzai Runners who made 200-mile runs in one hour in the night hours, or the cross-country Cannonball racers or all the other types of illegal auto sports. He was talking about good old-fashioned street dragging that was as traditional and normal an American pastime as sandlot baseball: 'I've done it. You've done it. Your father probably did it. My *mother's* done it.' The official sport had become too formalised with nit-picking technical regulations and the elements of mystery and 'prove it' removed. In serious street racing for money there were no classes, no display of elapsed times on the windows, secrecy and deceit were essential elements of the sport. There was a good deal of negotiation of the rules of the match beforehand, what fuel could be used, who was to get what handicap, what starting procedure would apply, etc., but, mechanically, anything went. Most matches were for $100–$300 but could go as high as $3,000 and there was a good deal of ancillary betting especially in drug-trafficking areas. They didn't want crowds and most areas had several venues on the streets they could race on and some had even set up their own 'strips': 'To give just one example: within earshot of the Baylands Raceway in Fremont, the street racers set up their own "track", complete with lanes, lines, and billboards, on one of the nearby back-bay roads.'[14] The main reason the street racers didn't come on to the strips was that they didn't come close to meeting basic, practical safety standards and there were no guard rails, no safety crews, no ambulances, often no fire equipment or traffic and crowd controls at these illegal gatherings. The solution was for police and townspeople to find street racers somewhere else to run and to try to incorporate them on to the strips with special grudge nights involving simple heads-up racing, very few rules and minimal technical inspection, something *Hot Rod* had been urging for some time.[15]

This article provoked some letters one of which reverberated across the decades back to the way readers defended the street sport in the 1950s, like those I set out in Chapter Two:

It is easy to to say 'If you want to race, do it at the track', but where are these tracks you speak of? You said it yourself in past issues of Hot Rod magazine: as land values escalate, dragstrips disappear and I fear the day when the local strip becomes as rare as a 50-cent gallon of premium. I belong to that large group of 'trackless' people who were left with only two options after Terminal Island Raceway and Orange County International Raceway were closed. My choices were to street race or stick the ol' Chevy on the shelf. I fail to see what damage is done when a dozen or so people migrate to a deserted industrial street for a quick, midnight race. I say to all of you at Hot Rod magazine hang in there, continue to give us the support that you've been providing for so long, but don't slap us on the wrist for keeping hot rodding alive. After all, where would you all be if it hadn't been for street racing?

Bill Ogg
San Pedro, California.

The editor's reply, that nothing could be more detrimental to the sport than reviving its lawless image, was standard, but his proferred solution – why didn't the writer use the time to prepare 'like a touring pro' for a once a month trip to a sanctioned track in Arizona – lacked some conviction.[16]

If from the mid-1970s the amateur sport changed and simplified and moved away from the grip of the associations, professional racing too found the going get tougher and the main problem was cost. This was in part a result of general inflation but mainly the way the 'top' of the sport had developed because of the way sponsors' contributions had been used and the set-ups they had encouraged. Even the editors of Hot Rod began to refer to it wryly as the 'drag racing business not sport'. From the mid-1970s support for another ban on the use of nitro was canvassed, partly for safety reasons, partly for noise abatement but mainly as a way of controlling costs, not just the cost of nitro itself but its effect in routinely destroying engines and other components: 'One racer related to SEMA officials that he spent $11,000 on nitro alone in 1974, with a corresponding expenditure of over $20,000 in replacement engine parts alone.'[17]

However, the worry was whether you could 'reverse progress' and maintain spectator appeal if speeds dropped without the use of nitro. Articles began to reappear about 'Better Racing Through Chemistry' and the 'black art' of using nitrous oxide, a fuel limited in use to the pros which not only made cars go faster but had the potential to damage engines severely and cause the driver to hallucinate. Discussion rumbled on through the 1980s with the NHRA putting a partial ban on nitrous oxide on safety and cost grounds in 1983 but there were always the threat that: '. . . a rocket fuel that some say makes nitrous look like Johnny's pop gun – could easily be substituted for nitrous and be very hard to detect'.[18]

Soon the sport appeared to be in a financial impasse. Professional drag raing seemed to be big business, every national NHRA event appeared on some kind of TV and it was estimated that a major event had a $2 million economic impact on the city in which it took place. In 1978 the prizes for the season-long NHRA points competition offered $141,600 to the professionals and $33,400 to sportsmen made up from $125,000 from the major sponsors (Winston cigarettes) and $50,000 from the NHRA. The IHRA, also benefiting from Winston, offered $75,200 to the pros and $49,800 to sportsmen. However, as Garlits estimated that in the same year it cost him $500 each time he ran down a drag strip, the purses did not seem commensurate with the costs. Garlits, with lifetime earnings of $4 million and named by the AHRA as 'drag racer of the century', estimated he earned $300,000 in 1978 but it had cost him $200,000 to do it and he was a *very* successful competitor. He argued that fewer and fewer cars would be able to afford to compete in the top fuel category which was the fastest and most spectacular of all.

The nub of the issue, as it had been in the early 1960s, came to be the relation of the sanctioning bodies, especially the dominant NHRA, to the professional group and who was making what out of the sport. Complying with the ever-increasing complexities of the competition classes put up costs. Then professional drivers looked at the National Association for Stock Car Automobile Racing (NASCAR) circuit and saw a much more overt attitude to making money out of sport and certainly higher rewards being paid to top drivers. Attention began to focus on the NHRA, its ambivalent relation with the professional group and whether it was holding back the sport from developing into a full-blown modern spectacle and a flat-out money spinner. The NHRA had the best tracks, publicity, honest times and links with manufacturers but, apparently, little cash. The NHRA constantly stressed that it was a non-profit-making organisation and could not increase purses. *Hot Rod*, celebrating an anniversary, put the official line:

> The NHRA is *still* a nonprofit organization. The intent 25 years ago and today is to use whatever revenues are generated by competition, advertising and promotion to better the sport of drag racing. There are no owners, no stockholders, no one to pocket the proceeds in those years when the NHRA operates in the black, which, unfortunately, is not every year. It exists for the regulation, promotion and betterment of the sport.

Though the NHRA liked to present itself as a: 'true philanthropist . . . reluctant to acknowledge its aid to many local tracks',[19] promotors and track operators were getting worried too. Regional events often were not profitable after the NHRA collected an automatic 25 per cent of takings as a service fee and as these offered only half the points of national events the crowd-pulling stars often did not take part. The NHRA's ideology, that the sport was essentially an amateur-based endeavour with a safety and public benefit stance, seemed to lack the commercial dynamism necessary to thrust drag racing on to a new plateau to satisfy all those who wanted to make money directly from the sport.

The NHRA's view was that, somehow, the boys would always come up with the funds to keep their cars on the track and that the NHRA's expanding TV coverage would help them to get sponsors to match the costs. *Hot Rod* published articles telling racers: 'What it Takes to Get a Sponsorship in Today's Business World.' These insisted: 'the racer's skills must extend beyond his machinery and into the sponsor's motives. He must talk as easily about ROI (return on investment) as he does about ET (elapsed time).'[20] The series tried to correct the racer's 'promotional illiteracy' and coach them in how to work-in promotional plugs in media interviews: 'Until the racer accepts, first that he or she is a potentially valuable commodity and, second, that his or her sport attracts a larger following of fans, that is, consumers, than, say professional baseball, then he or she is doomed to speaking in language foreign to the sponsor.'

Some professionals had chosen to run in the 'Funny Car' class instead of the dragsters because their bodies provided bigger billboards for sponsors but even sponsors began to baulk at the ever-increasing costs at the pinnacle of drag racing. By 1981 it cost a touring pro $500,000 a year to compete, and, apart from the handful of national events, fewer racers were performing less frequently at fewer strips and fewer spectators were willing to pay the high prices being charged to watch them. Characteristically, the NHRA, through Parks, tended to blame the professionals:

> I think for a sport that was created – and still is maintained – as a place to go out and do something that you like to do, anybody who puts that kind of money into it and expects to get it out is crazy. We've always felt that way. There's no way we can put a leash on how much money an individual can spend on his car, of course. In the last few years, it appears as if some of the racers are having a big contest to see who can spend the most money and come up with the most pretentious rig and equipment. We have increased purses probably on a scale of 10% a year, and we never pretended that the purses were going to be a source of professional, ensured income.[21]

He looked back to the days when the top runners improvised or made their own equipment and could afford to go out and run every weekend. Now there was a $5 million payout at NHRA-sanctioned strips alone but this was nowhere near enough to meet the expanded costs. His solution was that big money sponsorship was the key for professional racing.

However, the NHRA had got into an awkward position. Its additional televised national events on prime summer weekends both competed for attention with the local tracks the organisation sanctioned, and made their owners compete with the NHRA for appearances by star performers. They also cut down on the chances of professionals taking part in lucrative match races for which Prudhomme, for example, could get $2,500 a start in the late 1970s. Parks mused:

> it's a different world now, an expensive world that we've helped to create by getting involved in the business of promoting races and creating stars. We have a situation right now where it's very difficult for an independent track operator to be able to afford a reasonably sized field of professional racers. The primary reason is that the racers are just gradually pricing themselves right out of business. But I don't know of any way you can put a handle on the cost of any individual's operation in any kind of racing. Tracks blame us for the high cost of professional racers, yet since back in the early Sixties, we're the ones who used to try and preach against coming in and putting up too much in monetary awards; because we'll blow this thing out of the door and become too expensive for anybody, especially the racers, to afford. We have to this day never paid our first appearance money or guarantees at our major events.

The AHRA and the IHRA did but, Parks argued, if the NHRA did get involved in some type of guaranteed income to racers the professionals would need to be, as on the NASCAR circuit, exclusively pledged to the NHRA and other racers would not be allowed to compete.

Others attacked the NHRA for being plodding and held back by tradition, for being committee-bound and for not leading but simply following, often with obvious reluctance, changes and new ideas initiated by its smaller rivals. Parks clung to the NHRA's special position in the sport, of its being the national organiser, even though this opened it up to criticism from the various groups it sought to represent. The whole sport still had 'to be coordinated and organized and protected'. Or as another NHRA official put it:

> The one thing that myself and the company want to preserve is legal, legitimate, respectable drag racing, and that's the thing that concerns me now with some of these other circuits or shows. It's too much of a closed, bought-in deal, and I'd hate to see it come to where it's comparable to wrestling or roller derby; where you come in, you set up your clocks, and 'X' number of guys that are getting paid-in go out, they make their runs; they pack up, and they go down the road . . . NHRA puts on a good, safe, respectable show, and I still think that's what racing's all about. How long that can survive, I don't know.[22]

A response from Garlits argued that the future of professional drag racing was in jeopardy and that 'most championships are bought these days'. He believed that the sanctioning bodies certainly could act so as to cut the huge amounts that professional racers had come to spend in order to compete. In essence, he wanted the associations to alter certain rules so as to force a return close to 'run what you brung'. He advocated limitation of the replacement of components and engines that could be made during an event thus making all competitors more careful and less reliant on the wholesale substitution of power plants when, as it frequently did, something exploded or cracked.[23] In the mid-1980s the edges of all these issues got sharper as costs escalated. By 1984 professionals estimated it was costing them somewhere around $2,500 each time they ran down a quarter-mile, and the basic question remained one of whether enough sponsors would keep coming forward to fund what had become a very expensive vehicle for advertising.

In early 1988 Billy Meyer, wealthy Texas businessman, a competitor in the 'Funny Car' classes and owner of the latest supertrack, took over the IHRA in a multi-million dollar deal. The AHRA had rather faded away in the early 1980s in a contested change of ownership and the IHRA had become the NHRA's main rival. Meyer began trying to relocate drag racing in a completely new context: overt commercialism as in his outline plan to unite his IHRA with the NHRA in one profit-oriented corporation quoted at the start of this chapter. This challenge was a hard one for the NHRA to stomach as, through the years, it had barely publicly acknowledged the existence of the IHRA (or AHRA for that matter) and, as I have tried to detail, its relation to the commercial opportunities opened up by the the sport had always been mediated, opaque, refracted and apparently incidental. The public service, safety programme, little guys, low bucks ideology of the NHRA and, indeed, *Hot Rod* meshed uneasily with the big money brashness of the young entrepreneur.

Essentially Meyer wanted to restructure professional drag racing to make more money go to the tracks and racers and less to the salaries, perks and operations of the associations. His model was the much more overtly successful NASCAR circuit. What he wanted was to create that one national body which the NHRA had always claimed itself to be. Then there would be one 20–22 event season backed by the major sponsor Winston, running on the developing circuit of supertracks (he was building another in Detroit) with associated TV deals, an accent on more involvement from the Detroit companies and so on. The NHRA leaders rejected his proposed merger: 'We feel that drag racing is too important to be controlled by one man. We also feel that a profit making corporation cannot properly deal with the needs of the sport.'[24] They doubted whether there was all the extra sponsorship available that he imagined and they doubted that the money would trickle down deep down enough to ensure the survival of drag racing as a widespread mass activity as opposed to a mass spectator sport based in a few locations. What, they asked, was supposed to happen to all the NHRA sanctioned tracks that would never get a chance to run the big events? For the while, at least, the NHRA was content to compete with the noisy newcomer and try to maintain NHRA dominance with the IHRA in a useful but certainly secondary spot. Their Winston Drag Race Series was worth $1,076,600 in 1988 with three-quarters going to the professionals.

Meyer's view of the NHRA was:

> I don't have to throw stones. I know more about them than they know. It's just my way of doing business. I don't go into something blind. I have a bunch of stuff I could bring out – what you call skeletons, or bones, or whatever – but there's no reason to do that. I guess there's a paranoia there – that 37 years of never having to put up with an upstart like me has got them running around in circles. I hope they quit running around in circles, and finally figure out: let's start working for the betterment of the sport.[25]

At the time of writing it looks like the NHRA prevailed against this challenger, for in 1989 Meyer sold the IHRA though still retaining an interest in drag racing through holding on to the IHRA's journal, which was retitled *Drag Racing Today*. As ever, in this sport the specialist magazines are more than just ephemera for enthusiasts.

But the bucks stop here

As drag racing ran into big problems in the 1980s a certain nostalgia crept into the sport and enthusiasm as the apparatus began to reflect on its own history and, indeed, recreate it. Old racers started to argue in the press about who had beat whom where and which one had set what record. Of course, nostalgia offers new business opportunities in sport as in everything else. Examples of street racing in big box-office films formed part of a wider evocation of a simpler, easier and better America, as did, in fact, a hymn to the illegal sport by a major rock star:

> We take all the action we can meet
> And we cover all the North East states.
> When the strips shut down, we run 'em in the streets

From the fire roads to the Interstate.
Now some guys all just give up living,
And start dying little by little, piece by piece,
Some guys come home from work and wash up
And go racing in the streets.
Tonight, tonight, the strip's just right,
I wanna blow 'em all out of their seats.
We're calling out around the world.
We're going racing in the streets.[26]

A series of 'Nostalgia Graffiti Nites' aimed to live again the California of the early 1950s as hot rodders combined in organised cruises to the few remaining original hot dog stands and drive-ins. A Nostalgia Drag Racing Association began its Nationals in the 1980s where old drag racing machines raced against each other to get back to the feel of 'real drags', for modern racing was too efficient, too standardised and too professional. Articles appeared on how to restore the classic dragsters of the 1960s and 1970s and kits were marketed so enthusiasts could build reproduction Model A roadsters and the like. Plans were announced for a Drag Racing Hall of Fame and other hot rod and drag racing museums opened up such as Garlits's Museum of Drag Racing near Disney World in Florida. One of his famous machines, however, was donated to the Museum of American History of the Smithsonian Institution in 1988 and, to publicise an exhibition, the dragster's last roar rattled windows along the Mall in the heart of the capital of the USA.[27] Ironically, one of the variations on conventional drag racing that was promoted as local strips closed down was participation on the dry lakes as *Hot Rod* carried a succession of recommendations to people in California to go out to: 'El Mirage, which has experienced an incredible resurgence in '83'.[28] In 1984 it was hailed as: 'our roots, our Mecca, our Wailing Wall, our Blarney Stone . . . It's the ultimate, hard core experience'.[29] While in 1987: 'entry fees are cheap, the atmosphere is great, and just remember that this is where it all started'.[30] The SCTA was still running out there.

But if drag racing ran into troubles in the 1980s one of the main struts of the hot rod economy built upon it, enthusiast magazines, certainly did not. There was a proliferation of titles through the years, and I have not even mentioned most of them, but when *Advertising Age* listed the specialist automotive magazines' revenue leaders in 1981 some of the oldest titles were still out infront:

	Revenue (millions of dollars)
Car and Driver	23.7
Road and Track	22.9
Hot Rod	20.1
Motor Trend	18.0
Car Craft	10.0

The last three of these were published by Petersen Publications.[31] The owner of this private company appeared relatively often in the management literature of the 1980s as a compelling example of entreprenurial success based on leisure, hobbies and sport. As *Forbes* put it in 1983: 'Bob Petersen built a tiny hot rod magazine into a fortune on three rules: simplicity, simplicity and simplicity.' Actually, as even the article showed, it had been a bit more complicated than that since Petersen stressed the importance he attached to pursuing a 'show-how with know-how' approach across a whole range of leisure interests, how a new interest could be nurtured and developed in one magazine and then fragmented off into a totally new publication and how he sought to pull the reader round the life-cycle, on from the youthful hot rod to the more expensive automobile world featured in *Motor Trend*. *Forbes* estimated the whole Petersen Group would be worth $175 million to another publisher.[32]

In 1984 *Advertising Age* estimated that the company's total revenues the previous year were $140.5 million overwhelmingly from publishing, though the company also planned five major auto exhibitions in 1984.[33] Mr Petersen's lifestyle became a subject of mass media interest[34] and he achieved a more overt sporting prominence when he was chosen to be Commissioner for shooting sports at the Los Angeles Olympic Games, not just because he was a keen hunter, with a stuffed polar bear adorning his office, but because one of his successful thirteen or so monthly magazines was *Guns and Ammo* – an important outlet for the gun lobby, another of those neglected enthusiasms and sports of America. Possibly the oddest article ever to appear in *Hot Rod* came in 1982 when it published an 'Opinion' by the Chairman of the Board – Petersen – which was about the 'misguided fanatics' who were seeking to introduce an initiative in California to prohibit the sale of guns.[35] In 1985 *Advertising Age* showed Petersen Publications to rank seventy-sixth out of the top one hundred American media companies by revenue, quite close to, say, the much more sociologically discussed, Playboy Enterprises, $166 million to $142 million.[36]

As well as having a hand in the creation of the NHRA and SEMA, *Hot*

Rod and Petersen also helped to found the National Street Rod Association whose activities catered for the showier, non-racing side of the hot rod enthusiasm, and certain analyses of this aspect of rodding err by not detailing the orchestrating role that the magazine and Petersen Publications played here too. *Hot Rod* itself, which periodically had to insist that, despite what people said, it did not own the NHRA, nor did Petersen, nor did the NHRA own the magazine, claimed five million readers a month in 1987 and continued on its track with regular type articles on: 'Max Tork vs. Hi H-power', 'Chevy's Gripping Disc-brake Upgrade for Camaros', 'Part 1 of a Build-up on a Classic Carriages '32 Roadster' and so on[37]. In June 1988 Petersen Publications launched their latest monthly magazine, *Drag Racing*. So the net of ties between specialist magazines, the organisation of a sport and the ideologies of an automobile enthusiasm seem quite likely to gain in strength and complexity in the years to come.

All in all, despite all the enduring problems, in money terms at least, hot rodding had travelled a long, long way out of the white dust of those dry lakes of Southern California.

Notes

1 Billy Meyer, owner of the IHRA, interviewed in 'Meyerplex', *Hot Rod Magazine (HRM)*, 41, February 1988, pp. 72–6, 102.
2 S. Alexander, 'All over in 6 seconds', *Road and Track*, August 1974, pp. 73–8.
3 National Hot Rod Association pamphlet, 'Drag racing: understanding the eliminators', 1976.
4 *HRM*, 36, July 1983, p. 11.
5 *HRM*, 28, August 1975, p. 12.
6 *HRM*, 29, March 1976, p. 6.
7 *HRM*, 31, August 1978, pp. 24–5 and *HRM*, January 1977, pp. 32–3.
8 C. Clement, *ET. Bracket Drag Racing: Racing your Everyday Car, Truck or Motorcycle for Fun and Profit* (Cuyahoga Falls, Ohio, 1988).
9 *The Bracket Flyer*, March/April 1989, p. 9.
10 *HRM*, 37, October 1984, p. 113.
11 'Hot rodders: an endangered species', *HRM*, 34, April 1981, pp. 52–3.
12 'Drag strip survival: the Riverside saga', *HRM*, 37, January 1984, pp. 62–4.
13 See *California Traffic Safety Education Task Force Report* (Sacramento, 1977), pp. 152–4 and 'Illegal drag racing deadly and to some irresistible', *New York Times*, 28 September 1980, part iv, pp. 6–7.
14 P. Ganahl, 'Street racing', *HRM*, 38, August 1985, pp. 18–24.
15 E.g. 'The street meets: one drag strip is finally giving the street racers what they want', *HRM*, 36, August 1983, pp. 59–61.
16 *HRM*, 38, November 1985, p. 6.
17 'The nitro ban', *HRM*, 28, January 1975, p. 77.
18 *HRM*, 36, April 1983, p. 50 and see e.g. J. Baechtel, 'Better racing through

chemistry', *HRM*, 37, January and February 1984.
19 *HRM*, 29, July 1976, p. 28.
20 B. Vogels, 'Bank shot', *HRM*, 31, October, November and December 1978.
21 D. Wallace, 'The trouble with drag racing: part 2', *HRM*, 34, February 1981, pp. 52–4.
22 D. Wallace, 'The trouble with drag racing: part 3', *HRM*, 34, March 1981, pp. 70–3.
23 'Big daddy speaks out', *HRM*, 34, August 1981, p. 8.
24 *HRM*, 41, February 1988, p. 72.
25 Meyer *ibid.*, p. 74.
26 B. Springsteen, 'Racing in the streets', from the album *Darkness on the Edge of Town* (CBS 1978). Quoted with permission.
27 *The Smithsonian*, 1988.
28 *HRM*, 36, November 1983, p. 2.
29 *HRM*, 37, February 1984, pp. 62–5.
30 *HRM*, 40, August 1987, p. 80 which supplied an address for readers to write to the SCTA.
31 'Magazines of more than passing interest?', *Advertising Age*, 53, 25 October 1982, p. 60.
32 'Know thy reader', *Forbes*, 132, 29 August 1983, p. 54.
33 'Petersen's aim is right on target', *Advertising Age*, 55, 26 July 1984, p. 13.
34 'California lifestyles', *Los Angeles Times*, 21 September 1975, home section, pp. 62–7. Mr Petersen, here and elsewhere, attributed his success to adherence to the work ethic.
35 'Opinion' *HRM*, 35, October 1982, p. 4.
36 'Buyouts reshape 84 media rankings', *Advertising Age*, 56, 27 June 1985, pp. 1, 49–50.
37 *HRM*, 41 and 42, April 1988 and February 1989.

Chapter Ten
The shut down

Don't tell me you never rode in a hot rod or had a late date in the balcony?[1]

So that is hot rodding. It is quite a complex phenomenon and not, I trust I have shown, an uninteresting one. Rodding is a ubiquitous illegal activity, an amateur sport, a business enclave, a professional spectacular, unpaid labour and a mechanism for purveying ideologies about technology, work, America and modern life. I make no claim that it is unique or special as an enthusiasm, though the associated sports are, perhaps, rather unusual because through the length of hot rod history they have skidded along the edge of illegality. I do insist that it is an enthusiasm worth serious consideration because it neatly poses a number of issues which most social analysis chooses to avoid, those concerning the ramifications of the consumption of commodities. Both sociology and Marxism have concentrated on the automobile as *the* production item of the twentieth century but have more or less ignored it in use. The car on road or track, in garage and museum, on strip or in salesroom remains virtual terra incognita to the academic mind. This has to change, and my book has been an attempt to try to argue, through a detailed consideration of one automobile sport and enthusiasm, just why it might be worth while spending as much effort and intellectual energy in dissecting the automobile as an object in consumption as has been expended on it as an object in production. For example, if social explanation requires to be adequate at the level of meaning then, surely, there is a need to consider those parts of society in which Henry Ford is appreciated in ways which most social analysis would regard as quite peculiar: not as industrial magnate nor as the destroyer of skill but as the well-meaning supplier of sturdy cars and, even more tellingly, as the prototype self-taught mechanic and backyard tinkerer. A real roll-up-your-sleeves do-it-yourself kind of a guy, who wasn't afraid to put it on the line and compete. A shade tree hero, whose efforts brought solid

221

benefits to a lot of others, unlike the money men.[2]

When Henry Ford had the great River Rouge plant built in Detroit in the 1920s it was surrounded by 120 acres of parking lots for the use of employees. Social analysis has now told us what happened to just about every bolt ever made in the Rouge, but the cars of the men who worked there remain a mystery and so, relatedly, do their lives outside 'Fordism' for the most part. Indeed, often Gramsci's ridiculous few-page portrayal is held up as having said all that really needs saying about this topic.[3] At the moment there is a great academic interest in post-Fordism and post-modernism, both of which rest on a highly dubious evocation of 'Fordism'. While smart criticism here is turning on the way such broad sweeps stereotype 'Fordist' *production*,[4] I need to add that they also have not grasped the realities of capitalist *consumption*. The belief that mass production equalled standardised consumption both ignores the objective and subjective effects of the input of Sloanist principles[5] and the work that people have always done on their own cars.[6] Moreover, car plants and company displays were big tourist draws from the earliest years of this century, as big as any contemporary garden festival. Often, in such shows the Ford Company tried to illustrate how, if the automobile was still produced via the ways of old crafts, it would be far too expensive for the average person to purchase.[7] In short, assertion of the shock of the 'new' often merely indicates the lack of much appreciation of the history of modes of consumption and the ways these have been suffused with meanings.

This is a major failing of the emerging sociology of consumption. In contemporary capitalist society consumption activities have a great social and subjective importance, an importance which most orthodox social analysis has ignored. Unfortunately the new field is being rapidly colonized by sign bores whose attempts to examine consumption not only involve empirically dubious invocations of some 'new regime of accumulation' plus a muddled grip on the realities of social stratification, but also tend to provide highly generalised accounts of 'modern consumption' offering very few detailed studies. The editor of one recent book can claim: 'Fewer and fewer people in contemporary capitalism work at making things. More and more people work to make impressions.'[8] It is difficult to know where to begin pointing out all the errors in such attempts to encapsulate 'consumption' in strained epigrams and quick-fix labels. Empirical examples which are often proffered, from fast food and jeans through Disneyland to the mass media, are self-confirming ones which lend themselves to being easily encompassed through post-modern spectacles. While there is much *talk* of pleasure, excitement, desire, projects, identity confirmation, dreams etc. and much *lip service* is paid to 'the concrete analysis of the social process', all too often this boils down to providing yet another paraphrase of Barthes, Baudrillard or Bourdieu, or giving a whiff of the latest hallucinogen drifting out of the second *arrondissement,* rather than as the cue for detailed research especially of all the types of 'modern consumption' which have been virtually neglected up to now – driving a car for example. The situation is such that when the journal *Sociology* turned its attention to the new field in a special issue we got statements like: 'The overproduction of signs and reproduction of images and simulations leads to a loss of stable meaning, and an aestheticisation of reality in which the masses become fascinated by the endless flow of bizarre juxtapositions which take the viewer beyond stable sense.'[9] Well, not in my understanding of the hot rod enthusiasm they don't! Of course, it has to be said that to some analysts all the world's a sign. It's tiresome, but totally necessary, to insist that virtually all of the devil lies in the detail. The main problem with the rise of the soothsayers of signs is that really important works of scholarship like Pahl's and Campbell's[10] do not get all the attention *and* the criticism they deserve.

I have argued throughout this book that *one way* in which consumption and identities are structured and presented in advanced capitalist society is via institutions variously known as 'hobbies', 'subcultures', 'leisure activities' etc. which I have called enthusiasms and which can, in many cases, contain a sport as their core activity. In such institutions that complex of sages, hustlers, missionaries and artists, experts and traffickers, which Mills labelled the cultural apparatus are likely to be of great importance. They construct their own theories, philosophies, organisations, histories, practices and honours. But while the pressure groups of politics or industry are well-studied, those of modern culture and meaning are not. Their existence tends to be dealt with in the broadest of brush strokes, few nuances are allowed. So while almost everyone agrees that we now live in a 'consumer society' the sales effort of modern capitalism is quite neglected. Henry Ford has his scrutineers, Frederick Taylor his Braverman and hosts of lesser Boswells, but A. P. Sloan, Harley Earl, the styling studios, hire purchase businesses, marketing and sales promotion offices, public relations suites and dealer showrooms of Ford, General Motors etc. are all but ignored. Except for 'mass advertising', virtually all the modern sales and symbol-sorting professions have honour paid to their theories, practices and achievements only by their own kind. They tend to be invisible in social analysis yet they are the organic intellectuals of consumption. Their achievements are either ignored (as in most orthodox social analysis) or held to be grand and far-reaching (as in media studies and post-modernism). Either way, it seems, their activities do not require much investigation, apart from flip references to the 'power' of 'mass' advertising and 'mass' marketing.

I have reviewed the organisation and cultural apparatus of just one modern sport and enthusiasm, one related to the automobile in use, to try to suggest some of the complexities of the cultural, social and economic processes involved. At the end of my track I want to stress the significance of five points.

First, there are dynamic cultural processes in operation in such activities. Their local intelligensia, by no means always enamoured of *la vie bohemienne*, scrabble through the rag bag of general ideologies and codes, and 'grander' values, myths, and slogans are borrowed, stretched, repositioned, replayed and aligned to the preoccupations of the enthusiasm, including consumption activities. Through such intellectual labour 'old' and 'traditional' values are filled with new content and made more applicable in the reality of modern life. Examples of such 'translations' in this enthusiasm are the 'work ethic' and the nature of the true 'American genius', including the view that the very reasons for American success lay in the interconnections between personal inventiveness, backyard experimentation, tinkering, technology and the absence of state interference. Different commodities have different resonances and the automobile in *use* allows cultural brokers to use, without much strain, the sellotape of compelling metaphors about 'progress', 'mobility' and 'advance' to link the enthusiasm and the American way. For example, the competitive urge for speed and superior performance at the heart of the enthusiasm was seen, in *Hot Rod Industry News*, as relating directly to an entrepreneurial 'drive for profits' among dry lake veterans. In short, certain commodities facilitate particular manoeuvrings of meanings by their local apparatus and some of these involve 'reaching back' to some presumed, 'traditional', honest ideas. They affirm values which now seem displaced, old-fashioned, out of date, at odds with an unpleasant reality.

Second, such enthusiasms utilise a rhetoric of 'individualism' and 'community' within what is perceived, *by its cultural apparatus*, as an increasingly atomised and massified society. Kinship, community and recognition of individual ability are promised through involvement in the activities of the enthusiasm. In hot rodding important facets of this ethos were the notions of test through competition, the subjective significance of rare pieces of action, society's need for the self-reliant individual, etc. but so were the camaraderie of the 'insider' and the minutae of membership in a special world of knowledge. A place was offered to be someone based on a free choice not constraint. Petersen Publications sought to travel with their readers down life's highway, from hot rod to (by the 1980s) the motor home, though, it was averred, the ageing hot rodder still wanted to get a little more juice from his caravan than the 'average guy'.

Third, modern consumption is not to be equated with 'passivity', 'musing', 'stylistic display' or even 'illusory hedonism'. The hot rod apparatus certainly organised consumption, magazines and speed shops were pillars of the enthusiasm *and* sales outlets. But buying *and using* commodities was the essence of the activity. Self expression is not, and is not always presented in modern capitalism as being, the same as the absence of self-denial. What have to be investigated are the kinds of standards of excellence people are asked to judge themselves against and how people are asked to act so as to create their own pleasures. In the enthusiasm I have discussed, the emphasis was on involvement in personal projects, deferred gratification, measured performance, grazed knuckles, hard work through long nights, magic moments of accelerated experience. Dreams were to be made manifest and realised in the pur-chasing, modifying and use of objects over a long period of time or, at least, that is what the hot rod apparatus told people they should be doing. Of course, in the continuous and, only sometimes, impetuous activity of street racing, action not style is, ultimately, what counts.

Fourth, appeals to 'big business', 'commodification', 'capitalist provi-sion', 'the commercialisation of leisure', 'the pleasure industries' etc. can quickly become meaningless unless such terms are investigated in all their complexities including inherent conflicts of interests.[11] The intelli-gentsia of this enthusiasm fought to hold its own niche in the great market place based on clean enthusiast and community credentials. The hot rod apparatus struggled with the mass media, the state and truly big business to try and safeguard a sport and enthusiasm with its own activities, codes of conduct, and, of course, economic opportunities, against often well-meaning predators who sought to reduce this special world into a bland, regulated, standardised, homogenised, safe, ordina-riness. In doing so, these intellectuals offered a critique of aspects of up a relationship with their various audiences which was not just a straight, if sophisticated, sales pitch but stressed a concern for use-values and traditional rights. To this end, they warned their readers of the hollowness of the interest shown by big business, of the perils attendant on all-out economic exploitation and the danger of the constant encroachment of dull bureaucracies, who took a reasonable point far too far and trespassed upon the individual's right to choose and to be free.

Fifth, that the 'incorporation of activities', the main sensible way in which the issues I am concerned with have been dealt with in social analysis, is a very complex matter. Even such a sensitive scholar as Butsch simplifies the issues here when he argues: 'the hegemony of commercialized leisure is dependent for its existence upon its own incompleteness. Hegemony grows from a symbiosis between corporate capitalism and consumers. Consumers participate in shaping new products and practices, which corporations in turn shape into profits and 'mass culture.'[12] What I have tried to show is that any such symbiosis can be much more complex. Out of the tensions caused by commercialism and professionalism in the sport, and the interlocks between the sport, Detroit and the state, the hot rod apparatus did alter its stance but always promoted itself as standing for the little guy. It was constrained to do so. The truth is that some little guys (and gals) will always do something that a cultural apparatus can take up, spread and convince a much greater number that they do this or did do it once or might want to do it. But this cannot be reduced, flattened, changed or stripped down too much without incurring the wrath of the core devotees or losing its promise to *all* layers of enthusiasts that at least somewhere in modern life they can find an interesting world separate and distinct from the general grey, that they will be expert about something 'real' and 'useful' and will be associated with some activity through which they are likely to be able to gain status in whichever of their 'communities' their skill is relevant. Some complex core task and some body of knowledge has to remain for the devotees to practice and learn or the whole enthusiasm will lose its weight. Some do and become merely 'fads' but others endure as enthusiasms sustained, at least in part, by an urgent press and literature operating beneath (and often at odds with) the *mass* media, a specialist media which social analysis just cannot be bothered with. The papers, programmes and magazines of sports and enthusiasms require a lot more attention from any social analysis that really does want to grasp the subjectivities on offer and accepted in modern capitalism.[13]

The shut down

Of course, as critics are bound to point out, there's an awful lot more I ought to try to get clear. I haven't even got down everything that should be said about hot rodding or drag racing. It cannot all be done in one book and, in any case, any book is just the draft that gets printed. So I have to conclude in the hope that this text will prove provocative. I want it to provoke other people to carry out detailed studies of enthusiasms. I want to hear what other people have to say about the structures and cultural effects of hot rodding or other automobile sports or the use of cars or about enthusiasms more generally, including all the various relationships between sports and enthusiasms. At the moment, the ignorance, arrogance, condescension, traditions and reward structures of most social analysis make that quite a difficult path to travel. Still, the road is wide open for anyone who wants to join in the empirical examination of the importance of enthusiasm in society. It would seem like some kind of achievement if this text persuaded more people that it was worthwhile to take that trip and if it provided a few directions that helped them along in their own journeys.

Notes

1 Mamie van Doren to her teacher in the film *High School Confidential* (1958).
2 D. Lewis, *The Public Image of Henry Ford* (Detroit, 1976).
3 A. Gramsci, 'Americanism and Fordism', in D. Forgacs (ed.), *A Gramsci Reader* (London, 1988), pp. 275–95.
4 E.g. J. Lovering, 'A perfunctory sort of post-Fordism' and T. Elger, 'Technical innovation and work reorganization in British manufacturing in the 1980s', both in *Work Employment and Society*, additional special issue, May 1990; and S. Clarke, 'What in the Ford's name is Fordism?', paper delivered at the annual conference of the British Sociological Association, University of Surrey, April 1990.
5 E. Rothschild, *Paradise Lost: The Decline of the Auto-Industrial Age* (New York, 1973).
6 H. F. Moorhouse, 'American automobiles and workers' dreams', *Sociological Review*, 31, August 1983, pp. 413–14.
7 Lewis, *Public Image*, pp. 297–301; N. Bel Geddes, *Magic Motorways* (New York, 1940) and L. Sorenson, *The Ford Shows* (St. Helena California, 1976) especially pp. 216–22.
8 A. Tomlinson (ed.), *Consumption, Identity and Style* (London, 1990), p. 21.
9 M. Featherstone, 'Perspectives on consumer culture', *Sociology* 24, special edition on the sociology of consumption, February 1990, p. 7.
10 R. E. Pahl, *Divisions of Labour* (Oxford, 1984); C. Campbell, *The Romantic Ethic and The Spirit of Modern Consumerism* (Oxford, 1987).
11 See R. Butsch, 'Home video and corporate plans: capital's limited power to manipulate leisure', in R. Butsch (ed.), *For Fun and Profit: The Transformation of Leisure into Consumption* (Philadelphia, 1990) pp. 215–35.

12 *For Fun and Profit*, p. 19.
13 Consider how readily Lowenthal's research on magazines – highly socially and methodologically specific – has been accepted as showing a widespread consuming interest in passive pleasure, a promoted lack of patterning in the route to success etc., whereas what he finds is in many ways an artefact of where he looks. L. Lowenthal, 'Biographies in popular magazines', in P. Lazarsfeld and F. Stanton (eds.), *Radio Research (1942–3)* (New York, 1944).

Index

Adorno, T., 10–13, 21
Advertising Age, 169, 217–18
'alienation', 12–13, 145
American Dream, 10, 71, 170–97
American Hot Rod Association, 85,
 106, 117–19, 186, 200, 212–15
American Hot Rod Conference, 42,
 46–7, 50, 53
automobile sports, 7, 172
Automobile Timing Association of
 America (ATAA), 62, 66, 75,
 84–5, 101–6, 157

bracket racing, 201–6
Butsch, R., 13, 226

Campbell, C., 18–21, 223
Chinoy, E., 147
Colliers, 29, 31–2, 34, 175
commodification, 13, 92, 159, 225
consumption
 importance for social analysis,
  4–5, 15–16, 221–7
 sociology of, 7, 14–15, 18–21, 23,
  92, 147–9, 221–7
cultural apparatus
 concept, 15–18, 22, 167, 223–5
 hot rod, 38–40, 50, 58, 62, 68,
  83–5, 92–3, 119, 122–5, 132,
  144–5, 162, 171

Detroit, 60, 75, 77, 81, 87, 113–17,
 123–9, 135–6, 139, 141, 195–6,

 215, 222
drag racing sport
 championships, 117, 213–14
 commercial strips, 60–3, 75, 208
 crowds, 110, 129
 early history, 40, 45, 49–56
 prize money, 118–19, 211–12
 problems, 58–68, 87–90, 132–41,
  201
 sanctioning bodies, 83–4, 200–1,
  214–16
dry lakes sport, 26–9, 32–3, 36–41,
 45, 51–2, 93–6, 217

enthusiasm, 17–18, 21–3, 45, 92,
 221–7
Esquire, 65, 195

Forbes, 218
Fortune, 28, 71
fuel, 38–9, 88, 93–100, 211–15
fuel ban, 101–110

Garlits, D., 31, 102–3, 106–19, 164–5,
 177, 189, 211, 215, 217
Gramsci, A., 222

hedonism, 18–21, 147, 167, 225
hegemony, 9, 171, 226
Hoggart, R., 144, 159
hot rodding
 and gender divisions, 177–190
 and wars, 155, 174–77

229